Why Do You Need This New Edition?

If you're wondering why you need this new edition of *Rethinking California* here are five good reasons!

1. A discussion of the 2009 economic crisis analyzes the factors that led to the budget fiasco and looming bankruptcy of the state.

2. Simmering problems—an ideologically prepared legislature, widespread bureaucracy, underfunded schools, overcrowded prisons, and dilapidated infrastructure—and the demand for an overhaul of California's constitution to address these issues are covered in detail.

3. An analysis of the politics and mechanics of the recall of Governor Gray Davis and the election of Arnold Schwarzenegger is included.

4. A new chapter on direct democracy offers an expanded discussion of the initiative, the referendum, and the recall and considers why they figure so prominently in California politics.

5. A fresh array of contemporary and historical readings from literature, essays, and political biographies appear in each chapter, illustrating California's unique political culture.

PEARSON

Editor-in-Chief: Eric Stano
Managing Editor: Nancy Wolitzer
Marketing Manager: Lindsey Prudhomme
Production Manager: Ellen MacElree
Project Coordination, Text Design, and Electronic Page Makeup: GGS Higher
   Education Resources, A Division of PreMedia Global Inc.
Cover Designer/Manager: Wendy Ann Fredericks
Cover Photo: © Joseph B. Strauss/Corbis Yellow
Senior Manufacturing Buyer: Roy L. Pickering, Jr.
Printer and Binder: R. R. Donnelley & Sons, Harrisonburg
Cover Printer: R. R. Donnelley & Sons, Harrisonburg

Library of Congress Cataloging in Publication Data

Cahn, Matthew Alan
   Rethinking California: politics and policy in the golden state / Matthew Alan Cahn,
H. Eric Schockman, David M. Shafie. — 2nd ed.
      p. cm.
Includes bibliographical references and index.
ISBN-13: 978-0-13-184292-2 (alk. paper)
ISBN-10: 0-13-184292-7 (alk. paper)
1. Political planning—California. 2. Political culture—California. 3. California—Politics and
government. I. Schockman, H. Eric. II. Shafie, David M. III. Title.

JK8749.P64C34 2010
320.9794—dc22

2009021104

Longman
is an imprint of

1 2 3 4 5 6 7 8 9 10—DOH—12 11 10 09

ISBN-10:   0-13-184292-7
ISBN-13: 978-0-13-184292-2

www.pearsonhighered.com

RETHINKING CALIFORNIA
Politics and Policy in the Golden State

Second Edition

Matthew Alan Cahn
California State University, Northridge

H. Eric Schockman
California State University, Northridge

David M. Shafie
Chapman University

Longman

New York   Boston   San Francisco
London   Toronto   Sydney   Tokyo   Singapore   Madrid
Mexico City   Munich   Paris   Cape Town   Hong Kong   Montreal

Contents

Preface

Early in 2009, hundreds of citizens gathered in a hotel ballroom in Sacramento and calmly discussed a radical idea: a complete overhaul of California's constitution. The meeting came on the heels of a protracted budget crisis that left the state without cash for its payroll. Several state offices, including the Department of Motor Vehicles, were shut down temporarily to conserve funds, and employees were forced to take furloughs. The budget dispute eventually ended when Governor Arnold Schwarzenegger and the state legislature struck a deal to cut spending and raise some taxes and fees, but that solution did not satisfy the group of business and labor leaders, teachers, public interest group members, and concerned citizens that had gathered in Sacramento.

The group called for nothing less than a constitutional convention, to be initiated at the ballot box unless the legislature acted first. This had become necessary, they argued, because the state's executive leadership, bureaucracy, and ideologically polarized legislature had been unable to solve a host of simmering problems. Besides the budget fiasco, there were underfunded schools, overcrowded prisons, and an infrastructure in tatters. California's government was "broken," they declared, and the only solution was to throw out the 130-year-old document and begin anew.

The forum was a sign of the growing frustration over the failure of government institutions to meet the challenges of the largest and most diverse state, the largest agricultural producer *and* home to the largest urban population, a state with extreme concentrations of wealth and poverty, the world's eighth-largest economy. The once-utopian Golden State was facing serious problems.

Much has happened since the first edition of this book appeared. The recall election of Governor Gray Davis was the kind of spectacle that could happen only in California. Using the instrument of *direct democracy*, a well-funded group forced a special election to remove an unpopular governor less than one year into his second term, replacing him with a Venice Beach bodybuilder-turned-movie star. The record $43 billion deficit that Schwarzenegger faced at the end of 2008 was even larger than the gap in the state's finances that sparked the recall of his predecessor.

The second edition of *Rethinking California* features a number of additions, including a discussion of the politics and the mechanics of the recall. A new chapter on direct democracy includes an expanded discussion of the initiative, the referendum, and the recall, and it considers why they figure so prominently in California politics. Finally, this new edition features supplemental readings from a variety of sources. These selections from literature, essays, and political biographies in each chapter add lively contemporary and historical voices to our treatment of the subjects.

This book is dedicated to our families: Ann, Tara, Diane, Arlo, Tobin, Jonah, and Steven.

Matthew Alan Cahn
H. Eric Schockman
David M. Shafie

Acknowledgments

No book is the work of its authors alone. We would like to thank several people for their insights into the California experience. They include Tim Hodson at the Center for California Studies (CSU Sacramento), Jaime Regalado at the Pat Brown Institute (Cal State, Los Angeles), Fernando Guerra at the Center for the Study of Los Angeles (Loyola, Marymount), and Tom Hogen-Esch, Martin Saiz, and Larry Becker in the Department of Political Science at Cal State Northridge. We would also like to thank the reviewers who provided their scholarly analysis of this new edition: Damon Conklin (Golden Gate University) and Sean Q. Kelly (California State University—Channel Islands).

In addition, we would like to thank Rian Medlin, Christopher Johnson, Heather Wolfson, and Maggie Hanson for their research assistance with the second edition.

About the Authors

MATTHEW ALAN CAHN is professor and chair of the Political Science Department at California State University, Northridge. His research interests include California politics, urban environmental policy, and resource management. Dr. Cahn has been involved in several applied policy areas, ranging from transportation issues in metropolitan Los Angeles to the question of protected areas in the Channel Islands National Marine Sanctuary. He has authored and co-authored several books, including *Environmental Deceptions*, *Thinking About the Environment*, and *California: An Owner's Manual*. Over the years, Dr. Cahn has taught at San Francisco State, San Jose State, and UC Santa Barbara.

H. ERIC SCHOCKMAN teaches Public Policy at California State University, Northridge, and is president of MAZON: A Jewish Response to Hunger. In 2007, Dr. Schockman was named by Governor Arnold Schwarzenegger to serve on California's Commission on Higher Education. He has headed numerous policy think tanks and served as a consultant to the California legislature and the Los Angeles City Council and as a commissioner for the state of California's Little Hoover Commission.

DAVID M. SHAFIE is assistant professor of Political Science at Chapman University. His research interests include state and local politics, environmental policy, and media and politics. He has also been a journalist and has taught at California State University, Fullerton, Long Beach State, and Ohio University.

CHAPTER 1

The Three States of California: An Introduction

Featured Reading / Pages 7–10
Joan Didion
Notes from a Native Daughter

[Many people] have been to Los Angeles or to San Francisco, have driven through a giant redwood and have seen the Pacific glazed by the afternoon sun off Big Sur, and they naturally tend to believe that they have in fact been to California. They have not been, and they probably never will be, for it is a longer and in many more ways a more difficult trip than they might want to undertake, one of those trips on which the destination flickers chimerically on the horizon, ever receding, ever diminishing.

—Joan Didion, from *Notes from a Native Daughter*

California has always been considered somewhat different from the rest of the nation. It is, as Theodore Roosevelt pointed out, "west of the West." Yet California has emerged as a dominant trendsetter, establishing models and approaches that are emulated throughout the nation. California may be west of the traditional centers of power, but its size and influence have surpassed those of all other states. Stretching 825 miles from Crescent City to San Diego and 215 miles from Monterey to Mono Lake, California comprises 164,000 square miles and 36.5 million people—12.1 percent of the total U.S. population.[1]

Captured by the United States in 1846, with statehood bestowed in 1850, California was a latecomer to national politics. As a consequence of both its distance from the established power centers of the East and its "frontier" culture, California was seen more as a repository of rich natural resources than as a partner in policy. California was a terrain contested by three nations and dozens of Native American communities. Between Cabrillo's claims on the Pacific Coast in 1542 and the Mexican-American War in 1846, Spain, Mexico, and the United States maneuvered, battled, and manipulated to gain control.

Spanish colonization of California began in 1769, when Junipero Serra established El Camino Real, the Mission Trail—nine missions whose central function was to control Indian land on behalf of Spain and convert native civilizations to

Christianity. Spain actively recruited settlers from Mexico, drawing fundamentally from the poorest *mestizo* communities.[2] Spain's hold on California was weak, consisting of only 3,000 settlers—most of whom were Mexican. When Mexico became independent of Spain in 1821, California became a Mexican territory. City names like Mendocino, Sonoma, San Francisco, San Jose, Santa Cruz, Monterey, San Luis Obispo, Los Angeles, and San Diego reflect its Native American, Spanish, and Mexican heritage—and its ethnic ambivalence. The 46 original settlers of Los Angeles, for example, were *mestizos* of Indian, African, and Spanish ancestry.[3] This ambivalence runs deep in part because the U.S. claim on California was pushed by American squatters in what was then Mexico.[4]

THREE STATES

California is often characterized in singular terms, suggesting a common landscape and people. The stereotype of California as a collection of sun-drenched beaches, clogged freeways, dysfunctional celebrities, and self-obsessed citizens seems to inhabit the national psyche but does not in fact describe the state. All of these may exist to a greater or lesser extent, though they are only a small part of a complex mosaic. We believe that California is unique because of this complexity. Rather than think about the state as a single place, we prefer to think about California as a multitude of interrelated places—overlapping and interconnected like a Venn diagram that has spun out of control. This perspective is important in helping explain how California's communities, cultures, and economies are simultaneously independent and interdependent, contiguous and noncontiguous, similar and diverse. Though California is often thought of in mid-twentieth-century snapshots, we suggest rethinking California as it becomes its mid-twenty-first-century self.

Many observers have noted that California, with its complex network of communities and regional resources, may in fact be composed of three different states. If one were to explore how California's many communities related to each other, it would be possible to identify clear regional cultures within which unique subcultures interact. Politically, economically, socially, philosophically, and even ethnically, California is actually three different places: southern California (San Diego north to San Luis Obispo County), northern California (Monterey County up through Humboldt County), and the Central Valley (Kern and Inyo Counties north to Oregon). Each of these regions maintains unique economies, idiosyncratic political cultures, unique microclimates, and even distinct language patterns and cultural reference points. To fully understand California, one must understand its separate regional identities.

Southern California

Southern California can be characterized as densely populated urban coastline, particularly between Ventura and Orange Counties. With the notable exception of Los Angeles and Santa Barbara Counties, Southern California tends to vote Republican.

As a consequence of the large metropolitan areas, Southern California remains ethnically and religiously diverse. Traditional Southern California economic engines have been manufacturing and light industry. Since the 1970s, however, the Southern California economy has become more service oriented and corporate in nature. The archetypal Southern California job in the 1950s was industrial (shipyards, tire manufacturing). The archetypal Southern California job in the 2000s is service sector (low-paying jobs include food service and retail jobs; high-paying jobs include international banking and consulting jobs).

Add to these structural phenomena the unique architectural and cultural edifices, and the Southern California character is complete. Because the region grew extremely quickly—exponentially increasing in population between 1940 and today—effectively planning the infrastructure was impossible. The result is evident in both land planning and transportation. The mini-mall, a Southern California invention, has come to dominate the landscape. These strip malls, which typically include some combination of convenience store, donut shop, dry cleaners, and hair and nail shop, were in many ways predetermined by Southern California's geography. Quick growth and conservative politics tend to preclude land and architectural planning, warm weather encourages convenience shopping in open-air storefronts, the reliance on cars makes parking lots a necessity, and the relatively cheap land in outlying areas encourages the construction of multi-unit retail space (e.g., mini-malls) on speculation by small investors.

Southern California is defined in many ways by its freeways. This, however, was not always the case. As early as 1924, Southern California's Red Car system carried 100 million riders annually between San Fernando, Newport Beach, Pasadena, and San Bernardino—covering Los Angeles and outward for some 75 miles in all directions. The fate of mass transit in Southern California was doomed, however, for two reasons. First, the short-term success of the Red Car actually prevented long-term success because the system encouraged building out rather than building up, as in most Eastern cities. Home builders built large tracts of housing on cheap land, advertising "live in the country, work in the city." The Red Car made it possible to buy a house in an inexpensive area, while commuting into the city. However, as development grew beyond train stations in outlying areas, mass transit became less attractive. By the 1940s, home builders were advertising garages with driveways rather than proximity to train stations.

Second, as a relatively new urban area, Southern California's major investment in its transportation infrastructure came at a time when cars were increasingly inexpensive and roads were relatively uncongested. Related issues such as energy and air quality were not yet significant concerns. In 1926, when Angelenos were asked to vote on bond measures that would define Southern California's transportation infrastructure for the next century, rail construction lost out to freeway construction. This was perhaps preordained. Who in 1926 could have predicted the growth Southern California would achieve over the next 75 years?

In addition, Southern California's weather—with a year-round median temperature in the mid-70s and little rainfall—encourages an outdoor lifestyle. The architecture reflects this, as do the fashion and the vernacular. Housing tracts—with two-bedroom Spanish-style bungalows in the 1920s and 1930s; larger "modern" ranch-style houses boasting three bedrooms and two bathrooms in the 1940s, 1950s, and 1960s; and even larger Mediterranean styles in the 1970s, 1980s, and 1990s— suggest a Southern California style. Front yards are dominated by garages and drive-ways, with the notable absence of porches, suggesting a space of utility rather than socializing with neighbors. Backyards are dominated by "family space," including BBQ areas, swing sets, and dog runs.

The warm weather and proximity to a swimmable coastline ensures an enduring relationship with the beach and ocean. While the Aloha shirt may or may not be fashionable throughout the state, it has never lost favor in Southern California. Southern California vernacular has consistently included outdoor references. From the Annette Funicello/Frankie Avalon beach party movies to *Baywatch*, Southern Californians have long had to balance externally imposed stereotypes with organic, homegrown lifestyles. This hasn't been easy, in large part because the Southern California media persists in celebrating the *Baywatch* ideal and because of the high number of transplants who have flocked to Southern California in search of this idealized lifestyle. While many outsiders see Malibu or Santa Monica as quintessential Southern California, the real Southern California is a quilt of cultures, alive and well in places like Ventura and Oxnard, San Fernando, Inglewood, Monterey Park, San Pedro, Riverside, Long Beach, Santa Ana, and Oceanside.

Northern California

Mark Twain once commented that the coldest winter he ever spent was a summer in San Francisco. Whereas Southern California is often warm and dry, Northern California is often cold and damp. But the differences go far beyond weather. Northern California tends to vote Democratic, albeit with distinct enclaves of conservative voters. While architecture dominates the Southern California landscape, in Northern California, landscape dominates architecture. The "Little Boxes" that dot Daly City's residential tracts are necessitated by the urban density of the San Francisco peninsula. Bordered by the bay and the ocean, the available space to build is severely limited.

The earth tones of Marin architecture and the unobtrusive style of Big Sur architecture reflect the region's comfort with nature. This is a function of lower density and cooler weather. Southern Californians spend much of the year indoors to avoid the heat. Northern Californians spend much of the year indoors to avoid the rain. Each climate requires different architecture. Functional fashion may also be a result: Hiking boots and flannel make more sense in Humboldt than in San Diego.

Northern California may itself contain two very different regions. The Bay Area is distinctly different from the northern coast. The high-tech industries along the San Jose–San Francisco corridor lead the nation in new technology research and development and in high-tech manufacturing. The income generated in Silicon Valley is illustrated by a local housing market that is two to three times higher than in the Bay

Area generally. At the same time, the timber-based economy of the north is extremely vulnerable to recession. In 2004, median household income in Santa Clara County (including Silicon Valley) was $68,842. At the same time, median household income in Glenn County was $34,883.[5]

Northern California's urban centers mirror the cultural and ethnic diversity of Southern California, but its rural northwest does not. The Bay Area is extremely diverse, incorporating strong and politicized black, Latino, Asian, and Native American communities. Cities such as Oakland, San Francisco, and San Jose are among the nation's premier multicultural centers. At the same time, the northwest coast from Mendocino to Crescent City looks more like Oregon than California— predominantly white, modest incomes, and largely Christian.

If there is a Northern California vernacular, it may be due to politicized university students from Santa Cruz, Stanford, Berkeley, San Francisco, San Jose, Hayward, Sonoma, and Humboldt State. These institutions have a long history of activism, particularly with regard to environmental issues and civil rights. A case in point: The tired phrase *politically correct* originated on Northern California campuses, as an affectionate jab by campus leftists at their more programmatic colleagues. In a bit of Orwellian double-speak, it has since been hijacked by conservatives to marginalize progressive concerns.

The Central Valley

The Central Valley is California's heartland. It is primarily agricultural, with small cities separated by miles of farmland. Density is low outside its major cities. It is the home of the Central Valley Project, the primary delivery system for agricultural water diverted from the Sacramento Delta. The relatively narrow valley, bordered on the east and west by mountains, is home to a thick fog every winter. This tule fog is both an institution and a hazard. Most Californians know the Central Valley at 70 mph, as they drive between the Bay Area and Southern California along Interstate 5. Relatively few travel off the interstate, making the Valley unknown to most Californians.

The Central Valley includes vast rural areas, with growing urban areas in Bakersfield, Fresno, and, of course, the greater Sacramento area. Fresno and Sacramento are among the state's 10 largest cities, with populations of 471,479 and 457,514, respectively. Fresno County is one of the state's fastest-growing areas, predicted to grow from its current population of 891,000 to 2.5 million over the next 40 years.[6] And, while many small cities in the Central Valley are predominately white and Latino, the larger cities are extremely diverse. Bakersfield, Fresno, Stockton, and Sacramento reflect the diversity of the rest of the state.

Politically, the Central Valley tends to be split. The agricultural counties tend to vote Republican, the urban counties vote Democratic. The Central Valley's economic engine is primarily agricultural, from the farms in Kern, Kings, and Fresno Counties in the south up to the northern counties that unfold along the Sacramento River—Colusa, Butte, and Tehama Counties. Stockton and Sacramento remain active port cities, with light industry and related services. The Sacramento,

American, and Feather Rivers spill into the Sacramento Delta, a vast maze of bayous and tributaries, invoking the flavor of Louisiana in California.

If there is a "beltway" in California, it is Sacramento. With the large number of state offices and the influx of representatives, staff, lobbyists, and the public, Sacramento at times looks more like Washington than the sleepy Central Valley river town it once was. As the political nexus of the state, downtown Sacramento has been able to remake itself in the image of every Californian. This is remarkable, considering how different Californians are from one another. The warm weather and urban sprawl are familiar to Southern Californians, the heavy tree covering and lush gardens are familiar to Northern Californians, and to the Central Valley, Sacramento is—well, home.

HOW MANY CALIFORNIAS?

Some observers see even more than three states within California's borders. Philip Fradkin, for example, identifies seven.[7] Fradkin sees differing landscapes as critical determinants of cultural expression. Fradkin's first California is the deserts, along the southeastern corridor of the state, from Mono Lake south to the Salton Sea. The deserts are defined by drought, little population, untamed open space, and ghosts of past civilizations. His second California is the Sierra, encompassing the Sierra Nevada from Donner Pass to Bakersfield. This 430-mile-long mountain region is distinguished by vast wilderness, even fewer people, and characterized by a pioneer past. The Sierra Nevadas, while never tamed, had to be understood to allow westward immigration. The hard lessons of the Donner Party[8] underscore life in this California.

Fradkin's third California, "the Land of Fire," is the volcanic Cascade region in the northeasternmost section of the state. His fourth California, "the Land of Water," is the northwest coastal area from Crescent City to Point Arena. This California is dominated by forests, wind, fog, and rain. The population is centered in Crescent City, Arcata, Humboldt, and Eureka. Separated from the rest of the state by thick forests, there is a palpable sense of isolation. California number five is the "Great Valley." The central valley between Redding and Bakersfield is the state's bread basket, making up one of the largest regions of sustained agriculture in the nation. Population is greatest in the greater Sacramento area, inclusive of Stockton, and in the Fresno/Bakersfield area, which is the fastest-growing region of the state, but is distributed throughout the region. California number six includes the northern California coastline from Point Reyes to Point Conception. This "Fractured Province" is defined in large measure by the frequency of earthquake fault lines.

Finally, California number seven, Southern California from Point Conception to San Diego, is Fradkin's "Profligate Province." This region is the most populated and, in Fradkin's view, the most wildly extravagant. The cycle of earthquake, fire, and flood is somehow a function of Southern California's hubris. In this Fradkin anticipates Mike Davis' *Ecology of Fear*.[9] Whether one accepts the notion of multiple Californias or not, it is clear that regional differences have emerged as being important to California's diversity.

Urban California, Urban Peripheries, and Rural California

Some observers note that while there are different Californias, it is not geography that distinguishes them. Rather, the very different types of cities and towns throughout the state can be delineated by economic base, demographics, and size. More specifically, communities throughout the state can be divided into Urban California, Urban Peripheries, and Rural California. According to this analysis, cities of like size, demography, and structure have more in common than do cities that share a geographic region. San Francisco, for example, has much more in common with Los Angeles than with Willits, a small lumber town in Mendocino. Similarly, Vista, in northern San Diego County, has much more in common with Concord, in the Bay Area, than with San Diego.

Urban centers tend to share common concerns, as do urban peripheries and rural areas. Urban cores are concerned with race relations, economic revitalization, international commerce, crime, and crumbling school districts. Urban peripheries, those suburbs that ring urban cores, depend on the central city for economic sustenance, but struggle with issues of open space, zoning, and the retail "flavor" of boutique downtown areas. Crime is a major preoccupation, but typically in the context of containing "city crime" from spreading into the periphery neighborhoods. Rural areas share a concern for agricultural and timber resources, tend to oppose environmental restrictions, and fear "urban sprawl," where urban peripheries begin to extend into agricultural areas. At the same time, rural communities battle periphery cities over open space issues. Newly incorporated cities in outlying areas hope to preserve open space in perpetuity, while rural communities often assert a right to develop open space as the market dictates.

California Divide

Whether one agrees with Fradkin's borders or a more modest set of borders, there clearly are significant regional differences. It is often surprising how these 58 distinctive counties manage to interact as a common state. Intraregional relations, interregional relations, and region-to-state relations all depend on the unique cultures and politics that dominate the region. As we explore these relationships, we must keep an eye toward the regional idiosyncrasies that make California unique.

Notes from a Native Daughter   *Joan Didion*

It was very easy to sit at the bar in, say, La Scala in Beverly Hills, or Ernie's in San Francisco, and to share in the pervasive delusion that California is only five hours from New York by air. The truth is that La Scala and Ernie's are only five hours from New York by air. California is somewhere else.

Many people in the East (or "back East," as they say in California, although not in La Scala or Ernie's) do not believe this. They have been to Los Angeles or to San Francisco, have driven through a giant redwood and have seen the Pacific glazed by the afternoon sun off Big Sur, and they naturally tend to believe that they have in fact been to California. They have not been, and they probably never will be, for it is a longer and in many more ways a more difficult trip than they might want to undertake, one of those trips on which the destination flickers chimerically on the horizon, ever receding, ever diminishing. I happen to know about that trip because I come from California, come from a family, or a congeries of families, that has always been in the Sacramento Valley.

You might protest that no family has been in the Sacramento Valley for anything approaching "always." But it is characteristic of Californians to speak grandly of the past as if it had simultaneously begun, *tabula rasa*, and reached a happy ending on the day the wagons started West. *Eureka*—"I Have Found It"— as the state motto has it. Such a view of history casts a certain melancholia over those who participate in it; my own childhood was suffused with the conviction that we had long outlived our finest hour. In fact that is what I want to tell you about: what it is like to have come from a place like Sacramento. If I could make you understand that, I could make you understand California and perhaps something else besides, for Sacramento *is* California, and California is a place in which a boom mentality and a sense of Chekhovian loss meet in uneasy suspension; in which the mind is troubled by some buried but ineradicable suspension that things had better work here, because here, beneath that immense bleached sky, is where we run out of continent.

In 1847 Sacramento was no more than an adobe enclosure, Sutter's Fort, standing alone on the prairie; cut off from San Francisco and the sea by the Coast Range and from the rest of the continent by the Sierra Nevada, the Sacramento Valley was then a true sea of grass, grass so high a man riding into it could tie it across his saddle. A year later gold was discovered in the Sierra foothills, and abruptly Sacramento was a town, a town any moviegoer could map tonight in his dreams— a dusty collage of assay offices and wagonmakers and saloons. Call that Phase Two. Then the settlers came—the farmers, the people who for two hundred years had been moving west of the frontier, the peculiar flawed strain who had cleared Virginia, Kentucky, Missouri; they made Sacramento a farm town. Because the land was rich, Sacramento became eventually a rich farm town, which meant houses in town, Cadillac dealers, a country club. In that gentle sleep Sacramento dreamed until perhaps 1950, when something happened. What happened was that Sacramento woke to the fact that the outside world was moving in, fast and hard. At the moment of its waking Sacramento lost, for better or for worse, its character, and that is part of what I want to tell you about.

But the change is not what I remember first. First I remember running a boxer dog of my brother's over the same flat fields that our great-great-grandfather had found virgin and had planted; I remember swimming (albeit nervously, for I was a nervous child, afraid of sinkholes and afraid of snakes, and perhaps that was the beginning of my error) the same rivers we had swum for a century: the Sacramento, so rich with silt that we could barely see our hands a few inches beneath the surface; the American, running clean and fast with melted Sierra snow until July, when it would slow down, and rattlesnakes would sun themselves on its newly exposed rocks. The Sacramento, the American, sometimes the Cosumnes, occasionally the Feather. Incautious children died every day in those rivers; we had read about it in the paper, how they had miscalculated a current or stepped into a hole down where the American runs into the Sacramento, how the Berry Brothers had been called in from Yolo County to drag the river but how the bodies remained unrecovered. "They were from away," my grandmother would extrapolate from the newspaper stories. "Their parents had no *business* letting them in the river. They were visitors from Omaha." It was not a bad lesson, although a less than reliable one; children we knew died in the rivers too. . . .

Later, when I was living in New York, I would make the trip back to Sacramento four and five times a year (the more comfortable the flight, the more obscurely miserable I would be, for it weighs heavily upon my mind that we could perhaps not make it by wagon), trying to prove that I had not meant to leave at all, because in at least one respect California—the California we are talking about—resembles Eden: It is assumed that those who absent themselves from its blessings have been banished, exiled by some perversity of heart. Did not the Donner-Reed Party, after all, eat its own dead to reach Sacramento?

I have said that the trip back is difficult, and it is—difficult in a way that magnifies the ordinary ambiguities of sentimental journeys. Going back to California is not like going back to Vermont, or Chicago; Vermont and Chicago are relative constants, against which one measures one's own change. All that is constant about the California of my childhood is the rate at which it disappears. An instance: on Saint Patrick's Day of 1948 I was taken to see the legislature "in action," a dismal experience; a handful of florid assemblymen, wearing green hats, were reading Pat-and-Mike jokes into the record. I still think of the legislators that way—wearing green hats, or sitting around on the veranda of the Senator Hotel fanning themselves and being entertained by Artie Samish's emissaries. (Samish was the lobbyist who said, "Earl Warren may be the governor of the state, but I'm the governor of the legislature.") In fact, there is no longer a veranda at the Senator Hotel—it was turned into an airline ticket office, if you want to embroider the point—and in any case the legislature has largely deserted the Senator for the flashy motels north of town, where the tiki torches flame and the steam rises off the heated swimming pools in the cold Valley night.

It is hard to *find* California now, unsettling to wonder how much of it was merely imagined or improvised; melancholy to realize how much of anyone's memory is no true memory at all but only the traces of someone else's memory, stories handed down on the family network. I have an indelibly vivid "memory," for example, of how Prohibition affected the hop growers around Sacramento: The sister of a grower my family knew brought home a mink coat from San Francisco, and was told to take it back, and sat on the floor of the parlor cradling that coat and crying. Although I was not born until a year after Repeal, that scene is more "real" to me than many I have played myself.

I remember one trip home, when I sat alone on a night jet from New York and read over and over some lines from a W. S. Merwin poem I had come across in a magazine, a poem about a man who had been a long time in another country and knew that he must go home:

> . . . But it should be
> Soon. Already I defend hotly
> Certain of our indefensible faults,
> Resent being reminded; already in my mind

Our language becomes freighted with a richness

No common tongue could offer, while the mountains

Are like nowhere on earth, and the wide rivers.

You see the point. I want to tell you the truth, and already I have told you about the wide rivers.

It should be clear by now that the truth about the place is elusive, and must be tracked with caution. You might go to Sacramento tomorrow and someone (although no one I know) might take you out to Aerojet-General, which has, in the Sacramento phrase, "something to do with rockets." Fifteen thousand people work for Aerojet, almost all of them imported; a Sacramento lawyer's wife told me, as evidence of how Sacramento was opening up, that she believed she had met one of them, at an open house two Decembers ago. ("Couldn't have been nicer, actually," she added enthusiastically. "I think he and his wife bought the house next *door* to Mary and Al, something like that, which of course was how *they* met him.") So you might go to Aerojet and stand in the big vendors' lobby where a couple of thousand components salesmen try every week to sell their wares and you might look up at the electrical wallboard that lists Aerojet personnel, their projects and their location at any given time, and you might wonder if I have been in Sacramento lately. MINUTEMEN, POLARIS, TITAN, the lights flash, and all the coffee tables are littered with airline schedules, very now, very much in touch.

But I could take you a few miles from here into towns where the banks still bear names like The Bank of Alex Brown, into towns where the one hotel still has an octagonal-tile floor in the dining room and dusty potted palms and big ceiling fans; into towns where everything—the seed business, the Harvester franchise, the hotel, the department store and the main street—carries a single name, the name of the man who built the town. A few Sundays ago I was in a town like that, a town smaller than that, really, no hotel, no Harvester franchise, the bank burned out, a river town. It was the golden anniversary of some of my relatives and it was 110° and the guests of honor sat on straight-backed chairs in front of a sheaf of gladioluses in the Rebekah Hall. I mentioned visiting Aerojet-General to a cousin I saw there, who listened to me with interested disbelief. Which is the true California? That is what we all wonder.

Source: Joan Didion, "Notes from a Native Daughter," *Slouching Toward Bethlehem*. Copyright © 1966, 1968, renewed 1996 by Joan Didion. Reprinted by permission of Farrar, Straus and Giroux, LLC.

THE STRUCTURE OF THIS BOOK

This book explores the evolving role of politics and policy in California. To achieve this, the book seeks to do the impossible: to convey the taste, smell, and feel of the state at the dawn of the twenty-first century. As the most populous state, California has emerged as a leader of national and international politics, economics, and culture. The following chapters review California's unique institutional structure on both the state and local levels, as well as California's unique cultural legacy.

Part I provides an overview of California's unique history and culture, with special attention paid to political culture, people and diversity, and politics and economics. Part II introduces the institutional infrastructure. These chapters explore the constitutional makeup of California, the governor, state legislature, and state judiciary, as well as local governments. Part III focuses on the policy players—those individuals and organizations who work to influence politics and policy throughout the state, including interest groups, the media, parties, campaigns, and elections. Part IV assesses the major policy issues affecting the state, including education, environment, immigration, and civil rights. California's political culture is as vast and complicated as its terrain. It is its people that make it special and its natural resources that make it unique. The following pages will introduce you to the personalities and ideas that are essential to an understanding of the Golden State, from its early history to the controversies that shape political conflict in the present day.

NOTES

1. California Department of Finance, Population Research Unit, *California Statistical Abstract Report 2006* and U.S. Census Bureau Population Clock (www.census.gov/main/www/popclock.html).
2. Mestizos were subsistence farmers of mixed native and European ancestry.
3. Ronald Takaki, *A Different Mirror: A History of Multicultural America* (Boston: Little, Brown and Company, 1993) and Clyde Milner II, Carol O'Connor, Martha Sandweiss, eds., *The Oxford History of the American West* (New York: Oxford University Press, 1994).
4. Takaki, *A Different Mirror.*
5. Quickfacts, U.S. Census Bureau (http://quickfacts.census.gov/qfd/states/06/06021.html).
6. California Department of Finance, Population Research Unit, *California Statistical Abstract Report 2006.*
7. Philip Fradkin, *The Seven States of California: A Natural and Human History* (Berkeley: University of California Press, 1997).
8. The Donner Party was a group of California pioneers who were trapped in a blizzard in the winter of 1846 while transiting what is now Donner Pass in the Sierra Nevada range. Members of the party were rumored to have resorted to cannibalism in order to survive.
9. Mike Davis, *Ecology of Fear: Los Angeles and the Imagination of Disaster* (New York: Metropolitan Books, 1998).

CHAPTER 2

California's Political History

Featured Reading / Pages 19–23
Rubén Martínez
La Placita

What surrounds me is my history, I repeat to myself. The words become my mantra: I must have a history.

—Rubén Martínez, from *La Placita*

California has always been viewed as unique. Historian Carey McWilliams argues that the state is "exceptional" in its evolution—different from any other region of the globe and inhabited by a different breed of individuals. For McWilliams, California is "no ordinary state. It is an anomaly, a freak, the great exception among the American states."[1] The novelist Christopher Isherwood once called California "a tragic land—like Palestine, like every promised land."[2] Isherwood's comparison of California to the metaphoric New Jerusalem suggests both a biblical utopia, a cornucopia of natural resources and yet an unsettled and tragic land, consumed by the turmoil of its people. It may be the earthly representation of the Garden of Eden or the twisted torment of paradise. Critics may deride California, its unique culture, its diversity and unconventional politics. But dismissing California belies its cultural and political significance. The Golden State is a dominant exporter of ideas. California's popular culture is emulated from rural West Africa to the crowded capitals of the Pacific Rim. The state's policy debates—ranging from the sublime to the surreal—are exported to the rest of the United States as grassroots movements and policy innovations. Thus from tax revolts to gay rights, from affirmative action to immigration, from term limits to welfare reform, California is widely viewed as a cradle of cutting-edge social and political movements.

A DIVERSE HERITAGE

To understand California, it is necessary to place the state into historical perspective. There is evidence of human settlements in California dating back some 12,000 years. Nomadic tribes crossed the Bering Strait from Asia when the land bridge connected the two continents. The origins of California's diversity can trace its roots back to these indigenous peoples. James Rawls points out that the construct of the California Indian is a white invention: "It was created for the purposes of description and analysis, but it was also useful as a stereotype for whites overwhelmed by the diversity of the peoples encountered in the area."[3] The terminology also encapsulated an underlining assumption that all these diverse tribes were homogeneous and of one culture, language, and philosophy.

In reality, California's indigenous peoples were autonomous, nomadic, and diverse. Nearly 300,000 people lived in California before the first European explorers arrived. There were over 100 tribes, or "tribelets," averaging only 250 individuals; together they spoke over 80 distinct dialects. California's indigenous peoples may have had the greatest linguistic diversity in the world.[4] The Tolowa Modoc, Shasta, and Kavok tribes (of the Athabascan family), for example, lived on the border between Oregon and California; the Kawaiisu, Vanyume, Kitanemuk, Serrano, Tubatulabal, Miwok, and Monache tribes (of the Penutian and Shoshonean families) inhabited California's vast Central Valley region; and the Diegueno, Kamia, and Yuma tribes (of the Hokan family) dominated the southernmost part of the state, bordering Mexico.

These indigenous peoples evolved quite distinctly from their pre-Columbian cousins to the south. They had no common language, no regional confederation, and no permanent settlements—except for a handful of tribes such as the Mohave and Yuma that practiced agriculture. Nor were there great empires built like those of the Aztecs or Incas. California's earliest inhabitants were hunter-gatherers who roamed their territories, living off the abundant plants and wildlife. This was both a blessing and a curse. These communities were empowered with their own self-government and autonomy, but ultimately they were too small to collectively withstand the onslaught of Spanish conquest and colonization.

Conquest and Colonization

In 1542, a half-century after Christopher Columbus first came to the "New World," Spain claimed California as one of its possessions during the voyage of the Portuguese navigator Juan Rodriguez Cabrillo. The Spanish quickly lost interest in their new find, however. For almost two centuries, until the mid-1700s, Spain's western Pacific territory remained an outpost of limited commerce and settlement. By this time other European powers, notably France, Russia, and England, were exploring the region for potential new trading and commerce opportunities. Russian fur-trading posts were being established along the northern coastline above San Francisco (hence the name of Sonoma County's Russian River) and nearby Fort Ross.

In 1769 the Spanish ordered a small expedition headed by Gaspar de Portola as its military advisor and Father Junipero Serra as its Catholic missionary to move into "Alta California" to establish a series of missions, presidios (military bases), and pueblos in order to control the territory and convert the native population to Christianity. This process of "hispanicizing" the indigenous population was a unique settlement plan, in blunt contrast to the forced displacement of Indians by land-hungry immigrants common in other areas of the Spanish Empire.[5]

For the next 50 years, the Spanish colonizers built a string of missions running the length of California. They established California's first civilian settlements, or pueblos, in San Jose in 1777, and on September 4, 1781, they founded El Pueblo de Nuestra Señora la Reina de Los Angeles. Due in part to the Napoleonic wars and the remoteness of the colony itself, Spain was unprepared to devote much, if any, of its resources toward full colonization. It ruled the colony by proxy via its royal viceroy in Mexico City and at the height of its conquest had only about 3,000 subjects loyal to Spain living in California. Instead it used hispanicization and the indentured servitude of the native people to develop its missions. The Franciscan padres were used as the principle instrument of colonization. Accounts by the Spanish military troops housed in the presidios adjacent to the missions describe unusually harsh treatment by the Franciscans—surpassing even the cruelty of latter-day institutional slavery. By the end of the eighteenth century, some 13,000 Indians were held in 18 missions across California.[6]

The Spanish empire began to unravel by 1822, when Mexico broke from its colonial orbit. As Mexico moved to shed its clerical ties to the church, it secularized the California missions, giving civilian authority to its pueblos and introducing economic reforms. Mexico awarded large land grants for the development of *ranchos*—some up to a quarter of a million acres—as patronage to settlers strongly connected to governors sent from Mexico City. Emboldened by Mexico's weak administration, the rumors of a potential war between the United States and Mexico, and the onslaught of new American migrants flooding into California between 1830 and the mid-1840s, a short Yankee insurrection known as the Bear Flag Revolt began in 1846, led by John C. Fremont. The insurrection was soon to be overshadowed by the Mexican-American War.

The Mexican–American War

Following the Missouri Compromise, Texas applied for admission into the Union—as a slave state. This magnified the ongoing border dispute Texas had with Mexico, dating back to the 1830s. Against the backdrop of President James Polk's desire to fulfill "manifest destiny"—not only for the annexation of Texas, but also much of Utah, Colorado, Nevada, and all of California, Arizona, and New Mexico—the Texas boundary dispute was enough to launch the Mexican-American War of 1846. By January 1847, the U.S. military was in control of much of this territory, encountering little resistance and eventually capturing Mexico City itself. The provisional government signed the Treaty of Guadalupe Hidalgo in 1848 to cede these territories to the United States in exchange for a payment of $15 million and the recognition that Mexican Californians could become U.S. citizens if they so wished and that land titles issued by Mexico and Spain would be honored. One interesting provision of the treaty, later repealed in the state's second constitution, was the assurance that Spanish would remain one of California's official languages, along with English.

California's Boom

California's status as a sleepy possession of the United States under military rule ended with the discovery of gold at Sutter's Mill in January 1848. The gold rush brought in a quarter million settlers to the state between 1848 and 1853. Gold made California and the West a new promised land, first for miners, then for their suppliers, then for those who followed: ranchers, railroad tycoons, and land developers. Later, the discovery of "black gold," or oil, fueled an economic boom in Southern California. Offshore drilling of oil started as early as the 1920s off the coast of Santa Barbara. By the 1870s "green gold," or agricultural land, was to the Central Valley what gold was to Northern California and oil was to Southern California. By 1935 the great Central Valley, 100 miles wide and 500 miles long, was thriving due to the Central Valley Water Project, which created a grid of dams and channels to bring water to California's fertile fields.

As each of these "booms" hit, so did the arrival of new settlers armed with their own set of Yankee prejudices. They eventually outnumbered the original Mexican Californians, most of whom had pure or mixed Mexican blood. Land grants were compromised, businesses stolen outright, and quasi-legal maneuvers forced many into squalor. The native Indian population fared even worse. A de facto genocide was conducted against them from the time of the mission period. Ravaged by Western diseases, embattled by each wave of new colonizers, whole tribes became extinct: By the census of 1880, only 6 percent of the original 300,000 native Americans remained.

A smattering of symbols constantly reminds us of a previous civilization swept aside in the crush of Americanization. They are emblazoned on the street names as directional icons: Pico Boulevard and Olvera Street. They are assigned as names to jurisdictional counties and cities as if they were some trophy snatched away in the victory of a war: Modoc County, Shasta County, Mono County, San Francisco, Monterey, Santa Ana, and San Bernardino. They are evident in such architectural styles as Spanish Colonial and in the romance of the Old West celebrated in museums and festivals, symbolically preserving relics of a displaced culture even as its legacy was erased.

RAILROAD POLITICS

The Americanization of California could not have been accomplished without the arrival of the era's new technology: the railroad. The railroad transformed the demographics, commerce, and politics of the state. The Central Pacific Railroad, founded by Leland Stanford, Collins Huntington, Charles Crocker, and Mark Hopkins—the "Big Four"—transformed California during the 1860s from a remote island across the Sierra Nevada to an accessible destination. In six years California was linked by rail to virtually every major city in the United States. The heavy labor of building the rail lines and tunneling through the Sierras was done by a predominantly Chinese workforce, imported for their skill and willingness to work for a subsistence wage. Their impact on California's emerging commercial infrastructure is surpassed only by their impact on California's expanding cultural diversity.[7]

The Big Four's monopolization of the railroads and their commensurate control of the early political process would come to dominate California's economy and politics for the next 50 years. With shrewd politicking, they were able to convince state and federal taxpayers to fund their transcontinental railroad in the name of the "public interest." After Stanford became governor of California in 1862, he persuaded the state legislature to provide public subsidies and low-interest loans to the Central Pacific Railroad project, which was to be built from two directions, east and west, simultaneously. Another flow of funding came "voluntarily" from local cities and counties in the state, which were reasonably concerned that if they did not ante up, the railroad would simply be built around or away from their communities. When the city of San Bernardino refused to subsidize the Southern Pacific Railroad,[8] the company simply moved its proposed depot to a small town just southwest of the city—the town of Colton—where it served as the regional hub to move cargo and people into and out of the area.[9]

The last subsidy of the funding mosaic came from the federal treasury. For this, the Big Four relied on one of their own, Collins Huntington,[10] to be their point person and advocate in Washington. Through Huntington's East Coast political connections and his corporate position as vice president of the railroad, he was successful in getting Congress to pass the Pacific Railway Act in 1862. The federal government's financial largess was the final link: It provided large land grants from the public domain. Over the next century, Southern Pacific would become the largest landholder in the state, controlling over 11.5 million acres, or approximately 12 percent of all the state's land. The law also provided millions of dollars in long-term loans to subsidize the railroad. Upon completing the transcontinental railroad in 1869, the Big Four moved on to monopolize the state's entire transportation system. By the 1880s, these four men controlled 85 percent of all transportation in the state.

Business development closely followed the state's transportation growth. As a result of the Southern Pacific's deep ties to the state's economy, a vast political machine emerged on all levels of government in California. Political leaders, the state's major newspapers, and even the judiciary had a strong pro-railroad bias. When it came to the state's economic development, what was good for Southern Pacific was good for California. However, this marriage of corporate convenience was short-lived. The depression of the 1870s brought serious economic shifts to the state and consequently ushered in a more pessimistic mood, fueled by economic anxiety and manifesting in political activism and anti-Chinese xenophobia. The political empire built by the Big Four began unraveling, though the sustained power of Southern Pacific remained.

Xenophobia has been a common political feature in California since 1877. In September 1877, Dennis Kearney formed the Workingmen's Party in San Francisco, which was not only the first official opposition to the railroads but also one of the first organized xenophobic movements. The Kearneyites turned to the streets for mob action, denouncing not only the Big Four cartel but invoking the more potent rallying cry "The Chinese must go." Later, through more peaceful and traditional means of democratic change, they used the foil of the Workingmen's Party to organize a united front at the constitutional convention of 1878, which ultimately produced the second of California's two constitutions—the one in force today.

CALIFORNIA'S CONSTITUTION

The usual definition of *constitution* alludes to some framework of orderly systems and principles by which a diverse mass of citizens consent to be governed. This framework embodies not only "timeless" principles but also practical political compromises to resolve the power conflicts of the time in which they were written. California's two constitutions (1849 and 1879) are both lofty, visionary, and inspirational documents—as well as windows to the political currents of the historical periods during which they were drafted and ratified.

The First Constitution

To prepare California for admission into the Union in 1850, a constitutional convention was held in the fall of 1849. Nationally, the debate over California's admittance hung over the slavery controversy. Under the Missouri Compromise, California would be admitted as a free (non-slave) state. With this decided, the convention went about drafting the state's first constitution. The 48 delegates borrowed heavily from constitutions of other states, notably those of New York and Iowa, two states where many of the delegates had previously lived.

The constitution established a plural executive branch, whereby the governor, lieutenant governor, controller, superintendent of public instruction, attorney general, and surveyor general would all be elected separately by the voters. The legislature was bicameral—a senate and an assembly. The judiciary would be composed of lower courts and a supreme court. San Jose was chosen as the state capital. Perhaps most noteworthy, however, was the state constitution's explicit emphasis on basic civil liberties for its citizens. Article I, Section 1 of California's first constitution asserts: "All people are by nature free and independent and have inalienable rights. Among these are enjoying and defending life and liberty, acquiring, possessing, and protecting property, and pursuing and obtaining safety, happiness, and privacy." The U.S. Congress accepted the constitution, and on September 9, 1850, California was admitted as the 31st state in the Union.

The Second Constitution

The economic and social turmoil of the 1870s brought about the call for a new constitutional convention. The convention had a strong presence of Kearneyites and small farmers (represented by the Grange) who were allied in their pursuit to constitutionally limit the power of large corporations, banks, utilities, and the railroads. The delegates included strict regulatory oversights for these entities—although these have been gradually amended out of the constitution over the years. At the same time, there were other structural overhauls to the constitution. These included setting limits on taxing and spending by the legislature, refinement of the judicial branch, and the extension of civil liberties for some Californians. At the same time, pronounced anti-Asian (Chinese, in particular) exclusionary provisions worked to maintain a system of race-based employment and, later, housing discrimination. These became encrusted in the state constitution and were only repealed as late as 1952. Furthermore, the revised constitution took away the provision guaranteed in the Treaty of Guadalupe Hidalgo to place Spanish as one of the two official languages of California. The debates we have seen in California since the 1980s over English as the state's official language and over immigration reform are in fact longstanding political schisms that have challenged California's collective character for the past 130 years.

THE PROGRESSIVE MOVEMENT'S LEGACY

The Progressive movement emerged in California in the early 1900s, following a national trend, and brought about significant reforms in the way Californians viewed government. Every time we enter the voting booth to exercise our right to direct democratic initiatives to improve the living, working, and environmental conditions brought on by industrial and postindustrial society, we are participating in political reforms brought about by the Progressive movement. The Progressives were a professional, mostly white, middle-class reform movement that emerged as a response to the political corruption and excessive special-interest power that had been commonplace in major urban cities throughout the second half of the nineteenth century. They sought "progressive" reform, greater access to government, and greater control over "undesirable" classes—specifically working-class and immigrant populations. In California, that meant taking on the Southern Pacific Railroad. As the dominant corporation of its day, the Southern Pacific Railroad heavily influenced the legislature, courts, and most local and county offices.

The Progressives also fought for increased citizen participation and more accountability of elected officials. One of the defining variables that distinguished the California Progressives was their common distrust for centralized power and their desire to democratize every aspect of the decision-making process in order to incorporate more voices. As Chapter 7 discusses, the tools of "direct democracy" favored by the Progressives are still used today as an essential part of the electoral arsenal. Since the 1970s, a number of significant issues have reached the policy agenda through the initiative process, which was brought about by the Progressive movement. Proposition 13 (property tax reform), Proposition 187 (cutting basic services to undocumented immigrants), and Proposition 227 (banning bilingual education) owe their existence to the Progressive legacy.

The Progressives first organized the larger urban centers of California, and by 1907 had created the Lincoln-Roosevelt League within the Republican Party. The league was successful in fielding its own slate of reform candidates to the state legislature, and by 1908 they were in the statehouse, pushing for the dismantling of machine politics. They ended party nominations of future candidates by introducing the direct primary, allowing voters to directly choose their candidates. In 1910 Progressive Republican Hiram Johnson was elected governor, clearing the way for significant Progressive reform. His campaign theme was simple but effective: "Kick the Southern Pacific out of politics."

Between 1911 and 1913 the Progressives put into constitutional or statutory law the following reforms:

- The Public Utilities Commission was established to regulate the railroads and utilities (electricity, gas, and telephones).
- Women were extended the right to vote.
- Child labor laws were enacted.
- Worker compensation laws were enacted.
- Conservation and environmental regulations were passed.
- Party labels were removed to make local city, county, and special district elections nonpartisan. (This also applied to judicial and school board elections.)
- "Cross-filing" by candidates permitted them to seek nomination by any party.
- A civil service system for government workers broke the old patronage system.
- Perhaps the most enduring reform, the direct democracy tools of the initiative, referendum, and recall were created.

The Progressive Social Agenda

The Progressives were interested in more than political reform. They also pursued a nativist social agenda that sought to regulate class, cultural, and racial deviation from what they considered the white, middle-class norm. The message of the Progressives resonated and found saliency against a backdrop of large waves of immigration from western and southern Europe. The Progressive agenda became a national blueprint for business and upper-middle-class elites to close ranks against emerging ethnic constituencies and reframe the cultural debate in the language of electoral reform and government efficiency.[11] The Progressives led the national debate on more restrictive immigration reforms driven by the racism of "yellow-peril" hysteria. California was their testing ground. Noncitizens were forbidden to own land in the state. Chinese immigration was cut off by 1882 and Japanese immigration by 1924. Soon new "aliens" came from the South (Mexico) to feed the need of California growers for cheap agricultural workers. In this context, one can see that the current fight over California's social and cultural soul is only the latest onslaught in a century-long debate about what it means to be a Californian.

La Placita   *Rubén Martínez*

Newspapers, photos, diary notes, articles, stat sheets, and books—Christopher Isherwood's *A Single Man*, Rudy Acuña's *Occupied America*, Raymond Chandler's *The High Window*, Susan Kelly's *Mastering Word Perfect 5*—and family heirlooms surround me in a pile across what was once my father's bedroom. He stood at the picture window to my right during the air-raid blackouts of World War II, watching searchlights crisscross skies just like tonight's when a rusty-gray blanket hides the handful of stars that can survive the city glare.

   And I begin by lighting a votive candle emblazoned with the image of San Martín de Porres at the altar where I've gathered together the objects of the living and the dead: grandmother's finely molded hand mirror with the Deco engraving on the back (if I look into it now will I see her face instead of mine?); the wallet-sized photo of my girlfriend, her stare questioning my soul from three thousand miles away in Guatemala City where maybe I'd rather be; the brittle yellowed leaf from Palm Sunday at the Old Plaza Church, where Father Luis Olivares showered the thousands of Mexicanos and Centroamericanos surrounding him with holy water; the calling card that Hector Oqueli handed me three months before he was kidnapped and assassinated in Guatemala City; the cassette sleeve with the red-black-yellow slogans that Dago the ardent revolutionary gave me a month before a Salvadorian army bullet pierced his lung and he convulsed into his final breath during the FMLN guerrilla offensive of 1989 in downtown San Salvador.

   I continue by turning off the overhead light so that the candle flame transforms the shadow of the crucifix into a pair of outstretched arms. The faint, wavering light glows upon the photos of my late grandparents.

   I do this alone, in my grandparents' house in the L.A. neighborhood north of downtown known as Silver Lake. I do it because my grandmother once did it, each night with me before I said my prayers. I do this and many other things like it, here in this house, because I feel as if somehow my grandparents were living through me when I do. This is important—it is my history. There is much else that is my history, too; the things that pertain to my particular generation, which I experienced directly or indirectly and that make up my cultural and political vocabulary. Everything from Watergate to the Flintstones to Robert Kennedy's assassination and the time the white hippie from Marshall High spit on me, the brown scrub, while I walked home from Franklin Elementary; to the earthquakes and dozens of *noir* and war movies I watched with my father; to Rubén Salazar's death at the Chicano Moratorium and later on my own belated encounter with Revolution via Nicaragua and El Salvador and the subsequent disillusionments, and the sex, lies, and performance art of the eighties, and now The Walls Coming Down.

   And this is as close as it gets to home, right here in Silver Lake on this cool L.A. summer night looking down on a deserted Glendale Boulevard, a block above where my grandparents worked themselves into alcoholism and heart attacks at La Ronda, the Mexican restaurant they owned in the fifties and sixties and that now is a gay bar. "As close as it gets," because my home is L.A. and L.A. is an antihome. So, this journal is an attempt to gather together the strewn shards of my identity scattered like the beads of broken glass across the Golden State Freeway three miles north of here, where a few days ago a big rig hauling fifty thousand pounds of tomatoes crushed a trailer home, killing three of four members of a tourist family who'd come all the way from Canada to visit Disneyland.

   What surrounds me is my history, I repeat to myself. The words become my mantra: I must have a history.

"Baptism Souvenir," it says, in badly printed, kitschy cursive on the cardboard frame. "Our Lady Queen of the Angels (Old Mission Plaza)." A smiling kid swathed in virgin white, laid out horizontally before the silver-haired priest (horn-rimmed glasses, lips pursed), who the frame catches right at the moment he's letting the water fall on my head.

Our Lady Queen of the Angels Church, popularly known as La Placita, is the historic center of the city: where the city began, where I began. Every Sunday, at this modest mission founded in 1781, an average of 250 Mexicanos, Chicanos, and, increasingly, Centroamericanos, bring their babies to be baptized in the chapel christened Nuestra Señora la Reina de Los Angeles de Porciúncula—the original, overwrought Catholic name for L.A. They come, dressed to kill in rented suits and home-stitched silk dresses, and the photographers swarm around them, exactly as one George A. Pérez (whose name is printed on the back of the cardboard frame) accosted my family one Sunday twenty-eight years ago. I am cradled by my grandfather, whose hair is just beginning to turn gray. His aquiline, northern Mexican nose gives him an air of dignified *mestizo*-ness, right on the border between the *indígena* and the Spaniard; my grandmother (softer feathers, light-complected, large eyes, less *indígena*) holds my hand.

It is 1962, just before the October Missile Crisis. My grandparents' restaurant has taken shape on Glendale Boulevard. Elvis Presley stopped by not long ago (my grandparents had no idea who he was) and wrote, "Nice place, great food. Elvis Presley," on a napkin that is now my younger sister's prized possession.

My father is doing litho work at a place called Rapid Blue Print, making very good money ($1.50 an hour) for a first-generation Mexican. He likes to slick his hair but he is not a *pachuco*—he's proud to speak an accentless English as well as a perfect Spanish. And, as he will still say thirty years later, is proud to be better off than the *chusma*, the recently arrived immigrants who gather in squalor in the barrios to the south and to the east of La Placita. My mother's English is still awkward and heavily accented; she's doing her best at playing the classic housewife, watching a lot of TV (which inspires her to do her hair up Jackie Kennedy-style), singing nursery rhymes to me in Spanish in the afternoons, and probably still thinking a lot about her native El Salvador, which she left only a few years before.

My parents live in their newly built house in Silver Lake (only five minutes away from my grandparents). It's all very idyllic and I'm the model firstborn son; my parents have representatives of the fledgling Latino middle class over to the house often for martinis and cha-cha dancing, the men with Brylcreamed hair wearing sharp suits and thin ties and the women with knee-length solid-colored or polka-dotted dresses and teased, Roman-arched hair.

Father must work eighteen, sometimes twenty hours a day, and this begins to take its toll on my mother. Late one night, alone in the house with her son fast asleep, the isolation, her longing for the comfort of the large family she left behind in El Salvador and the vastness of a city she doesn't understand bring her to the verge of a breakdown. She locks herself in the bathroom. My father comes home and finds her still there, shaken and wordless, in the early morning hours. From this moment on, I begin to have nightmares about monsters lurking outside in the darkness of the city, poised to leap out and tear my family apart.

Nearly thirty years later, I'm still hanging out at La Placita. Something in or about that baptism water.

Today, a pierced blue sky. The famous "Santa Ana winds" have returned with their dry cowboy heat and blown the smog out to sea. Y.—who is here for a month before she returns to Guatemala—and I awake, slightly hungover, in my father's old bedroom. (Father told me recently that sleeping with a woman who is not my wife in my grandmother's house is probably enough to make her turn over in her grave.) . . .

We straggle out of bed and arrive at La Placita just in time for the eleven-thirty mass. La Placita today is not the church it was before the arrival in 1981 of Father Luis Olivares. Back then, it still leaned toward a touristy quaintness and was mainly attended by the Chicano and Mexicano middle class. Today, shrines paying tribute to the various Latino communities that make up the parish adorn the walls of the church—*El Cristo Negro de Esquipulas* (Guatemala), *El Santo Niño de Atocha* (El Salvador), *El Señor de los Milagros* (Peru), and, Olivares's favorite, the expressionistic lithograph depicting the assassination of Salvadorian archbishop Oscar Arnulfo Romero. Surrounding the church and in the internal patio, Olivares has allowed dozens of Latino street vendors to sell their wares, everything from bootlegged cassettes, tamales and *champurrados* to blinking plastic roses. The vast majority of the parishioners are recent arrivals—Mexicanos and Centroamericanos who came to La Placita because they already knew of the church and its controversial pastor long before they began their dangerous journeys north. La Placita has become a mythic haven on the well-trodden path to the American Dream; hundreds sleep in the church's shelter every night. In 1985, Olivares declared La Placita—in public defiance to the Immigration Reform and Control Act—a "sanctuary" for Central American refugees and the destitute undocumented from Mexico.

Whether or not La Placita will remain a haven for the poor is now in question, however. Months ago, Olivares's superiors of the Claretian Order announced that he would be transferred to a Fort Worth parish. And then, only two weeks before his scheduled departure, he fell gravely ill with what was initially diagnosed as meningitis with complications.

This Sunday was to have been his farewell. We enter the church, squeezing in with the typical overcapacity crowd. To everyone's surprise, Olivares is at his usual post, beneath the large image of the Vírgen de Guadalupe to the left of the altar. His head is bowed with exhaustion, and he is still wearing a hospital I.D. bracelet (his condition is listed as "serious" at Cedars-Sinai Hospital, and he will be rushed back immediately after the service). All eyes are fixed upon the now-fragile Olivares, whose voice once boomed out from the pulpit, challenging his parish to confront its enemies: the *migra*—the Immigration and Naturalization Service agents who flash their badges and ask for green cards—the LAPD, the U.S. government. He cradles his head in pain.

Associate pastor Michael Kennedy officiates the mass, but when it comes time for the homily, he hands the microphone to Olivares, who is so weak he can barely hold it. His voice begins in a weak whisper, but soon he is weaving a powerful and emotional sermon. He confides that the doctors have given him one or two years of life. "But I do not fear my death, my brothers and sisters. One must accept the will of God. If He wants me to stay on in this, this," he says, summoning a weak somewhat ironic smile before going on, "vale of tears, then I will stay. If He wishes me to leave, I will leave."

Father Luis Olivares bids La Placita farewell with these words: "Like John the Baptist called . . . so each of us, upon being baptized, is called to be a prophet of love and justice. I ask the Lord for a special blessing for this community that has fought so hard for justice, not only here and in Central America, but all over the world. May it continue to do so, to live out the true meaning of the Gospel." After saying this, he sinks back into the wheelchair, exhausted.

After the recitation of the Lord's Prayer, and during the traditional mutual offering of peace, an old Mexicana painfully canes her way up to the altar to touch Olivares. Next, a communion-aged boy does the same. Soon, a steady stream of parishioners is tearfully laying hands upon him. But suddenly a tall, attractive blond woman who has been standing near Olivares . . . puts a stop to this. Towering over the children and *ancianos* with tears in their eyes, she tells them to go back, "No más, no más," in a thickly accented Spanish.

Five days later, during my morning ritual at the Silver Lake house, I open the front door and pick up the morning edition of the *L.A. Times.* I scan the Metro section. . . . That page is now torn out, gathering dust on the floor along with all the other clippings:

Activist Priest Says He Has AIDs

Father Luis Olivares, the activist Roman Catholic priest and long-time champion of Central American refugees who had been hospitalized for the past month with meningitis, revealed Thursday that he has AIDS. Doctors said they believe that he contracted the disease from contaminated needles while undergoing treatment for other ailments while traveling in Central America. . . .

L.A. history begins at La Placita, and ends at La Placita. . . .

Source: Rubén Martínez, "La Placita," in David Reid, ed., *Sex, Death, and God in L.A.* Copyright © 1992 by Random House, Inc. Compilation copyright © 1992 by David Reid. Reprinted by permission of Pantheon Books, a division of Random House, Inc.

SUMMARY

California is no ordinary state. Its politics stem from the unique blend of circumstances and personalities that molded its history. Diverse groups—from California's original inhabitants to the early Europeans, to the Mexican conquest and the early gold prospectors, to the great post-World War II migration and its contemporary immigrants—have been arriving for generations in pursuit of opportunities, a pristine environment, and a better quality of life. Difficulties and growing pains notwithstanding, this great blending of peoples continues to be a testimony to the Golden State and its open arms.

NOTES

1. Carey McWilliams, *California: The Great Exception* (Westport, NY: Greenwood Press, 1971), p. 24.
2. Christopher Isherwood, as quoted in Leonard Michaels, David Reid, Raquel Scheer, eds., *West of the West: Imagining California* (Berkeley: University of California Press, 1989), p. 310.
3. Quoted in Sucheng Chan and Spencer C. Olin, *Major Problems in California History* (New York: Houghton Mifflin Co., 1997), p. 30.

4. Philip L. Fradkin, *The Seven States of California: A Human and Natural History* (Berkeley: University of California Press, 1997), p. 3.
5. James N. Gregory, "The Shaping of California History," in Sucheng Chan and Spencer C. Olin, *Major Problems in California History* (New York: Houghton Mifflin Co., 1997), p. 18.
6. David Lavender, *California: Land of New Beginnings* (Lincoln, NE: University of Nebraska Press, 1972), p. 69.
7. The State Railroad Museum in Sacramento's Old Town is a superb testament to the contribution Chinese Americans made to California's emerging importance as a political and economic power.
8. The Southern Pacific Railroad was acquired by the Central Pacific to provide regional rail links with the state, and it eventually became the namesake of the entire corporate identity.
9. Ward McAfee, *California's Railroad Era: 1850–1911* (San Marino, CA: Golden West Books, 1973), p. 123.
10. By the 1850s in Los Angeles, the Huntingtons were constructing a vast inter-urban streetcar system known as the Pacific Electric Company and constructed some 1,200 miles of track for their streetcars, which would feed the new main railroad depot built as Central Station.
11. See H. Eric Schockman, "Is Los Angeles Governable?" in Michael J. Dear, H. Eric Schockman, and Greg Hise, eds., *Rethinking Los Angeles* (Thousand Oaks, CA: Sage Publications, 1996), pp. 57–75.

CHAPTER 3

Political Culture and Politics in Postwar California

What thoughts I have of you tonight, Walt Whitman, for I walked down the side-streets under the trees with a headache self-conscious looking at the full moon.

In my hungry fatigue, and shopping for images, I went into the neon fruit super-market, dreaming of your enumerations!

What peaches and what penumbras! Whole families shopping at night! Aisles full of husbands! Wives in the avocados, babies in the tomatoes!—and you, García Lorca, what were you doing down by the watermelons?

I saw you, Walt Whitman, childless, lonely old grubber, poking among the meats in the refrigerator and eyeing the grocery boys.

I heard you asking questions of each: Who killed the pork chops? What price bananas? Are you my Angel?

I wandered in and out of the brilliant stacks of cans following you, and followed in my imagination by the store detective.

We strode down the open corridors together in our solitary fancy tasting arti-chokes, possessing every frozen delicacy, and never passing the cashier.

Where are we going, Walt Whitman? The doors close in an hour. Which way does your beard point tonight?

(I touch your book and dream of our odyssey in the supermarket and feel absurd.)

Will we walk all night through solitary streets? The trees add shade to shade, lights out in the houses, we'll be lonely.

Will we stroll dreaming of the lost America of love past blue automobiles in dri-veways, home in our silent cottage?

Ah, dear father, graybeard, lonely old courage-teacher, what America did you have when Charon quit poling his ferry and you got out on a smoking bank and stood watching the boat disappear on the black waters of Lethe?

—Allen Ginsberg, "A Supermarket in California,"
from *Reality Sandwiches*. Reprinted by permission.

The term *political culture* describes shared beliefs, values, and attitudes about how government should function. Researchers have sought to explain how political cul-ture accounts for variations in the behavior of individuals and institutions, as well as the public policies of states and nations. American political culture emphasizes the values of classical liberalism, including individualism, freedom, equality, democracy, and capitalism. But these values often collide, as they did in the California tax revolt of the 1970s. Debates over public spending often mask conflict over more fundamental values.

Contemporary ideologies such as liberalism and conservatism represent popular belief systems that emphasize competing values within the same political culture.[1] They offer a prescription for the appropriate role of government in society. Liberals tend to place more of an emphasis on equality, tolerance, and aid to the disadvantaged, for example, while conservatives tend to emphasize order, economic growth, and preserving what they perceive as "traditional values." Even when accounting for variations in the variables that explain voting patterns such as race, income, education and religion, Californians are more likely to hold liberal views on social issues than residents of other states.[2]

Individualism is a central tenet of California's political culture. Since statehood, California history has been written by an eclectic cast that includes frontier explorers and exploiters, opportunity-seeking migrants, and progressive reformers with a strong belief in the active, virtuous citizen of the polis. This unique history has produced a political culture that encourages policy innovation by politicians, mistrust of large traditional organizations such as political parties and big business, and a strong belief in direct democracy. The political successes—and failures—of state government between the 1940s and 1990s reflect California's iconoclastic, and often conflicted, political culture.

THE POSTWAR ERA

After World War II California's political culture was transformed as the two major parties adapted to changing conditions. Rapid growth and change upset the balance of state politics, invigorating the Democratic party and ending the dominance by moderate Republicans such as Earl Warren and Goodwin Knight. In the late 1950s, California's post-Progressive, nonpartisan politics gave way to the more competitive, ideologically charged politics of two-party rivalry.

California experienced unprecedented growth in the postwar period. The promise of prosperity attracted migrants from all over the country and the world. Here they found warmer climes, inexpensive housing, and well-paying jobs in a booming economy, particularly in the Cold War defense and aerospace industries. By 1962 California had become the most populous state in the nation. During this period, increasing ideological polarization of the parties upset the equilibrium in state politics that had rested on a consensus on several bipartisan issues, including government efficiency, weak parties, citizen participation, and popular New Deal social programs. Bipartisan support was instrumental to the success of Republican Governors Warren and Knight, since Democrats held a substantial voter registration edge from the time of the Great Depression. The Republican party had dominated state government for most of the century, from the Progressive Era until 1957.

During this time, Republicans had the winning edge in all but one election for governor. They also controlled both houses of the legislature, except for a brief period in the 1930s when Democrats controlled the assembly.

One factor that impeded the Democrats' success was cross-filing, a reform mechanism left over from the Progressives. Cross-filing was based on the logic that voters of California should have the right to elect the most qualified individual for an office and not be swayed by the candidate's party label. A single ballot was distributed in California primaries, allowing candidates from one party to seek the nomination of another party. Under this confusing system, Democrats could run as Republicans and vice versa, and nominations were consequently won on the basis of a candidate's ability to spend on his or her campaign. This sometimes had odd results. In 1952, for example, Republican Senator William Knowland was the nominee of both the Republican and Democratic parties.[3]

Although registration numbers favored the Democrats, party loyalty was weak. It was a common strategy for Republican candidates to appeal to Democratic voters. The system of cross-filing was modified by a 1952 statewide initiative, requiring candidates to list their party affiliation on the ballot. A sunset provision ended cross-filing altogether in 1959.[4]

Republican Governor Earl Warren was elected in 1942, carried into office by his commitments to restoring the nonpartisan spirit of the Progressive tradition and reforming state government. Warren was less conservative than his Republican predecessors, bringing to Sacramento what seemed like a Democratic agenda (although it could be called a "nonpartisan" agenda), including such statutory priorities as unemployment insurance, better pensions, and increased health insurance coverage. Thus, Warren had established himself as a moderate-to-liberal executive even before he was tapped by President Eisenhower to join the Supreme Court. As Chief Justice, Warren was criticized by some conservatives for controversial decisions in cases ranging from school desegregation, to school prayer, to the rights of the accused.

Eisenhower's appointment of Warren more than midway through his third term as governor left the incumbent lieutenant governor, Republican Goodwin Knight, to assume the governorship. Knight governed as a moderate, supporting legislation popular with labor and other Democratic constituencies, while keeping much of Warren's agenda alive. He successfully preserved his predecessor's bipartisan electoral base, winning election in 1954 in his own right. With increasing party polarization, however, Democrats turned out in force at the next election to send Democratic state Attorney General Edmund G. "Pat" Brown to the governor's office.[5]

THE PAT BROWN LEGACY

The 1958 election was a turning point in California's political history. Pat Brown's victory and Democratic majorities in the legislature began an era of Democratic dominance of state politics. The professionalization of the state legislature bolstered the party by bringing in candidates with working- and middle-class backgrounds, who would never have run as candidates in a part-time, or "amateur," legislature that favored wealthy candidates and those with outside sources of income. The effect of this reform was to help Democrats attract better candidates and retain good legislators by making politics a practical career alternative.

This era was marked by an ideological struggle between two competing strains of liberalism. Long excluded from governing, California's liberals now saw an opportunity to fulfill the promises of the New Deal, which they felt had been compromised by a generation of Republican leadership. However, conditions had changed since the 1930s, and there was little agreement on exactly how the New Deal should be applied in the more prosperous—and populous—California of the 1950s and 1960s.

The intraparty tension over competing visions of the proper role of government was personified by the political rivalry between Brown and the assembly's powerful speaker, Jesse M. Unruh.[6] Brown represented the traditional view of liberalism in California: the need for an activist government to invest in the state's future through large-scale capital projects and social programs. Unruh, on the other hand, was a pragmatist concerned with the future of the Democratic party in a post-New Deal world. Brown's ideology was an "emotive," or "soft" liberalism, strongly committed to advancing the agenda of the New Deal, while Unruh represented more of a "rational," or "hard" liberalism designed to sustain the party's majority by adapting the New Deal agenda to contend with changing realities.[7]

Pat Brown's Soft Liberalism

Pat Brown may best be remembered as the "master builder" of modern California. He pushed for a large bond measure funding the construction of the State Water Project to bring Northern California water to the aqueducts of the Central Valley and to the cities and suburbs of Southern California. The measure passed by a slim margin. The Brown administration wrote the "Master Plan for Higher Education," expanding college admissions to all qualified children of California residents, as well as expanding the physical infrastructure of the entire system by building more accessible regional campuses for the University of California and the California State University systems. As the process of suburbanization took hold, Brown oversaw the transfer of federal transportation dollars to the state, aiding in the construction of hundreds of new miles of freeways and the funding of public transit. Brown signed the Unruh Civil Rights Act, a state version of the 1964 U.S. Civil Rights Act, preventing discrimination in public accommodations, employment, and housing. At great political peril, he also opposed a ballot measure to repeal the 1964 Rumford Fair Housing Act, a law banning racial discrimination in the sale of homes. The repeal passed overwhelmingly, only to be declared unconstitutional by the courts.

Jesse Unruh's Hard Liberalism

Unruh stood for a new liberalism that was less interventionist and less generous than many of his fellow Democrats wanted. He recognized that it was becoming increasingly problematic for Democrats to adhere to an ideology that vilified big business and greedy capitalists in an age when workers enjoyed unprecedented economic opportunities and a rising standard of living. It was also problematic because of the numerous partnerships that had developed between government and business during the Cold War. Furthermore, he understood that the depression era logic of appealing to the interests of the disadvantaged and minorities could no longer guarantee enough votes to win elections in a large state. So many people had benefited from postwar prosperity that the old Democratic strategy seemed like a recipe for failure.

A World War II veteran and son of a sharecropper, Unruh was elected from an assembly district representing Inglewood and south-central Los Angeles and ascended quickly to the leadership. After becoming speaker in 1961, Unruh became known as the "Boss" and the "Big Daddy" of California politics because of his strict control of the assembly and his use of the institution as a vehicle for his own legislative agenda. His strategy was to manage the state's panoply of programs as efficiently as possible, while continuing to champion the working poor. Thus, Democrats could claim for themselves the banner of "good government," which had been the property of the Republicans ever since the Progressive era.

In contrast to the expansive policy proposals of the past, Unruh's Democrats advanced a much more limited, incremental policy agenda. Even as he shepherded Brown's legislative agenda through the assembly to build aqueducts and universities, Unruh himself favored a more modest role for government. Through progressive civil rights and consumer protection legislation, Unruh sought to make life easier for "the common man."[8]

Unruh's brand of liberalism created tension among the party faithful. In particular, Unruh's approach was at odds with the volunteers of the California Democratic Council (CDC). The CDC was a political club founded by Alan Cranston to overcome the confusion of cross-filing by endorsing candidates, providing Democratic voters with information and direction prior to election day. The CDC favored stronger bonds between organized labor and the party, as well as an activist role for government, including an expanded welfare state and détente with the Soviet Union. While Brown was content to enlist their support, Unruh sought to curtail the influence of CDC volunteers in state Democratic politics, fearing that their presence might jeopardize the party's appeal to the mainstream.[9]

Pat Brown lost his bid for a third term in 1966. Though Brown had defeated former Vice President Richard Nixon to be reelected in 1962, he lost four years later to a Hollywood actor named Ronald Reagan by more than a million votes. At the time, the state and nation were undergoing profound social and economic changes. The Democratic party was wounded politically by civil unrest, including opposition to the war in Vietnam and racial strife in urban enclaves such as the Watts neighborhood of Los Angeles and San Francisco's Hunter's Point. While the election was in some part a referendum on the social turmoil of the late 1960s, the voters were losing their taste for the government activism that Brown symbolized.[10] Two years later, the Democrats lost their majority in both houses of the legislature. After more difficult lessons at the polls, the hard liberalism of Jesse Unruh would come to be embraced as the dominant ideology of the party. This conversion took place both in California and nationally, as Democratic leaders from Dianne

Feinstein to Bill Clinton took up the cause of "good government," calling for fiscal conservatism while advancing modest legislative agendas designed to make life easier for the average working person. Unruh himself would play little part in the party's changing ideology. He served the remainder of his political career as California's state treasurer after losing his own bid for governor in 1970—to the incumbent Ronald Reagan.

CONSERVATISM MEETS POPULISM: THE REAGAN REVOLUTION

Part of Ronald Reagan's appeal was that he appeared to be an outsider unsullied by Sacramento politics, much like his early predecessor Hiram Johnson. An effective manipulator of symbols, Reagan emulated the cowboy heroes of his western films, riding into Sacramento for a showdown with big-spending Democrats in the legislature. With the Republican success in the 1968 election, driven in part by Californian Richard Nixon's successful bid for the presidency, Reagan was able to partner with a Republican-controlled legislature. But that Republican majority was short-lived.

Reagan's style of conservatism was as different from the Progressive and Eisenhower era Republicans as Unruh's liberalism was from the New Deal Democrats. Like his Republican predecessors, Reagan supported conservative causes such as low taxes, deregulation, anticommunism, and self-reliance over government aid. He also tapped a reservoir of frustration by railing against government itself, criticizing lawmakers and the bureaucrats in public service as contributing to the problems they purported to solve. He gave voice to popular frustration with the state's rapidly expanding welfare system, striking a moral tone in his attacks on recipients of Aid to Families with Dependent Children (AFDC). Reagan's mean-spirited attack on AFDC recipients as financially irresponsible and sexually promiscuous "welfare queens" polarized the discourse. The "welfare queen" stereotype reinforced a populist view that welfare recipients were not like you and me and were undeserving of government largess. After his loss to Reagan, former Speaker Unruh predicted that conservative politicians would have an easy time dividing the white working class in future elections.[11]

Reagan had some success in trimming the state budget. Much of this was accomplished by passing on the demands of the growing population through unfunded mandates, or requiring county governments to provide services without offering financial assistance to pay for them.[12] By the end of his two terms as governor, however, California's taxes and the state budget had increased dramatically. Even if he lost those battles, Reagan eventually won the war. His fusion of conservatism and populism became the dominant ideology of the right wing in state and national politics. After leaving office in 1974, Reagan mounted a strong primary challenge to President Gerald Ford. Later, Reagan's populist-conservative message resonated nationally, helping him win two terms as president.

THE POLITICS OF DIVIDED GOVERNMENT

The election of Reagan as governor in a year when Democrats retained their majority in the legislature began what seems to have become a permanent fixture of contemporary California politics: divided government. When no single party controls the apparatus of state government, either during a particular legislative term or over the long haul, internal divisions make policy innovation extremely difficult. Control of California's executive and legislative branches of government has often been divided. Except for the periods of unified Republican government (1969–1971) and unified Democratic government (1975–1983 and 1998–2003), California has lived with divided government since 1967. For much of the past four decades, there has been a Republican governor and a Democratic majority in at least one chamber of the legislature.

California is not unique in this respect. Since the 1950s, divided government has become an increasingly common outcome of state and national elections.[13] Divided government disappeared temporarily in California after 1974, a banner election year for Democrats. The Watergate scandal had not only brought down the Nixon administration, but Republican candidates nationwide were wounded politically in the fallout. When Governor Reagan decided not to seek a third term, Lieutenant Governor Ed Reinecke hoped to succeed him but was indicted (and later acquitted) for perjury in a scandal of his own over campaign finance. Amid a powerful anti-Republican tide, the Republican nominee, State Controller Houston Flournoy, lost by just 180,000 votes to Edmund G. (Jerry) Brown, Jr.

THE JERRY BROWN YEARS

The son of former Governor Pat Brown, Jerry Brown represented a new generation of Democratic leaders. His philosophy of government was more akin to the hard liberalism of Jesse Unruh than the soft liberalism of his father. Unlike Democrats of an earlier era, Brown rejected traditional big-government approaches to public problems, although he shared their commitment to the values of fairness and equality. Brown's campaign for governor received a boost by a wave of popular support for campaign finance reform in the aftermath of Watergate. As secretary of state, he drafted the political reform initiative Proposition 9, which appeared on the 1974 primary ballot. This measure required full disclosure of contributions to and expenditures by campaigns for state and local office, as well as campaigns for ballot initiatives. The successful linkage of his candidacy to the creation of his popular "citizen's initiative" captured the sentiments of the time and would come to be a model for many subsequent candidates and other ambitious politicians in California.

Brown, who had studied for many years as a Jesuit seminarian, thought in global and environmental terms and connected well with those traditionally marginalized from the political process. He understood the plight of the United Farm Workers and helped move the legislature in establishing the Agricultural Labor Relations Board as a state arbitrator between the rights of field laborers and the production goals of agribusiness. He opened the door to executive appointments for women and people of color on state boards, commissions, and the judiciary. He worked hard for the expansion of education, the health and safety concerns of all workers, and the environmental movement. But his efforts to balance his policy agenda often put him at odds with his traditional allies. In the name of environmental protection, Brown cut the state transportation budget for highway construction, diverting funds instead into mass transit development, and even bicycle paths. And, though a strong proponent of higher education, Brown earned the ire of state university professors by suggesting that their intellectual satisfaction with their work constituted a type of "psychic income," making an actual salary increase less necessary than for other state employees.

TAXPAYER REVOLT

The 1970s saw an extended period of high inflation, economic stagnation, and high unemployment in California and elsewhere around the nation. Ironically, as the state's fiscal health deteriorated, the tax system continued to reap large surpluses. Property taxes soared during the mid-1970s, as average property values in the state increased at an annual rate of 12 percent. As consumer prices and salaries increased, so too did revenues from sales and income taxes. By 1978, the state budget had accumulated a $6 billion surplus. Property tax reformers Howard Jarvis and Paul Gann read the popular frustration with this state of affairs and successfully petitioned to have Proposition 13 placed on the June 1978 primary ballot. The initiative cut property taxes by 60 percent and limited future taxes to 1 percent of assessed real estate value. Governor Brown backed a more moderate proposal, which failed at the ballot box. Proposition 13 passed by a two-to-one margin.

Proposition 13 represented a contest over political culture as much as it was an effort to provide taxpayer relief. Under the surface of the tax revolt were deep-seated attitudes about the proper role of government in society. As Table 3.1 suggests, the strongest support for Proposition 13 came from white, middle-aged, fully employed male homeowners. Minorities and the poor were less likely to support the initiative, even though they were the most likely to suffer the effects of high taxes. Supporters were more likely to believe that there was a problem with government waste, and this view was strongly related to a desire to cut welfare and other public assistance programs for the poor. At the same time, supporters were against cutting fire and police protection, education, mass transit, and mental health services. This paradox suggests that the support for the tax revolt was motivated, in part, to restrict government activism in specific unpopular policy areas. This observation led researchers David Sears and Jack Citrin to term the movement a "revolt of the haves."[14] As we will see in Chapter 5, Proposition 13 led directly to the reduced capacity of California's local governments to provide services to its burgeoning population.

Jerry Brown's two terms in office stand as proof that political paralysis and tension can be a problem even when the governor and both houses of the legislature are of the same party. One of Brown's strengths during his first term was connecting

TABLE 3.1 SUPPORT FOR PROPOSITION 13, BY DEMOGRAPHIC GROUP, MAY 1978

GROUP	% IN FAVOR	GROUP	% IN FAVOR
INCOME		*AGE*	
Less than $10,000	52	18–24	49
$11,000–$20,000	59	25–34	56
$21,000–$30,000	67	35–49	62
More than $30,000	69	50–64	71
		65+	69
EDUCATION			
Less than high school	74	*SEX*	
High school	68	Male	66
Some college	64	Female	59
College grad	69		
Beyond college	49	*ETHNICITY*	
		White	66
RESIDENCE		Hispanic	60
Bay Area	64	Black	18
Other Northern California	59		
Other Southern California	58		
LA & Orange Counties	66		
Homeowners	69		
Renters	46		

Source: May 1978 California Poll, reprinted in Sears and Citrin, 1982. Entries are the percentage of respondents from each demographic group expressing support for Proposition 13.

directly with the voters and bypassing the established rules and leadership of the legislative establishment. By his second term, this became a liability, as his relationship with his Democratic colleagues soured. His opposition to Proposition 13 and his administration's philosophy of imposing an "era of limits" added to this tenuous relationship. His campaigns for the presidency in 1976 and 1980 left his supporters feeling abandoned. Brown made some noteworthy achievements, yet he could have done more if he had worked to cultivate the support of his own party in the legislature, rather than grandstanding alone for policy change. His popularity waning, Brown was defeated by San Diego Mayor Pete Wilson in a 1982 bid for the U.S. Senate seat being vacated by Republican S. I. Hayakawa. Brown remained active in politics, including a third unsuccessful run for the Democratic presidential nomination. Later, after two terms as Mayor of Oakland, Brown was elected to his father's old job of Attorney General in 2006.

RETURN TO DIVIDED GOVERNMENT

Republican Attorney General George Deukmejian ran a strong law-and-order campaign and squeaked into the governorship in 1982, defeating Los Angeles Mayor Tom Bradley by fewer than 100,000 votes out of approximately 7.8 million cast. In a surprising rematch four years later, Democrats again fielded Tom Bradley against the incumbent Deukmejian. This time, Deukmejian won a smashing landslide over Bradley, by more than 1.7 million votes. It was in many ways a battle of ideological extremes: Bradley, a liberal African-American big-city mayor against Deukmejian, a conservative, law-and-order veteran of the Sacramento "beltway." The governor was helped by a high turnout of conservative voters, drawn to the ballot box to defeat a gun control initiative. With Proposition 62, an enhancement of Proposition 13's property tax reform, also appearing on the ballot, the gun lobby and the tax reform lobby were given a strong incentive to mobilize conservative voters.

A former attorney, Deukmejian had a style that was rather bland compared to his charismatic predecessors, Reagan and Brown. But he possessed important managerial skills necessary for the chief executive of the nation's largest state. At times his leadership style could be partisan, as when he battled for the creation of a redistricting commission (Proposition 39) to oversee the state reapportionment process then controlled by the Democratic legislature. On the issue of the judiciary, he was uncompromising. He successfully campaigned for a ballot initiative for the recall of California Supreme Court Justices Rose Bird, Cruz Reynoso, and Joseph Grodin (all appointed by Jerry Brown) for their reluctance to enforce the death penalty. Following their removal by the voters, he was given a windfall opportunity to name three new justices who reflected his own judicial philosophy. All the same, Deukmejian at times found common ground with Democrats and the legislative leadership. He signed legislation for a bold experiment to mandate new welfare-to-work rules by establishing the GAIN (Greater Avenues for Independence) workforce program. An American of Armenian heritage and personally sensitive to issues of human rights, Deukmejian also pushed for a $5 million state allocation for the Los Angeles–based Museum of Tolerance to educate future generations about ethnic diversity and genocide.

The mood of the electorate in 1990 was one of dissatisfaction, if not rage. California's economy was sliding into recession, and several state legislators were implicated in scandals such as "Shrimpgate."[15] The most visible response by voters was the passage of Proposition 140, which created a constitutional amendment to limit legislators' terms of office, end pension benefits for future legislators, and cut legislators' personal office budgets by 40 percent.[16] Proposition 140 was an unambiguous expression of the public's displeasure with the legislature, both for the ethical breaches of individual members and for their collective inability to get things done. Term limits as an instrument for enacting better public policy and getting "new blood" into the system will be discussed in detail in Chapter 7.

In 1990 Republicans nominated U.S. Senator Pete Wilson to replace the retiring George Deukmejian. Wilson went on to defeat the Democratic candidate, former San Francisco Mayor Dianne Feinstein, by 3 percentage points (49 to 46 percent) after she survived a bruising primary battle with Attorney General John Van de Kamp. Initially, Wilson's election as governor in 1990 was marked by some Democratic lawmakers with a sigh of relief and as the end to gridlock partisan politics in Sacramento. Wilson was known in his party as a "traditional moderate," a pragmatic middle-of-the-roader, pro-business and pro-choice. Early in his first term as governor, Wilson demonstrated his willingness to work with Democrats. For example, faced with unrelenting budget crises, he agreed to a round of new taxes. Wilson also supported policies protecting the rights of gays and lesbians. He supported legislation that prohibited discrimination by private-sector employers, and he continued an executive order, first issued by Jerry Brown, to protect state government workers from discrimination based on sexual orientation.

But by 1994, with his public approval plummeting, Wilson had moved from the center to the right and adopted a more confrontational style. He frequently clashed with the Democratic state legislature. He battled over reapportionment, threatening to veto any plan that he found unacceptable.[17] He also pushed controversial initiatives on hot-button issues including crime (e.g., Three Strikes (Proposition 220), illegal immigration (Proposition 187), and affirmative action (Proposition 209)).[18] Wilson won reelection by a wide margin over the Democratic challenger, State Treasurer Kathleen Brown, a victory he parlayed into a brief campaign for the Republican presidential nomination. Although much of Wilson's tenure in office was marred by a recessionary fiscal crisis, a booming economy in his second term freed up resources to repair the state's infrastructure. When the state received an unprecedented $4.4 billion windfall, Wilson called for more spending on education, public works, and social programs.[19] Wilson directed new state dollars to education to reduce class size (see Chapter 13) as well as to augment the state's child care budget, in anticipation of lifting poor, single working women out of welfare by providing support for their children while they are at work.

Wilson's successor for his party's nomination in 1998, Dan Lungren, hoped to capitalize on the successes of the Wilson years but was unsuccessful. A conservative Republican, Lungren had trouble drawing support beyond his ideological base. An additional liability for the Republican standard-bearer was Wilson's support for Proposition 187 (illegal immigration), which angered many Latino voters. As attorney general, Lungren had led the state's appeal of the controversial initiative after its most restrictive provisions were struck down in state court. After 16 years, the Democrats recaptured the Governor's mansion when Lungren lost by a 20-point margin to Lieutenant Governor Gray Davis. A former chief of staff to Governor Jerry Brown, Davis emerged as the last candidate standing after a bruising primary battle with two strong opponents, and then sailed to victory in the fall election.

CALIFORNIA POLITICS IN THE TWENTY-FIRST CENTURY

By the close of the twentieth century, California was no longer the conservative bastion that launched the careers of Nixon and Reagan. Decades of population growth and social change had produced a more diverse electorate, which seemed to favor moderate leaders. In every way, Gray Davis seemed to be the right kind of politician for this new California. His centrist politics evoked the hard liberalism of an earlier generation of California Democrats. Davis campaigned on a strategy of "triangulation," positioning himself in between the Republicans and the more liberal members of his own party in the legislature.[20] Davis avoided ideological fights and polarizing issues, although his support for California's controversial "three-strikes" law and the death penalty, as well as his neutrality on Proposition 187, irked many liberals but won support from moderates and independents.

At the dawn of the new century, the state was facing serious problems, and the safe approach to politics that Davis favored had fallen out of favor. A perfect storm of the sagging economy, the energy crisis, and an exploding budget deficit was already brewing before his reelection victory over Republican Bill Simon. As conditions worsened, Davis failed to reassure the voters that he could effectively deal with the state's problems. Just eight months after he was reelected, the bland, experienced, and cautious Davis was recalled and replaced with someone who was in many ways his opposite, Republican Arnold Schwarzenegger. The former bodybuilder and action-movie star was no conventional politician, but his ascent was the latest example of a tradition of outsider-governors in California. Like Ronald Reagan in the 1960s, Schwarzenegger traded on his celebrity name from the movie industry and rode a wave of voter discontent with the state's handling of social and economic problems. Like the Progressive Republican Hiram Johnson, Schwarzenegger promised sweeping reforms in Sacramento; and he came into power with the help of one of the instruments of the Progressives—the recall election. (The recall will be discussed at length in Chapter 7.)

POLITICAL CULTURE AND POLITICS IN POSTWAR CALIFORNIA

Political culture in California is a contested terrain. The policy approaches emerging over the past 50 years are as much about defining the cultural nature of politics as they are about mitigating specific problems. Republicans from Reagan to Wilson have worked to reduce the scope of governmental regulation in the lives of Californians, arguing consistently that most problems are better resolved in the private sector. Democrats from Pat Brown to Gray Davis have sought to build statewide consensus on traditional liberal values such as public education, infrastructure investment, civil rights, and broad social safety nets. There are different approaches—from the New Deal approaches of Brown to the cautious approaches of Unruh and Davis—but Democrats continue to see an important role for government in meeting the state's challenges. Schwarzenegger, the outsider, has fluctuated between conservative and liberal approaches to solving public problems.

SUMMARY

This chapter has shown that California politics is as much a contest over values as a vehicle to solve problems. As the state experienced phenomenal growth and change, the centrist, non-ideological politics of postwar California gave way to competitive, highly partisan politics by the 1960s. Then, for several years, Republicans were largely on the sidelines as Democrats battled over two competing visions of liberalism. The emotive liberalism of Pat Brown envisioned an active government to preserve and advance the New Deal agenda in a new age, while the bureaucratic liberalism of Jesse Unruh envisioned a limited government, one with more modest goals, which would still protect the interests of the disadvantaged. Before this debate was settled in favor of Unruh's vision, a new generation of California Republicans emerged with a drastically different prescription for the role of government. By infusing conservatism with populism, politicians such as Ronald Reagan promoted an appealing new style of conservatism, more "anti-government" than the old "good government" philosophy of previous Republicans. This anti-government sentiment was felt in the passage of Proposition 13, which severely curtailed activism by local governments. The tension between these competing strains of political ideology redefined the boundaries of the state's political culture. And yet, the contest remains unfinished. It is likely that Californians will continue to use the apparatus of state government to push specific visions of political culture. And, as the state's demographic makeup continues to shift, this contest is likely to become even more passionate.

NOTES

1. See Herbert McClosky and John Zaller, *The American Ethos* (Cambridge, MA: Harvard University Press, 1984).
2. Robert S. Erikson, John P. McIver, and Gerald C. Wright, Jr., "State Political Culture and Public Opinion," *American Political Science Review* 81 (1987): 797–813.
3. For more on the problems associated with cross-filing, see James R. Mills, *A Disorderly House* (Berkeley, CA: Heyday Books), pp. 204–205.
4. Cross-filing re-emerged in 1998, in the form of the blanket primary, after voters approved Proposition 198.
5. Republican U.S. Senator William Knowland decided he wanted to win his party's gubernatorial primary, rather than defer to Knight, the incumbent, who had expressed interest in running for re-election. Hoping to avoid a political bloodbath, a "big switch" deal was brokered by another native-son Californian, Vice President Richard Nixon. Knight would simply run for the Senate seat, and Knowland would run for the governorship. The switch failed, and neither Republican won election, handing the statehouse to Brown.
6. For a broader account of the political feud between Brown and Unruh, see Ethan Rarick, *California Rising: The Life and Times of Pat Brown* (Berkeley: University of California Press, 2005).
7. Garrin Burbank, "The Ambitions of Liberalism: Jesse Unruh and the Shape of Postwar Democratic Politics in California," *Southern California Quarterly* 21 (1997): 487–502.
8. James Mills, *A Disorderly House: The Brown–Unruh Years in Sacramento* (Berkeley, CA: Heyday Books, 1987).
9. Ibid.
10. Of course, other factors contributed to Brown's loss. These included a falling out with the party's left wing over his handling of antiwar protests on college campuses, the refusal of the CDC and organized labor to endorse him, and a primary challenge by Los Angeles Mayor Sam Yorty, which weakened him politically.
11. Burbank, "The Ambitions of Liberalism."

12. Before the passage of Proposition 13, the counties still had the capacity to absorb some of these additional expenses.
13. For an analysis of this phenomena at both the national and state levels, see Morris Fiorina, *Divided Government* (New York: Macmillan, 1992).
14. David O. Sears and Jack Citrin, *Tax Revolt: Something for Nothing in California* (Cambridge, MA: Harvard University Press, 1982).
15. Shrimpgate was an FBI sting operation that created a fictitious shrimp-packing company willing to trade money for members' votes. Several Sacramento lawmakers and lobbyists were snared. In its aftermath, the public became much more pessimistic about the state's campaign finance system and about state politics in general. See Steve Scott, "The Legacy of the Capitol Sting," *California Government and Politics Annual 1995–1996* (Sacramento: California Journal Press, 1995), pp. 35–38.
16. See Chapter 6 for a complete discussion of Proposition 140.
17. A. G. Block, "The Reapportionment Failure," *California Journal* 22, no. 11 (November 1991): 503–505.
18. See Chapter 6 for a full discussion on these initiatives.
19. Dan Morain, "Upbeat Wilson Sees More School Spending," *Los Angeles Times*, 15 May 1998, A1.
20. Dan Walters, "Davis Again Needs Help from Liberals He Once Shunned." *Sacramento Bee*, July 21, 2003, A3.

CHAPTER 4

People, Diversity, and Culture

Together, we have created what Gloria Anzaldua celebrated as a "borderland"—a place where "two or more cultures edge each other, where people of different races occupy the same territory." How can all of us meet on communal ground? "The struggle," Anzaldua responded, "is inner: Chicano, *indio*, American Indian, *mojado*, *mexicano*, immigrant Latino, Anglo in power, working-class Anglo, black, Asian—our psyches resemble the bordertowns and are populated by the same people. . . . Awareness of our situation must come before inner changes, which in turn must come before changes in society."

Such awareness, in turn, must come from a "revisioned" history. What Gloria Steinem termed "revolution from within" must ultimately be grounded in "unlearning" much of what we have been told about America's past and substituting a more inclusive and accurate history of all peoples of America. "To finally recognize our own invisibility," declared Mitsuye Yamada, "is to finally be on the path toward visibility." To become visible is to see ourselves and each other in a different mirror of history. . . .

By viewing ourselves in a mirror which reflects reality, we can see our past as undistorted and no longer have to peer into our future as through a glass darkly. The face of our cultural future can be found on the western edge of the continent. "California, and especially Los Angeles, a gateway to both Asia and Latin America," Carlos Fuentes observed, "poses the universal question of the coming century: How do we get along with each other?" Asked whether California, especially with its multiethnic society, represented the America of the twenty-first century, Alice Walker replied: "If that's not the future reality of the United States, there won't be any United States, because that's who we are."

—Ronald Takaki, from *A Different Mirror: A History of Multicultural America* (Boston: Little, Brown and Company, 1993).

THE MULTICULTURAL STATE

California is neither a melting pot nor a salad bowl. From the first Native American communities, through the period of Spanish conquest and the cultural imperialism of the missions, to the period of Mexican settlement, and ultimately the mass white migration of the 1870s and 1880s, California has evolved into an often uneasy jigsaw of competing interests. California's complex network of urban, suburban, and rural areas make up what is now the nation's most diverse population, representing hundreds of distinct cultures and communities. Ethnicity is arguably the most salient cleavage in American politics. Yet a striking trend in California's demography is the rate at which the present plurality ethnic group, non-Hispanic whites, is moving from the majority to become the largest minority. In 1940 whites comprised 89.5 percent of California's population; Latinos, 6 percent; Asians, 1.9 percent; African Americans, 1.8 percent; and Native Americans, 0.2 percent. By 2000, non-Hispanic whites made up only 46.7 percent. As Table 4.1 shows, California has become far more diverse than the nation as a whole. Latinos grew to 32.4 percent of the state population, Asians and Pacific Islanders collectively rose to 10.9 percent, African Americans to 6.7 percent, and Native Americans, 1 percent.[1]

But these numbers tell only part of the story. Births among California's communities give us a glimpse of the state's evolving ethnic character. Latinos represent 50.5 percent of new babies born in the state; whites, 29.2 percent; Asian Americans, 11.4 percent; African Americans, 5.3 percent; Native Americans, 0.5 percent; and Pacific Islanders, 0.5 percent.[2] More than 30 distinct ancestries are now represented by populations of 100,000 or more.[3] The list of the largest national groups appears in Table 4.2. In addition, immigration brings more than 200,000 people a year into the state, increasingly from Latin American countries, Asia, and eastern Europe. By 2040, California's population is expected to be 50 percent Latino, 32 percent white, 12 percent Asian, and 6 percent African American.[4]

California's diversity reaches well beyond ethnic differences. Geography is playing an increasingly important role in cultural definition. In 2000, 94.4 percent of Californians lived in urban areas, up from 80.7 percent in 1950, 52.3 percent in 1900, 20.7 percent in 1860, and only 7.4 percent in 1850.[5] California has been the most urbanized state in the nation since 1980. This urbanization, however, is split among classically urban cities—such as San Francisco, Oakland, Sacramento, Los Angeles, and San Diego—and growing suburban areas—such as Sonoma, Fresno, Orange, Riverside, and Ventura Counties. The residents of suburban areas remain suspicious of urban cores, while residents of urban areas see suburban growth as the abandonment of cities by the upper middle class. Add to this the rural Californians in the San Joaquin Valley and northern portion of the state, and geography comes into focus as a second dimension of California's cultural mosaic.

TABLE 4.1 DEMOGRAPHIC CHARACTERISTICS OF THE UNITED STATES AND OF CALIFORNIA, 2000

	POPULATION	WHITE (NON-HISPANIC)	BLACK	LATINO	ASIAN	AMERICAN INDIAN
United States	281,421,906	75.1%	12.3%	12.5%	3.6%	0.9%
California	33,871,648	46.7%	6.7%	32.4%	10.9%	1.0%

Source: U.S. Census Bureau, 2000 U.S. Census.

TABLE 4.2 CALIFORNIA POPULATION BY NATIONAL ANCESTRY, 2000

ANCESTRY	POPULATION	% OF STATE POPULATION
Mexican	8,455,926	24.9
German	3,332,396	9.8
Irish	2,611,449	7.7
English	2,521,355	7.4
Italian	1,450,884	4.3
Chinese	980,642	2.9
Filipino	918,678	2.7
French	782,083	2.3
Scottish	541,890	1.6
Polish	491,325	1.5
Swedish	459,897	1.4
Vietnamese	447,032	1.3
Norwegian	436,128	1.3
Dutch	417,382	1.2
Russian	402,480	1.2
Korean	345,882	1.0
Portuguese	330,974	1.0
Asian Indian	314,819	0.9
Japanese	288,854	0.9
Salvadoran	272,999	0.8
Danish	207,030	0.6
Armenian	204,631	0.6
Arab	192,887	0.6
Welsh	188,414	0.6
Spanish	162,214	0.5
Iranian	159,016	0.5
French Canadian	145,370	0.4
Guatemalan	143,500	0.4
Puerto Rican	140,570	0.4
Hungarian	133,988	0.4
Greek	125,284	0.4
Swiss	115,485	0.3

Source: U.S. Census Bureau, 2000 U.S. Census. All groups over 100,000.

Urbanites are concerned with rebuilding aging city infrastructure, as well as improving social and economic conditions, including minimizing crime, improving urban schools, bringing jobs back into urban cores, and improving public transit. Suburbanites are fundamentally concerned with keeping urban problems out of their neighborhoods, although increasingly the suburbs are facing similar challenges. Rural residents are concerned with maintaining their rural economies—whether based on agriculture or timber products—and with battling encroaching urbanization. The interaction of these three Californias creates a heady mix of politics that is exacerbated by the racial undercurrent: Because urban cores are increasingly African American, Latino, and Asian, and suburban and rural areas are generally white, racial tensions accent the claims of competing geographic interests.

Income represents a third dimension of California's diversity. As Table 4.3 demonstrates, uneven income distribution across the state—and across ethnic lines as well—adds further tension to California's cultural mosaic. While the median household income statewide is $50,046, median incomes across counties vary markedly. For example, Marin County, just across the Golden Gate Bridge from San Francisco, enjoys a median household income of $88,934, the highest in the state. The arid agricultural region of Imperial County is ranked near the bottom, with a median household income of $35,226. The median household income in California's urban counties is far lower than in the largely suburban counties, while the rural counties are lower yet. For example, Los Angeles County (the state's most urban) has a median household income of $46,452, while neighboring Ventura County (largely suburban) has a median household income of $65,285, the highest in Southern California. At the same time, the rural counties in the northernmost portion of the state are significantly lower: Trinity County has a median household income of $34,343, Siskiyou County of $36,890, and Modoc County of $35,978.[6] Looking at income across ethnic lines reveals that while 8 percent of white families live below the poverty line, 13 percent of Asian families live below the poverty line; 22 percent of black families and 22 percent of Latino families live in poverty.[7] Personal economic security has become a contentious issue throughout the state.

Beyond the three dimensions—ethnic differences, geography, and income— there are several communities of interest that face unique problems and present distinct pressures on politics and policy. The issues reflected in these communities include religion, gender equality, sexual identity, age, and employee rights. Religion continues to play a major role in California. Urban Jews and Catholics, for example, continue to vote overwhelmingly Democratic. In several areas the religious right has targeted local school boards in an effort to influence curricula. Gender politics has remained a dominant influence throughout the state as organizations such as NOW (National Organization of Women) and CARAL (California Abortion & Reproductive Rights Action League) fight for women's issues, from equal rights to abortion rights. Gays and lesbians have organized to pursue equal rights and to combat homophobia and hate crimes. Much of the passion in the fight over gays in the military and the current battle over same-sex marriages originated in California's powerful gay communities in Los Angeles and the Bay Area.

Over the past 20 years, age has emerged as a defining characteristic in identifying communities of interest. Seniors have organized in interest groups such as AARP (American Association of Retired Persons) to balance the strong influence of the baby boomer generation. This group flexed its political muscle in 2005, when it mobilized to shut down President Bush's efforts to privatize Social Security, a proposal that had slightly higher support among the more risk-tolerant baby boomers.

TABLE 4.3 MEDIAN FAMILY INCOME AND POPULATION BY COUNTY, 2000

COUNTY	MEDIAN INCOME	RANK	POPULATION
Alameda	65,857	6	1,443,741
Alpine	50,250	23	1,208
Amador	51,226	19	35,100
Butte	41,010	38	203,171
Calaveras	47,379	25	40,554
Colusa	40,138	40	18,804
Contra Costa	73,039	4	948,816
Del Norte	36,056	51	27,507
El Dorado	60,250	14	156,299
Fresno	38,455	44	799,407
Glenn	37,023	48	26,453
Humboldt	39,370	41	126,518
Imperial	35,226	53	142,361
Inyo	44,970	30	17,945
Kern	39,403	42	661,645
Kings	38,111	45	129,461
Lake	35,818	52	58,309
Lassen	43,398	34	33,828
Los Angeles	46,452	28	9,519,338
Madera	39,226	43	123,109
Marin	88,934	1	247,289
Mariposa	42,655	36	17,130
Mendocino	42,168	37	86,265
Merced	38,009	46	210,554
Modoc	35,978	51	9,449
Mono	50,487	22	12,853
Monterey	51,169	20	401,762
Napa	61,410	11	124,279
Nevada	52,697	17	92,033
Orange	64,611	8	2,846,289
Placer	65,858	5	248,399
Plumas	46,119	29	20,824
Riverside	48,409	24	1,545,387
Sacramento	50,717	21	1,223,499
San Benito	60,665	12	53,234
San Bernardino	46,574	27	1,709,434
San Diego	53,438	16	2,813,833
San Francisco	63,545	9	776,733
San Joaquin	46,919	26	563,598
San Luis Obispo	52,447	18	246,681
San Mateo	80,737	3	707,161

(continued)

TABLE 4.3 *(continued)*

County	Median Income	Rank	Population
Santa Barbara	54,042	15	399,347
Santa Clara	81,717	2	1,682,585
Shasta	40,491	39	163,256
Sierra	42,756	35	3,555
Siskiyou	36,890	49	44,301
Solano	60,597	13	394,542
Sonoma	61,921	10	458,614
Stanislaus	44,703	31	446,997
Sutter	44,330	32	78,930
Tehama	37,277	47	56,039
Trinity	34,343	54	13,022
Tulare	36,297	50	368,021
Tuolumne	44,327	33	54,501
Ventura	65,285	7	753,197
Yolo	51,623	18	168,660
Yuba	34,103	55	60,219
State median	50,046	Total	33,871,648

Source: U.S. Census Bureau, 2000 U.S. Census. All figures in 1999 dollars.

The baby boomers (those born during the surge of births following World War II, between 1945 and 1964) are now the generation in power in most economic, political, and social institutions. And, like previous generations that have attained positions of influence, boomers have pursued political and economic agendas that maximize their generational interests.

Unlike previous generations, however, boomers have developed extraordinarily high levels of power. This is a result of two phenomena. First, having come of age during a period of unprecedented economic growth, boomers have attained unprecedented wealth. Second, the sheer number of boomers relative to the general population has given them a distorted sense of self-importance. Partly in response to the boomer generation and partly in response to the issues that have always affected older citizens, seniors have become uniquely politicized and efficiently organized. AARP has emerged as one of the strongest interest groups in the state and nationwide, providing a counterbalancing interest to the boomers. The oldest of the baby boomers are just now approaching retirement age. There could be a convergence of interests between the generations as AARP is changed by the boomers or as the boomers are changed by retirement.

The most recent generation of Americans to come of age is only now beginning to develop a cohesive political identity. The children of the baby boomers, the so-called millennial (or dot-net) generation, can expect to earn less than their parents while facing significantly higher costs for housing and durable goods. In short, this post-boomer generation will absorb most of the costs while enjoying few of the benefits of

America's postwar economic growth. As a generation, the millennials are more politically independent. They are less likely to identify with a major political party, and they are moved to participate in politics less by partisanship than by issues. Turnout among younger voters (ages 18–24) is below that of the overall population, but people of this age group are more inclined toward other forms of civic engagement, such as volunteer work.[8] There are even signs that this generation is embracing traditional political participation in greater numbers. Between 2000 and 2004, turnout among young voters increased by 11 percent. Chief among the issues that move young people to participate are the consequences of policies enacted by their parents' generation. From the War in Iraq to the stifling national debt, millennials are facing the prospect of assuming the burdens of the previous generation's decisions and paying the previous generation's bills. There are also generational differences in views on key issues. In 2006, 4 percent of 18- to 24-year-olds agreed with the view that the United States relied too much on military force to fight terrorism, compared to 50 percent of all voters.

There are, of course, a variety of other communities of interest that exist within California. Organized labor continues to be a major influence in policy debates. Public sector unions such as SEIU (Service Employees International Union) have gained membership and influence, even as union membership in the state has dropped overall by 1 percent since the mid-1990s.[9] In a stunning display of union strength, SEIU and the Justice for Janitors movement organized a strike in 2000 to demand higher pay from the 18 contractors that paid workers an average wage of $6.80 per hour for cleaning downtown Los Angeles office buildings. Previously, contractors had been known to fire workers for demanding higher than the minimum wage, but a new workforce consisting mainly of Central American and Mexican immigrants were more enthusiastic about organizing. Altogether, more than 8,000 janitors took to the streets and secured pay raises. In addition, environmentalists as a community are gaining influence, presenting challenges to traditional power centers in timber, agriculture, and industry throughout the state. These communities of interest are increasingly adding demands to the policy discourse. In response to this ever-increasing diversity in ethnic, social, and economic interests, the state has developed a unique equilibrium-based politics with an ever-shifting center of balance.

Culture as Politics

Each of the communities discussed in the preceding section contributes to California's complex political environment. The multitude of political and demographic subcultures in California has led to an amazingly fluid, and often conflicted, political culture. California is not merely heterogeneous, it is full of crosscutting schisms and overlapping memberships in communities of interest. These communities share some common experience and values, giving rise to unique political subcultures.

Culture can be understood as a set of experiences and symbols that frame community cognitions. Language, history, rituals, and values all give focus to the way one sees the world. Political culture, therefore, can be understood as the set of experiences and symbols that focus political cognitions. California's diverse population represents a complex web of political subcultures, making the state a mosaic of cultural influences and political pressures rather than a single culture. The result of these competing influences is an extremely passionate pluralistic process. Ultimately, though, it is California's diversity that may give the state its greatest strength.

FEAR AND LOATHING IN CALIFORNIA'S CHANGING POPULATION

Political leaders have accepted and even embraced California's multicultural character as part of the political landscape. At the same time, many voters have been less tolerant, even fearful, of California's changing population. In recent years, the voting public has often used the direct democracy provision of the state constitution to roll back opportunities for non-whites. Examples include Proposition 63 (1986), Proposition 187 (1994), and the anti-affirmative action "California Civil Rights Initiative" (1996). This has been possible because the impressive numeric strength of California's minority communities has not yet translated into proportional political clout. By 1998, there were no African-American state legislators representing districts outside the Los Angeles metropolitan area. Many Latinos and Asian Americans, the two largest minority groups in the state, are ineligible to vote either because they are not yet citizens or because they are too young. For example, Latinos constitute more than one-fourth of the state's population, but only one out of thirteen voters is Latino.[10] Consequently, Latinos are severely underrepresented at the state and local levels of government.

A striking trend since the 1990s is the political incorporation of Latinos, lower rates of political participation notwithstanding. An early milestone occurred in 1991, when a Mexican American Legal Defense and Education Fund (MALDEF) lawsuit forced the Los Angeles County Board of Supervisors to draw new district lines. In the next election, the county's First District elected Democrat Gloria Molina after having been represented for many years by Pete Schabarum, a conservative Anglo Republican. Changing demographics and the introduction of term limits—as well as turnover in leadership posts—enhanced opportunities for Latinos in the legislature, as well.

In the state Assembly, the progress of African American and Latino politicians is reflected at the top. Willie Brown had led Assembly Democrats as speaker for several years before Republicans briefly took control of the chamber in the 1990s. In 1996, Democrat Cruz Bustamante became the Assembly's first Latino speaker, and he was succeeded by Antonio Villaraigosa. Another milestone was reached in 2005, when Villaraigosa became the first Latino elected mayor of Los Angeles since the nineteenth century. One of Villaraigosa's successors was Fabian Nunez, who served as speaker until he was termed out in 2008, and succeeded by Karen Bass, the first female African American to hold the post.

Proposition 63

In 1986, the same year Monterey Park passed and then rescinded its "official English" law, a similar proposal appeared in the form of an initiative on the state ballot. Proposition 63 was designed to "protect" the English language through an amendment to the state constitution, declaring English the common language of the state. It directed the legislature to make no law that diminishes the role of the language and granted citizens standing to bring suit against the state to enforce the law.[11] Despite opposition from state political leaders, including Governor Deukmejian, California voters passed Proposition 63 by nearly a three-to-one vote. Statewide, 73 percent voted for the initiative. The vote margin was more narrow in Monterey Park, where only 53 percent voted "yes" on the initiative. Two years later, voters in Florida, Colorado, and Arizona passed similar initiatives. It is no coincidence that the four states with the highest proportion of non-English-speaking minorities were the first to consider "official English" initiatives on their ballots.

California Civil Rights Initiative

The California Civil Rights Initiative (CCRI) sought to dismantle the state's longstanding commitment to affirmative action. The law states the following:

> The state shall not discriminate against, or grant preferential treatment to, any individual or group on the basis of race, sex, color, ethnicity, or national origin in the operation of public employment, public education, or public contracting.[12]

The initiative has stirred controversy because it targets equity programs that are largely responsible for giving traditionally underrepresented communities (e.g., women, blacks, Latinos, Asians) access to education, business, and the professions. Critics argued that CCRI is somewhat disingenuous, arguing that such discrimination is already banned by federal civil rights laws and pointing out that the third clause of the initiative presents an explicit attack on the protections against sexual discrimination ensured by Title X of federal Civil Rights law. The third clause of CCRI declares:

> Nothing in this section shall be interpreted as prohibiting bona fide qualifications based on sex which are reasonably necessary to the normal operation of public employment, public education, or public contracting.[13]

What "bona fide qualifications" are "reasonably necessary" has not been defined. Because public safety agencies (e.g., police and fire departments) have traditionally used this line of argument to exclude women, this language has elicited protest.

Proposition 187

In 1994, California voters approved Proposition 187, which essentially denied most public services to illegal immigrants. The measure sought to deter undocumented immigration into the state by requiring that "all persons employed in the providing of (public) services shall diligently protect public funds from misuse" by excluding anyone who has not been "verified" to be in the country legally. Further, the law states:

> If any public entity in this state to whom a person has applied for public social services determines *or reasonably suspects*, based upon the information provided to it, that the person is an alien in the United States in violation of federal law, the

following procedures shall be followed by the public entity: (1) The entity shall not provide the person with benefits or services. (2) The entity shall, in writing, notify the person of his or her apparent illegal immigration status, and that the person must either obtain legal status or leave the United States. (3) The entity shall also notify the State Director of Social Services, the Attorney General of California, and the U.S. Immigration and Naturalization Service of the *apparent* illegal status, and shall provide any additional information that may be requested by any other public entity.[14] (*Emphases added.*)

The policy reflects the growing frustration within the state and represents an exaggerated response. Proposition 187 was controversial because it evolved against the backdrop of Latino immigration and because it precludes due process. For example, according to the law, a child can be denied medical attention in a county facility based on a clerk's *suspicion* that the child is undocumented. With constant media messages focusing on Latino immigrants, the practical implication is de facto suspicion, and potential exclusion, of Latinos generally. Ultimately, California's courts struck down Proposition 187 after a series of legal challenges by the MALDEF and the League of United Latin American Citizens (LULAC). The state appealed the ruling, but following the election of 1998 and a change of administration, Governor Davis eventually abandoned the appeal.

A decade after Proposition 187 divided Californians on the immigration issue, a new backlash began in California and spread nationwide. A retired accountant and anti-illegal immigration activist from Orange County, Jim Gilchrist, founded the Minuteman Project in 2004. Termed a vigilante group by President Bush and the American Civil Liberties Union (ACLU) alike, the Minutemen organized their own citizen patrols of the Mexican Border. The group found a national following, with Minuteman chapters springing up in such unlikely places as Pennsylvania and North Carolina.

The immigration debate's impact at the ballot box was apparent in 2006, when it emerged as the central issue in a special congressional election in San Diego County. Republican Brian Bilbray was running to succeed another Republican, Randy "Duke" Cunningham, who had been convicted on bribery and corruption charges. Bilbray campaigned on a strong anti-illegal immigration platform, proposing to ban illegal immigrants from Social Security benefits and a "fence from the Pacific Ocean to the Gulf of Mexico."[15] Bilbray narrowly defeated his Democratic opponent, who ran on cleaning up corruption, even though the corruption issue cost the Republicans their majority in the fall election.

"Official English," Proposition 187, and CCRI are all examples of policies that reflect the ethnic tensions within the state. Frustrated by the perception that ethnic minorities were getting more than their share, voters bypassed the legislature to enact new policies designed to hasten the assimilation of new immigrants, limit immigration, and restrict opportunity for certain groups. As with ballot initiatives in other policy areas, California's controversial responses to diversity have been adopted nationwide. The success of California's Proposition 63 ignited a national "English-only" movement as activists raced to qualify similar initiatives for their own state ballots. Interest groups throughout the nation have introduced legislative proposals and ballot initiatives that mirror provisions of CCRI and Proposition 187 with varying degrees of success. As California goes, so goes the nation.

MONTEREY PARK: A CASE STUDY IN DIVERSITY

Ten miles east of downtown Los Angeles, drivers on the freeway will notice a sign welcoming them to "Monterey Park, All-American City." This middle-class suburb made national news in the 1980s, as it struggled to maintain a sense of identity after years of change and growth. After World War II, it was a mostly white bedroom community where Laura Scudder used home recipes to begin her peanut butter and potato chip business. By 1990, the city had a population of 61,000 and was home to a thriving retail center. A significant factor in this transformation was a change in demographics due to a rapid influx of Asian residents. Asians comprised only 3 percent of the city's population in 1960. This group was mostly of Japanese heritage and native born. In 1990, 56 percent of the population was Asian, due mainly to migration by ethnic Chinese from downtown Los Angeles, mainland China, Taiwan, Hong Kong, Vietnam, and other Southeast Asian nations. Of the Chinese immigrants living in Monterey Park, more than 65 percent arrived in the 1980s. During that decade, more than 30 times as many U.S.-bound immigrants from Taiwan reported Monterey Park than San Francisco as their destination.[16]

Monterey Park became known as "Little Taipei," replacing downtown LA's Chinatown as the center of Chinese cultural activity in Southern California. Surrounded by the predominantly Latino neighborhoods in the San Gabriel Valley, Monterey Park also saw its Latino population grow from 12 percent to 31 percent during this time. At the same time, non-Hispanic whites became a minority compared to the newcomers, dwindling from 85 percent of the population to just 12 percent. The Chinese did not fit the traditional pattern of immigration. Earlier waves of immigrants to the San Gabriel Valley—from Japan, Mexico, and Central America—had arrived gradually and had initially occupied the bottom rung of the economic ladder in the community. The Chinese community arrived rapidly in large numbers and reflected significant economic diversity.[17]

Ethnic tensions increased during the 1980s, as white residents began to perceive the rapid growth and changing character of the neighborhood as a threat. The city council, representing an "old guard" of established whites, passed an ordinance making English the city's "official" language and requiring English wording on all business signs. The council rescinded the law after public outcry. Nonetheless, a coalition of progressive Asian and Latino activists waged a campaign in 1987 to recall the three city council members who were behind the English ordinance. The recall failed, although the council members were voted out in subsequent elections.

The confluence of the issues of ethnic diversity and development allowed many residents to support nativist candidates and positions in the name of "slow growth," without appearing to be racist. Whites could oppose ethnic candidates as the agents of development interests. Thus, electoral politics were essentially deadlocked between multicultural, pro-growth forces and nativist antigrowth forces. Even though the majority of the city's residents were Asian, with whites comprising a small minority, this impasse kept the old guard in control of city hall. In 1988, a breakthrough occurred when a Chinese-American slow-growth advocate, Judy Chu, won election to the city council in a contest where ballots were printed in Chinese, English, Japanese, Spanish, and Vietnamese.[18]

The election of Chu was the watershed event in the city's transformation from a stronghold of nativism to a model of multiculturalism. Chu successfully forged a multiethnic coalition by appealing to Asians, Latinos, and whites who wanted to control growth, yet were dissatisfied with the nativist sentiments of local white politicians. Asian Americans had been elected to city government previously, but only with heavy support of white voters. The effect of the English-only controversy and the recall drive was to politicize the immigrant and minority communities in Monterey Park, which led to large-scale ethnic voting in local elections. Even in San Francisco, a city with a significant Asian population, no Asian was elected to city office before Supervisor Mabel Teng in 1994.

SUMMARY

California's social and cultural diversity reflects a dynamic tension that is organic to the state. The multiplicity of communities, cultures, and interests contributes to an engagingly pluralistic process of assessing public problems and determining public solutions. Such hyperpluralism plays against the backdrop of California's competing political cultures—ethnic, geographic, economic, and otherwise. California is the most diverse state in the nation. As of the 2000 Census, whites are no longer a majority of the population. Soon they will no longer be even a plurality, as Latinos are expected to become the largest ethnic group by 2015. As one of the largest states, California often experiences geographically based political conflict among urban, suburban, and rural interests. Some of the most extreme examples of opulence and poverty in the nation are found in California's upscale suburbs and poor agricultural communities—highlighting the sharp economic differences between California's households. And because the population is younger on average than in other states, there is also potential for sharp intergenerational conflict as the emerging minority–majority population reaches voting age and begins participating in higher rates.

NOTES

1. California Department of Finance, *Population Research Unit, Report 88 P-4, 93 P-1.*
2. California Department of Health Services, *Vital Statistics*, 2004.
3. U.S. Bureau of the Census, 2000 U.S. Census.
4. California Department of Health Services, 2004.
5. California Department of Finance, *Report 86, P-3* and California Department of Health Services, 1994.

6. California Franchise Tax Board, 1995.
 7. Alejandra Lopez, "Race and Poverty Rates in California" (Stanford: Center for Comparative Race and Ethnicity, November 2002).
 8. Cliff Zukin, Scott Keeter, Molly Andolina, Krista Jenkins, and Michael X. Delli Carpini, *A New Engagement? Political Participation, Civic Life, and the Changing American Citizen* (Oxford, UK: Oxford University Press, 2006).
 9. Harold Myerson, "Enter the Janitors." *LA Weekly*, April 14, 2000.
10. Leo Estrada, "Latinos in California's Future," *California Journal* (January 1995): 45–49.
11. Jack Citrin, "Language Politics and American Identity," *The Public Interest* 99 (Spring 1990): 96–109.
12. Ballot text of the California Civil Rights Initiative (1996), clause 1, lines 1–3.
13. Ballot text of the California Civil Rights Initiative (1996), clause 3, lines 5–7.
14. Ballot text of California's Proposition 187 (1994).
15. Campaign website for Brian Bilbray. http://bilbrayforcongress.com/ Accessed April 11, 2006.
16. Immigration and Naturalization Service statistics reported in Timothy P. Fong, *The First Suburban Chinatown: The Remaking of Monterey Park, California* (Philadelphia: Temple University Press, 1994).
17. John Horton argues that it was the absence of gross economic inequality that may be the reason Monterey Park was spared much of the turmoil of the 1992 Los Angeles riots. See John Horton, *The Politics of Diversity: Immigration, Resistance and Change in Monterey Park, California* (Philadelphia: Temple University Press, 1995).
18. For a detailed account of the recall and subsequent elections in Monterey Park, see Horton, 1995.

CHAPTER 5

California's Political Economy

Featured Reading / Pages 59–64
Jocelyn Lippert
Rancho de Los Arcos

Over the past century California has evolved from a sparsely populated frontier state to the most populous state in the nation. The state's size, strong economy, cultural influence, and diversity have propelled it to becoming a dominant player in national affairs. California's manufacturing base has long been critical to the nation's military, and its lead in aerospace and high technology has positioned the state for continued growth throughout the twenty-first century. In addition, California's entertainment industries—film, music, and television—have served to export a cultural self-image that, while somewhat artificial, has served to foster the evolution of popular culture throughout the nation.

California's status as an economic powerhouse is due in part to its capacity to exploit its location, encouraging open economic borders, open markets, and an open labor pool. Based on gross domestic product alone, California would be one of the world's largest economies—ranking seventh behind such giants as Japan, Germany, and the United States itself, as Table 5.1 illustrates. The state's attractiveness as a global production center is linked not only to a highly developed, culturally diverse internal labor and consumer market but also to the state's position as a springboard to the Pacific Rim and Latin American external markets. Its improved competitiveness is linked to the state's focus on investment, its role as a gateway for diffusing technology, and its bolstering of the export and import markets.

CALIFORNIA AND THE U.S. ECONOMY

California leads the nation in several sectors of the national economy. It remains a leader in the computer, film and animation, multimedia, biotechnology, semiconductor, and aerospace industries, and it has been incubating a new manufacturing base in the apparel and furniture-making industries. Over the past several years, the state has

TABLE 5.1   COMPARATIVE GROSS DOMESTIC PRODUCT

2005	GDP (IN BILLIONS)
United States	$12,397.9
Japan	4,549.2
Germany	2,786.9
United Kingdom	2,229.2
France	2,136.4
Italy	1,769.7
California	**1,622.1**
Canada	1,131.8
Spain	1,126.0
Korea	791.4
Mexico	768.0

Source: Organisation for Economic Co-operation and Development, *Annual National Accounts Database*, 2007, www.oecd.org. Shown in 2005 dollar equivalent exchange rate.

further diversified its economy, making it more resistant to fluctuations in the global market. The growing service industry accounts for approximately one-third of the state's workforce (see Table 5.2). The rapid growth in this sector, with its low to moderate wage scale, has raised some concerns about how the economy will make the adjustment from one dominated by a shrinking manufacturing sector, which traditionally employed moderate- to high-wage workers.

California's economy thrived for many years in part because of Cold War defense policies. Federal largesse had subsidized the Golden State in the form of military bases, defense contracts, and other defense-related industries that created high-paying jobs. With the end of the Cold War, however, California was targeted for more base closures than any other state. After two earlier rounds of base closings in 1989 and 1991, a devastating third round in 1993 shut down eight major military installations statewide. Six of these facilities were located in the San Francisco Bay area, and the region lost more than 30,000 jobs as a direct result of the shutdowns.[1] In Southern California, major base closings in the early 1990s included the San Diego Naval Training Center, the El Toro Marine Air Station, and the Long Beach Naval Hospital and Shipyard. Thousands of indirectly related service jobs were expected to evaporate due to the closures.

The defense cuts jolted California's economy beyond base closings. The reduction in federal defense contracts meant heavy losses in aerospace and high-tech civilian jobs. In Los Angeles County alone, employment in these two sectors dropped by more than half between 1988 and 1995.[2] During this period, nearly every defense contractor in the state downsized. Many of those laid off were middle-aged, working to support families, and highly paid—aerospace workers made an average salary of $18 per hour.[3] These workers have largely been unable to find work at the same level

TABLE 5.2   WAGE AND SALARY WORKERS IN NONAGRICULTURAL ESTABLISHMENTS BY MAJOR INDUSTRY, CALIFORNIA, 1939 TO 2002 (IN THOUSANDS)

YEAR	TOTAL b,c	MINING	CONSTRUCTION d	MANUFACTURING	TRANSPORTATION AND UTILITIES	WHOLESALE TRADE	RETAIL TRADE	FINANCE INSURANCE, REAL ESTATE	SERVICES	GOV'T e
STANDARD INDUSTRIAL CLASSIFICATION SYSTEM: SIC										
1939	1,812.2	40.0	78.8	384.4	185.1	— 504.7 —		93.9	274.7	250.3
1940	1,931.8	40.0	92.1	440.2	190.3	— 524.2 —		98.3	280.4	266.3
1941	2,264.9	40.1	138.5	593.6	213.0	— 572.1 —		102.4	297.4	307.8
1942	2,689.6	33.8	155.5	876.0	233.8	— 588.1 —		97.2	321.3	384.1
1943	3,083.6	29.4	140.3	1,165.5	250.8	160.2	435.9	94.9	341.5	465.0
1944	3,116.4	29.9	135.9	1,109.7	268.0	156.3	457.7	93.2	355.2	510.6
1945	2,961.3	30.6	139.0	860.8	279.5	167.6	486.7	97.8	365.7	533.7
1946	2,972.6	33.5	177.7	706.7	295.5	189.2	547.9	116.9	405.0	500.2
1947	3,080.0	34.2	209.0	721.8	312.6	203.5	571.2	125.8	418.9	483.0
1948	3,162.8	35.6	232.7	734.2	317.9	213.3	577.2	132.3	418.7	500.9
1949	3,088.1	34.4	204.4	701.5	306.0	207.7	559.5	134.2	415.6	524.6
1950	3,209.4	32.3	235.0	759.7	307.1	211.7	571.5	142.1	416.8	533.3
1951	3,518.3	35.0	250.9	892.5	327.1	221.8	599.1	150.3	441.7	599.9
1952	3,737.8	35.9	250.6	994.6	336.3	226.6	626.0	157.9	469.0	640.9
1953	3,880.7	37.3	261.5	1,060.8	346.6	234.3	646.8	166.7	480.4	646.4
1954	3,866.1	36.1	255.0	1,048.6	336.5	235.7	641.5	170.4	487.8	654.5
1955	4,082.9	36.8	284.0	1,121.1	347.4	244.4	671.2	180.4	516.5	681.2
1956	4,352.3	37.0	302.3	1,218.0	364.9	259.9	703.2	193.2	549.2	724.6
1957	4,525.2	36.5	287.5	1,283.8	372.8	272.5	714.4	203.7	593.1	760.9
1958	4,498.6	33.4	286.7	1,217.4	353.7	268.8	704.2	212.6	623.2	798.6
1959	4,774.8	32.4	308.4	1,312.6	354.8	282.5	748.3	226.2	677.2	832.4
1960	4,896.0	30.6	294.8	1,317.2	356.9	292.2	775.4	243.2	711.7	874.0
1961	4,996.1	30.3	294.4	1,318.0	351.2	296.3	784.3	253.0	748.3	920.3
1962	5,217.7	30.2	307.7	1,382.5	357.0	303.3	818.1	265.4	790.7	962.8
1963	5,412.3	29.6	329.0	1,394.3	360.3	311.9	857.1	281.0	847.5	1,001.6
1964	5,606.5	31.0	340.4	1,389.4	371.0	320.0	904.5	296.7	910.0	1,043.5
1965	5,800.3	31.7	323.7	1,411.2	387.1	330.5	939.2	306.7	964.8	1,105.4
1966	6,145.2	32.3	305.6	1,531.3	410.3	345.4	983.9	310.6	1,029.1	1,196.7
1967	6,367.6	31.9	275.2	1,594.0	428.7	352.7	1,006.0	319.3	1,085.5	1,274.3
1968	6,642.1	32.5	290.7	1,639.7	440.7	361.8	1,056.3	337.8	1,146.8	1,335.8
1969	6,931.5	32.6	310.6	1,661.3	460.7	377.0	1,116.0	358.4	1,223.2	1,391.7
1970	6,946.2	31.4	303.0	1,558.0	459.1	— 1,529.3 —		374.5	1,266.2	1,424.7
1971	6,917.0	30.4	301.5	1,473.2	452.6	— 1,545.2 —		386.8	1,281.0	1,446.3
1972	7,209.9	29.2	312.4	1,542.7	454.1	409.6	1,199.0	409.3	1,361.0	1,492.7
1973	7,621.9	30.5	333.4	1,660.7	467.0	441.6	1,261.9	431.6	1,470.6	1,524.8
1974	7,834.3	32.7	317.8	1,701.3	470.7	460.6	1,291.4	444.8	1,529.1	1,586.0
1975	7,847.2	33.9	285.9	1,593.7	458.1	465.9	1,320.4	446.4	1,572.4	1,670.6
1976	8,154.2	34.7	301.3	1,659.8	463.9	485.3	1,390.2	468.7	1,654.6	1,695.6
1977	8,599.7	35.6	350.4	1,737.8	476.5	507.5	1,474.9	505.4	1,770.9	1,740.7

TABLE 5.2 (continued)

Year	Total	Mining	Construction[d]	Manufacturing	Transportation and Utilities	Wholesale Trade	Retail Trade	Finance, Insurance, Real Estate	Services	Gov't[b]
1978	9,199.8	37.1	401.9	1,884.6	506.4	534.3	1,591.7	553.2	1,937.4	1,753.1
1979	9,664.6	39.3	448.7	2,012.7	534.7	564.1	1,659.7	595.9	2,074.6	1,735.0
1980	9,848.8	43.5	428.3	2,018.2	546.3	583.7	1,683.2	623.1	2,158.8	1,763.9
1981	9,985.3	49.2	407.6	2,032.3	554.8	590.6	1,710.9	642.9	2,240.5	1,756.4
1982	9,810.3	50.4	349.0	1,957.7	542.8	582.1	1,693.1	642.4	2,257.7	1,735.2
1983	9,917.8	47.7	366.9	1,927.0	531.9	600.7	1,731.1	653.8	2,334.4	1,724.3
1984	10,390.0	47.6	407.4	2,004.1	540.0	634.6	1,838.5	677.8	2,492.7	1,747.4
1985	10,769.8	47.8	435.8	2,024.2	553.5	660.4	1,914.7	697.3	2,643.3	1,792.8
1986	11,085.5	40.7	450.0	2,039.1	568.4	672.3	1,982.5	728.6	2,765.1	1,838.8
1987	11,472.6	37.3	487.2	2,060.1	583.2	688.0	2,067.9	755.1	2,910.2	1,883.7
1988	11,911.5	37.7	529.2	2,096.7	588.4	733.5	2,154.1	773.0	3,064.8	1,934.1
1989	12,238.5	37.3	560.0	2,107.0	598.2	758.2	2,193.9	789.0	3,196.2	1,998.7

NORTH AMERICAN INDUSTRY CLASSIFICATION SYSTEM: NAICS

Year	Total[b,c]	Natural Resources and Mining	Construction[d]	Manufacturing	Trade, Transportation and Utilities	Information	Financial Activities	Professional and Business Services	Educational and Health Services	Leisure and Hospitality	Other Services	Gov't[e]
1990	12,499.8	36.3	644.5	1,959.8	2,419.6	390.6	821.9	1,516.0	1,116.3	1,104.5	415.6	2,074.8
1991	12,358.9	34.6	561.8	1,885.2	2,380.7	395.5	809.0	1,512.0	1,154.3	1,119.4	415.7	2,090.6
1992	12,153.5	31.7	495.2	1,787.0	2,354.0	387.5	790.3	1,507.6	1,182.6	1,114.6	407.4	2,095.6
1993	12,045.4	29.8	458.9	1,695.2	2,337.6	386.2	787.0	1,541.6	1,195.8	1,124.6	408.2	2,080.6
1994	12,159.5	27.1	475.3	1,683.8	2,351.3	395.8	770.3	1,586.4	1,212.0	1,143.8	420.5	2,093.2
1995	12,422.0	26.1	498.8	1,714.9	2,398.2	415.9	742.3	1,667.8	1,238.9	1,181.5	430.6	2,107.0
1996	12,743.4	25.9	515.3	1,772.4	2,449.8	432.8	742.9	1,763.9	1,264.5	1,223.5	439.2	2,113.3
1997	13,129.7	25.9	554.5	1,825.1	2,516.0	461.7	744.3	1,888.5	1,291.7	1,236.0	445.2	2,140.7
1998	13,596.1	27.5	614.0	1,857.2	2,584.8	482.8	774.0	2,037.0	1,330.0	1,262.9	460.0	2,166.1
1999	13,991.8	26.3	682.9	1,829.9	2,645.1	517.4	793.2	2,119.2	1,368.3	1,297.1	473.2	2,239.3
2000	14,488.2	26.5	731.0	1,857.5	2,721.4	575.4	795.1	2,246.0	1,398.0	1,332.6	486.7	2,318.1
2001	14,602.0	25.6	779.0	1,785.7	2,746.6	551.5	835.2	2,186.5	1,446.9	1,364.1	499.0	2,382.1
2002	14,476.5	23.1	772.6	1,641.2	2,730.5	498.0	849.9	2,126.0	1,499.6	1,381.8	505.7	2,448.1

[a] The historical data based on the Standard Industrial Classification (SIC) system is provided for research purposes only. These data will not be updated. The NAICS and SIC data are not comparable.

[b] Excludes employers, own-account workers, unpaid family workers, domestic servants, and agricultural workers.

[c] Detail may not add to totals due to rounding.

[d] Includes employees of construction contractors and operative builders; does not include force-account and government construction workers.

[e] Includes civilian employees of federal, state, and local governments, regardless of activity in which engaged.

[f] Includes repair and maintenance, personal and laundry services, and religious and civic organizations.

Source: Employment Development Department, Labor Market Information Division (www.labormarketinfo.edd.ca.gov).

of skill and pay. But, devastating as they were, federal budget cuts were not the only shock to the flagging economy of the early 1990s.

The Golden State had lost much of its luster by the early 1990s, as national economic growth slowed, post-Cold War defense cuts, and a series of natural and social disasters plunged the region deeper into recession. The recession of 1991–1994 was preceded by a prolonged drought and the deadly 1989 Loma Prieta earthquake. The Los Angeles riots of 1992, which were precipitated by the acquittal of the four Los Angeles police officers who beat Rodney King, resulted in 55 deaths and more than 1,000 injuries and cost the state approximately $1 billion.[4] Floods, fires, and the 1994 Northridge earthquake put further stress on the state's infrastructure.

BUDGET CRISIS POLITICS

The recession, federal budget cuts, and natural disasters exacerbated an ongoing fiscal crisis in California. Accelerated emigration and a shrinking tax base were enough to push the state into a recession in the early 1990s. The migration from California reached an all-time high in 1992, with 580,000 people moving away from the state.[5] The ongoing recession brought an unprecedented crash on tax revenues, causing California's worst fiscal crisis since the Great Depression. By July 1992, the state was out of funds, leading the state controller to issue IOU warrants. Many banks honored the warrants for only the first month. Both Democrats and Republicans used the fiscal crisis as a vehicle to push their favored agendas. Democrats, who at the time controlled both the senate and the assembly, pushed for a tax increase to protect the state's social safety net. Governor Wilson and his Republican colleagues in the legislature sought deep spending cuts. The deadlock persisted for 63 days, as the state limped along without a budget. Ultimately, a $57.4 billion budget was passed. While the governor received most of his demands, the legislators minimized the damage to their favored programs.

The struggle to balance the budget occurred against the backdrop of a sluggish economy, the taxing and spending restrictions of Proposition 13, and the abolition of such revenue sources as the state inheritance tax and business inventory tax. Thus, from fiscal years 1991–1992 through 1994–1995, the total budget shortfall was $38 billion, which was met by revenue increases of $10.4 billion and expenditure reductions of $27.6 billion. The state's population grew 10 percent during those four years. Purchasing power for persons receiving state subsistence during those years fell by 10 percent. Californians on disability took a 20 percent cut in their monthly state disbursements. To help balance the budget, University of California students paid 134 percent higher tuition fees, and California State University students paid 103 percent higher fees. The 1994–1995 state budget in real dollars was 17 percent less than the 1990–1991 budget.

The cumulative impacts of the recession and budget crisis of the 1990s were most visible at the county level. The Tax Revolt of the 1970s restricted the ability of the counties to raise new revenues to meet the growing demands for services by their own residents, as well as the services required by the state. For more than a decade after Proposition 13 went into effect in 1978, the counties managed to avoid the full impact of its taxing and spending limitations. The same year, a sympathetic legislature in Sacramento provided relief in the form of AB 8, a comprehensive finance law that stabilized funding to school districts, cities, counties, and special districts in the wake of Proposition 13. This approach succeeded until the 1990s, when the state began experiencing a perennial budget crisis of its own. Governor Wilson and the legislature compensated by passing a series of temporary half-cent sales tax increases. This forced a shift in the way local government was financed, from property taxes to sales taxes. Anticipating some of the unintended consequences of this shift, Democratic State Senator Mike Thomson of Napa dubbed the 1993 budget the "Factory Outlet Act of 1993."[6]

Because Proposition 13 reduced property tax revenues by as much as 60 percent, several California counties were in financial distress by the early 1990s. Rural counties were hurt the most because of their dependence on property taxes and the lack of alternative revenue sources. Butte County avoided becoming the first county in the nation to file for bankruptcy, thanks to three consecutive state bailouts.[7] Rural counties from Siskiyou in the north to Imperial in the southeast found themselves strapped for cash, unable to raise the necessary revenue to meet their expenses. These fiscal crises were not limited to rural counties, however. In 1995, Los Angeles County was teetering on the edge of insolvency when President Clinton came to its aid with a federal bailout.

The Crisis Hits Suburbia: Municipal Bankruptcy in Orange County

In stark contrast to Los Angeles County, with its urban problems, and Northern California, with its budgetary woes, suburban Orange County was perhaps the one place most insulated from these fiscal pressures. Orange County is known as the home of Disneyland, aerospace and high-tech industries, good school districts, and a stronghold of conservative politics. Just days after the 1994 election ushered in a Republican congress on a platform of fiscal restraint, the county reluctantly announced that it had lost more than $1.6 billion in risky investments. When its lender banks began to seize Orange County securities as collateral, the county filed for Chapter 9 bankruptcy.[8]

The pages and airwaves of the national news media were filled with explanations of mismanagement by Orange County Treasurer Bob Citron. Citron borrowed twice as much money as he had on deposit, nearly tripling the size of the county's investment pool, to purchase high-risk, high-yield securities. When the Federal Reserve raised interest rates in 1994, however, the value of these investments crashed. When the county filed for protection from its creditors in December, the Orange County fiasco became the largest municipal bankruptcy in U.S. history. The county was in real danger of defaulting on a $1 billion debt, a sum far greater than the total debt of all 362 municipal bankruptcies since 1937.[9]

Even though Citron received the lion's share of the blame for the disaster, the conditions that made it possible were in place well before the people of Orange County elected him to office. Three factors made the fiscal crisis possible: political fragmentation, voter distrust, and state austerity.[10] Political fragmentation (that is, the capacity of multiple government entities to pursue competing goals simultaneously) is a common characteristic of the growing suburbs. There is a lack of accountability as political power is diffused between a large number of small cities and county supervisors, who tend to focus on their own districts. In Orange County, this arrangement left Citron to act as a relatively autonomous figure, without much oversight.

A second factor, voter distrust, has been especially intense in suburbs such as Orange County. Voters have become more likely to view government as costly, inefficient, and they have begun to demand increasingly high levels of service with low taxes. Middle-class suburbs have tended to elect government officials who share the same small-government, anti-tax views. Ever since the Tax Revolt of the 1970s, elected officials have been reluctant to make the case for tax increases. The refusal of a majority of the county's voters to approve a modest tax increase after the bankruptcy was interpreted as an expression of their lack of confidence in government to use the money wisely. In 1996, even after the effects of the bankruptcy were publicized, the county's voters overwhelmingly voted for Proposition 218, reaffirming and extending the limitations of Proposition 13. Affluent suburbanites want their cake.

The third factor leading to the crisis was the state's fiscal austerity. The state revenue shortfalls of the early 1990s reduced the aid coming in from Sacramento. The state reduced the local governments' share of property tax revenues, increasing pressure on the county treasurer to make up for the lost income with investments. Furthermore, the state's dire fiscal condition also precluded the possibility of a bailout.

The bankruptcy lasted 18 months, but its effects will be felt for a long time to come. The county was forced to lay off nearly 600 employees and slash some administrative budgets by as much as 30 percent.[11] Public health and services for the poor sustained the deepest cuts. Despite the threat of deep cuts to their school budgets and other public services, Orange County voters shocked observers elsewhere in the nation by defeating Measure R, a half-cent sales tax increase designed to bail the county out. With neither the state, the federal government, nor the voters willing to come to their aid, county leaders adopted a strategy of "suing their way out" of the predicament. Twenty-seven lawsuits were filed against Wall Street brokers that had advised Citron in his risky investments. By 1998, settlements of many of these cases helped the county recover $639 million, about 39 percent of the $1.6 billion lost.[12]

THE RETURN TO BUSINESS-AS-USUAL

High-tech industries powered an economic turnaround in the late 1990s, and for a while, deficits became a thing of the past. Governor Davis began his term in 1999 with proposals to invest the state's new wealth in education and infrastructure projects. However, the collapse of technology stocks, an energy crisis, and a nationwide post-9/11 recession brought these lofty visions back down to earth. By 2003, the state faced a record deficit, and Davis was recalled by the voters that October.

Governor Schwarzenegger arrived in Sacramento, promising to be a consensus builder. In his first months in office, he was praised by members of both parties for his ability to make deals with leaders of interest groups and Democratic leaders to pass legislation. Many such accords were brokered personally in his personal smoking tent on the capitol lawn. Schwarzenegger's first true test came midway through 2004, when he failed to meet his promise to deliver the state budget on time. As the July 1 deadline approached, there appeared to be agreement on the $103 billion budget, until Republicans in the legislature made their votes conditional upon Schwarzenegger's support for a proposed bill making it harder for workers to sue their employers and another one opening the way for public schools to contract for school bus drivers and cafeteria workers.[13] Budget talks stalled as Schwarzenegger assumed a more confrontational stance. He campaigned for the bills around the state and appropriated movie and television clichés, calling the leaders of the legislature "girlie men" and threatening to "terminate" them. The tough talk did nothing to prevent a new generation of long, hot summers in Sacramento. The stalemates continued, and in 2008 Governor Schwarzenegger approved a state budget that was a record 85 days overdue.

Rancho de Los Arcos   *Jocelyn Lippert*

He is used to getting up early, but this morning it is all he can do to drag himself out of bed. He picks up the jeans and jacket he had laid out the night before. They bulge out in odd places because of the wads of money stitched into the seams: under his belt, in his collar, around the cuffs of his pants and shirt. He stuffs some more into the toes of his boots before putting them on. Twelve hundred dollars makes a lot of bills, even in American money.

He usually eats a simple breakfast of milk and honey wafers, but this morning, March 3, 2001, his wife is up to cook him something substantial. She knows this will be his last meal for two days. His five children are subdued as they congregate in the kitchen. His son sits down at his place beside his father. Even though he is only 16 years old, he will be the head of the family for the next nine months, taking care of the 100 pigs on the family's farm, as well as working on a larger 10,000 hog farm nearby to earn extra money.

Diego Velez has dark hair and blue eyes that crinkle up at the corners when he laughs. This morning, however, there is no laughter in the Velez house. Velez gets up from the table and bends down to say goodbye to his children. His daughter puts her arm around her daddy's neck and kisses him on the cheek. Velez takes his worn black sombrero off the hook by the door, leaving the leather one he saves for special occasions to await his return in nine long months.

The Crossing

Velez is leaving home to meet his *coyote*, the wily guide who will lead him across the mountains and desert to California. Velez has made this journey many times since he first crossed the border in January 1986. By now he knows the system. He knows he must eat a lot before he leaves because he will have to go without food or water for the next two days and nights. He knows he must rest before the trip because the walk is exhausting. He knows to tell the coyote that he has an aunt in California who will pay the $1200 for his fee so that the coyote won't think that he has cash on his person. And he knows he must sew the real money into the seams of his clothes to prevent robbers, other crossers, and the coyotes from stealing it along the way.

Unlike Velez, most Mexicans cross the border without knowing where they will work when they get to the United States. Many find jobs once they get to the US through family members or friends.

The owner of one organic farm in Southern California says she picked up her team of Mexican workers off the street. "They're not educated at all," she says. "They don't even have basic hygiene."

She calls her operation a "model farm." She says she treats her workers well and starts their wages at $7.00 an hour, 25 cents above California's minimum wage. All of her workers cross the border illegally. None of them have papers or authorization to work.

"They die crossing that border," she says. "Usually once [my workers] find me, they stay. I'm kind of like the pot at the end of the rainbow." And yet, she says, because they don't have housing, two of her seven workers are now living in bushes.

One Farm's Seemingly Perfect Recipe

Diego Velez is one of the luckier ones this time around. He has a job and a room waiting for him in California, at an organic farm called XYZ Organics[*].

XYZ Organics farm uses only natural methods of pesticide and weed control. The farm workers spray garlic and fish mixtures on the plants to deter insects, and pull out the weeds by hand. The crops, which range from tomatoes to peaches to asparagus to carrots, are planted in alternating rows to discourage bugs, which tend to thrive in industrial mono-cropping farms. XYZ limits its use of gasoline-powered machinery because of the air pollution caused by burning fuel. The farm takes pride in what it views as a moral commitment to chemical-free, sustainable farming. It sells its produce at nearby farmers' markets and from a roadside stand on the property, as well as to restaurants around California. The owners of these restaurants express their gratitude for the quality and flavor of the fruits and vegetables with glowing praise and free meals for the farm managers.

XYZ's Secret Ingredient

XYZ Organics employs eight Mexican field workers. Each man has a resident alien card. Three of the cards are authentic. Five are not. The false cards cost anywhere from $40 to $100 to purchase, about the same price college students pay for fake IDs they use to get into clubs or to buy liquor. Velez and the other four unauthorized workers have fake social security cards as well, with fake social security numbers.

Jim McCann[*], the farm's personnel manager, checks the workers' cards and papers each year, as required by law. "But," says the farm's long-time manager, Peter Collins[*], "we know or sense that there are a few of our crew members where documentation is not real or has been purchased."

Collins says there is a false perception that, unlike conventional farms, organic farms don't hire illegal Mexican migrants.

"In the organic movement," Collins says, "it's a dirty little secret."

But Sam Hammond[*], XYZ's current market manager, says the secrecy extends well beyond the borders of organic farming.

"[Labor] is a taboo topic," Hammond says. "It's like the unspoken issue in farming that no one wants to talk about."

The National Agricultural Workers Survey is the most comprehensive survey on matters of migrant farm labor. The most recent NAWS, published in 2000, reported that 52 percent of farm workers interviewed nationwide were unauthorized, or "illegal." Howard Rosenberg, a specialist in agricultural labor issues at the University of California at Berkeley, says the number has only continued to increase since that time. Rosenberg says the hiring of ineligible farm workers was once thought limited to border states, but that in the past 10–15 years the phenomenon has been evident throughout the nation. "We used to think this was a little secret in places like California and Texas," Rosenberg says. "But the national survey showed that we exceeded 50 percent ineligible in the farm workforce all around the country."

Feeding a Nation

Americans enjoy some of the cheapest food in the world, due in part to the inexpensive labor Mexican workers provide. Mexican-born workers, both legal and undocumented, made up 91 percent of the California agricultural work force, and 77 percent of all US agricultural workers, according to the 2000 NAWS and the Department of Labor. "The cost of food is a reflection of how much can be paid to the workers," says Sam Hammond from XYZ Organics.

Jocelyn Sherman, a spokeswoman for the United Farm Workers union, says the agricultural system in the US is just plain unfair. "These [workers] are the people who put food on our table," Sherman says, "and many cannot feed their own children."

In a report entitled "Living at the Edge: Mexican Origin Farm Workers in Rural California," Don Villarejo, Ph.D., writes, "Foreign-born workers are now recognized to be the secret ingredient of one of the most perplexing puzzles of the unprecedented US economic boom of the last decade."

. . .

It is 5:00 A.M. on Monday, May 30, 2001. The fog that rolls in from the Pacific Ocean at night still hangs over the fields in the pre-dawn haze. Pedro Montano[*] comes out of his trailer room to put on his shoes. Montano, a jolly man from Oaxaca with a jovial laugh and a thick salt and pepper mustache, is one of the five undocumented men on the XYZ crew. He has been working on farms in California for over 20 years, returning to Mexico every year or two and making the trek back over the mountains with a coyote in the springtime.

Slowly the other workers emerge from their trailers. On Mondays and Thursdays, the men get up before dawn to begin harvesting string beans. They head to the field, quiet in the pre-dawn stillness and still sleepy until the sun climbs into the eastern sky. They each take a row in the front field of the farm, or "rancho." For the next four hours their bodies bend over the knee-high plants in human arches—"arcos," they call themselves—as they pick the beans, and place each handful in their white plastic buckets. They joke that the farm should be called not XYZ, but "Rancho de Los Arcos."

Living on the Farm

Eight Mexican men, two women, and three children live at XYZ in the cluster of trailers between the avocado orchard and the asparagus fields.

The kitchen trailer in the workers' quarters is used by five of the men. The men at XYZ each pay the farm $80 a month for utilities in the trailers. There is no bathroom. All thirteen people share one outhouse near the road at the other end of the farm. The outhouse is cleaned once a week. A bathhouse, which was begun last year, is still under construction. There is no heat in any of the structures, despite the fact that winter temperatures can drop to the low forties.

Wages at XYZ start at California's minimum wage of $6.75, which was raised from $6.25 in California in January 2002. Working 50-hour weeks for nine months of the year at minimum wage, the men at XYZ would make about $12,150 a year. Velez wires $300 a month back to his family in Mexico. The other men whose wives and families live in Mexico do the same. Taxes and social security are deducted from the wages pre-paycheck. Because their numbers are false, those who are unauthorized will probably never receive their social security benefits.

The Farmer's Dilemma

Collins says he feels that farmers like himself are caught in a vise. He says he cares about his workers and wants to make their experience working on his farm as positive as possible. He believes the Mexican migrants who work on farms in California and around the country should be treated as members of the community who are doing valuable work. But, he says, it is often a struggle to make ends meet at the farm.

"That place survives on a miracle every month. You try to make the situation as good as you can within the constraints of the resources you have."

Collins says that as far as he is concerned, it is impossible to get his workers legal papers. "Essentially, as a nation we guard the borders to keep out the very people whose hands grow our food."

Sam Hammond, XYZ's marketing manager, says he feels that in both the environmental and labor aspects of the farm, XYZ makes compromises.

"Like many other farms, we are operating on a shoestring, and it's pretty tricky to pull it off and pay people a living wage." He adds that farms like XYZ struggle to compete with larger agri-business operations. "In terms of why XYZ hasn't made leaps and bounds in terms of labor issues, it comes down to the fact that we're competing with farms that aren't making any leaps or bounds."

At Whose Expense?

California agriculture brought in $27 billion in revenue in 2000. If California were an independent nation, it would be the world's sixth largest economic power. Yet many of the men and women who work on California farms toil for minimum wage—and sometimes less. Dean Fryer of the Division of Labor Standards Enforcement in California says as far as his office is concerned, it doesn't matter if a worker is documented or not. "If you work here, you've got to get paid according to the law," Fryer said. "It doesn't matter where you're from, what papers you've got." But, Fryer says, a lot of workers are being paid less than the $6.75 required by California state law.

In addition, agricultural workers are exempt from the federal law requiring overtime pay after 8 hours of work in a day or 40 hours a week. In California, field workers are allowed to work 10 hours a day and 60 hours a week before being paid for overtime.

. . .

Whispering for Help

Juanita Martinez[*] had been bleeding for twelve days. Martinez, a beautiful woman with long silky hair, lives on the farm with Emilio and Antonio's nephew, Pablo Diaz[*]. Martinez, who is 16, gave birth to Pablo Diaz's son Daniel when she was 14 years old.

On the thirteenth day, Martinez went to take her shower. The shower on the farm is part of the shed, separated from the tool room by a shingled partition. A fluorescent outdoor patio light attached to one of the rafters sheds a dull pallor over the dank space. Martinez undressed Daniel and washed him and then herself, noticing that the bleeding had still not stopped.

When Martinez saw that Anna Morello[*], Sam Hammond's girlfriend who worked at a health care clinic, had come to the farm to drop off Hammond, Martinez approached her and quietly explained her problem. Morello referred Martinez to a clinic nearby and told her how to get there by bus.

Martinez and Diaz, like most Mexican farm worker families, do not have health insurance. Martinez, who came across the border in the line with false papers, is an illegal resident, as is Diaz. There is an option in Diaz's wage plan with XYZ to deduct a monthly amount for medical insurance but, like most farm workers, Diaz chose to wave his insurance option. Collins, XYZ's board president and longtime farm manager, says he has tried to encourage his workers to utilize the health insurance option.

"Originally we had two people, Jorge and Pablo, but they didn't stay with it because the reality is they don't feel comfortable . . . taking part in any formal system," Collins said.

The clinic where Anna Morello worked has a large number of Mexican migrant worker patients. Morello says there were people coming in all the time without insurance. The health care fees are often extremely burdensome for people making little more than minimum wage. "The [fee] without insurance to just get seen is $50 to $80," Morello says. "If they then have to go to a pharmacy for medication, who knows how much that could be."

Jorge Ines[*], a 58-year-old unauthorized worker who lives with Diego Velez, was diagnosed with diabetes two years ago. Because he is afraid a paper trail might lead to his deportation, he does not have health insurance and spends $400 a month on medication.

The doctors, Morello explained, do their best to help their patients. Some dispense doses of sample medications they get from pharmaceutical companies for free. The workers hear through word of mouth about the clinics where the doctors and nurses speak Spanish and won't ask questions. Morello says she could often tell when the papers and identifications were false. "It happens a lot," Morello explains. "But you learn to treat everyone as an individual and take what they say as the truth. You're there to help them with their health care needs and that's your only job."

. . .

Tres Meses en el Cielo

In about the middle of June, Diego Velez begins counting down the days. Each passing week is a week closer to his "tres meses en el cielo"—three months in heaven—that he spends with his family between November and March. The men at XYZ get tired of sleeping alone, tired of getting up early six days a week, tired of brushing their teeth with a bottle of water. More than anything, though, Velez just misses his family.

"At home," Velez says, "my daughter comes up to me and puts her arm around my neck and kisses me on the cheek. 'Papi,' she says. And here, nothing. Nobody."

Velez has left XYZ early a few times, returning home to Mexico before autumn comes to California. "Diego is such a sweetheart," Collins says of his employee. "He gets very lonely. He would bail out early, and it was too bad for the farm, but we understand of course."

Collins says he hopes some day all the families will live at XYZ in straw bale cottages. He says it's made him happy to have the two families currently living there.

But the dreams of the workers are a little different. All of the unauthorized workers say they would like to have paperwork that enables them to cross the border legally to work. Then they would also be able to visit their families during the year. Emilio Diaz says he would like to be able to make enough money on his farm in Mexico so he doesn't have to come to the US. Velez has already spent a cumulative $15,000 on building himself a house in Mexico. He would like to live there all year round.

This year, Velez stuck it out in California until November, returning home on the 29th with most of the XYZ crew. The day they leave California is a day full of anticipation for the men at XYZ. They pack small suitcases, leaving some of their belongings on the farm for their return next spring. They are thinking of the time they will get to spend with their loved ones back in Mexico, catching up on the year's events in conversations that are impossible using prepaid phone cards on public telephones.

Diego Velez takes down his sombrero from the hook by the door. He is wearing his Sunday clothes, a striped black and red shirt and black jeans. He wants to look nice when he sees his family. He puts the faded black hat on his head and closes the wooden door, picks up his bag, and walks up the hill without looking back.

Source: Jocelyn Lippert, "Rancho de Los Arcos" *AmeriQuests*, Volume 1, No. 1, 2004.

SUMMARY

Californians lived for many years under the myth that the state's economy was recession-proof. It must have appeared to many people that the economic infrastructure laid down after World War II, with its unrealistic reliance on federal dollars and the defense establishment, would continue forever. That perception changed with the crisis of the early 1990s. The recession was costly in terms of ruptured human lives, jobs, and prestige. Declining confidence in government had prompted voters to pass such measures as Proposition 13, restricting the discretionary power of elected leaders to such an extent that they were unable to cope with the fiscal crisis effectively. The costs of the downturn were passed first from the national level to the state level and, ultimately, to the local level. The counties continue to cope with the twin pressures of reduced revenues and a high demand for services. And, as county governments are forced to make hard choices, it is often those constituencies who are least able to fight for their fair share who are most severely affected.

NOTES

1. Mary Beth Barber, "When Johnny Comes Marching Home," *California Journal* 25 (January 1994): 19–25.
2. Steve Scott, "The Morphing Economy," *California Journal* 28 (July 1997): 14–20.
3. Mary Beth Barber, "Can You Make a Buck When Peace Breaks Out?" *California Journal* 25 (January 1994): 27–28.
4. Cost estimate from Rebuild L.A., quoted in "Rebuilding South Central," *California Journal* 28 (July 1997): 20.
5. Lou Cannon, "The Abiding Dream," *California Journal* 26 (January 1995): 7–10.
6. Mary Beth Barber, "Local Government Hits the Wall," *California Journal* 24 (August 1993): 13–15.
7. A. J. Block and Claudia Buck, eds., *California Political Almanac* (Sacramento, CA: State Net Services & Publications, 1999), p. 80.
8. Mark Baldassare, *When Government Fails: The Orange County Bankruptcy* (Berkeley: University of California Press, 1998).
9. Ibid.
10. Ibid.
11. E. Scott Reckard and Michael Wagner, "Broker to Settle with O.C. for $439 Million," *Los Angeles Times* (June 3, 1998): A1.
12. Ibid.
13. George Skelton, "It's Time to Act Like a Winner and Terminate Budget Battle" *Los Angeles Times* (July 19, 2004): B6.

CHAPTER 6

California's Constitution and Constitutional Officers

Featured Reading / Pages 76–78
Daniel Weintraub
The Un-California

> My son asked me what I hoped to accomplish as governor. I told him, essentially, to make life more comfortable for people, as far as government can. I think that embraces everything from developing the water resources vital to California's growth, to getting a man to work and back fifteen minutes earlier if it can be done through a state highway program.
>
> —Edmund G. "Pat" Brown, Sr., Governor of California, 1959–1967[1]

This chapter examines the executive branch of state government, as established by California's constitution. That document contains the framework of a plural executive, and the following section discusses the multiple and independent responsibilities of the state's constitutional officers and the executive bureaucracy.

CALIFORNIA'S CONSTITUTION

The state constitution outlines the structure of government, establishing the rules of the policy process, which government officials must apply and interpret. Like the U.S. Constitution, the state constitution codifies the rights of the state's people: Article I—the Declaration of Rights—addresses concrete issues as well as high principles, much like an elaborate version of the U.S. Constitution's Bill of Rights. Unlike the U.S. Constitution, the California constitution explicitly addresses several questions of institutional design, going into great detail about the size and function of specific public agencies. This attention to detail makes California's cumbersome constitution one of the longest of any state or nation. It was adopted in 1879 and has grown significantly in length, thanks to nearly 500 amendments.

Though it is possible to overhaul the state constitution through a constitutional convention, the delicate balance of power in the state makes such an event extremely unlikely.[2] It is more common to change the constitution either by constitutional amendment or through a constitutional revision commission. Most constitutional amendments are initiated through the legislative process. A constitutional measure must be approved by a two-thirds vote in both houses of the state legislature. It is then placed on the next statewide ballot and becomes constitutional law if approved by a majority vote of the electorate. Citizens may also bring about a constitutional amendment in the form of an initiative, bypassing the state legislature altogether. This process is discussed at length in Chapter 12.

A third way to change the state constitution is for the legislature to set up a constitutional revision commission composed of citizen appointees. These blue-ribbon commissions mainly "tinker-at-the edges" rather than systematically overhaul the document. Once the commission's recommendations are finalized, they are submitted back to the legislature for a two-thirds approval vote before they are sent on to the voters. Some modernizing efforts, such as the Sumner Commission (headed by Judge Bruce Sumner) in the 1960s–1970s made it to the voters and were approved. The Constitution Revision Commission issued several recommendations in 1995 to overhaul state government, including a unicameral legislature, having the governor and lieutenant governor run for office together as a single ticket, reducing the number of elected constitutional offices to simplify the state ballot, and switching from an annual budget to a two-year budget.[2] The structure of California's government has changed little in spite of such recommendations.

THE CONSTITUTIONAL OFFICERS

In order to govern the nation's largest state, California has developed an elaborate executive branch and an expansive bureaucracy. Some of this growth can be attributed to new offices created through reform efforts. Because California's constitution is easier to amend than that of other states, it has been relatively easy to pass initiatives creating new constitutional offices.[3] California's executive branch is populated with eight elected offices. In addition to the governor, voters choose candidates for seven other constitutional offices, including the lieutenant governor, attorney general, controller, secretary of state, state treasurer, superintendent of public instruction, and insurance commissioner. These officers each serve four-year terms, with a Proposition 140 limit of two terms in any one office.

The Governor

California's governor must share, and in some cases bow to, the constitutional authority of seven other statewide independent elected officials who exercise executive power. In this way California has a "plural executive" rather than a strong governorship, as Governor Deukmejian found in 1987 when state Attorney General John Van de Kamp refused to support his challenge to the state's toxics initiative, Proposition 65. California's governor has remarkably few cabinet and commission appointments, compared to other states, largely because most of these high administrative positions are nested within the protective civil service realm and are insulated from being politicized. Despite this, the governor is the focal point of state politics. Because California has the largest economy and population, as well as the most electoral votes of any state, its governors are often significant figures on the national political scene. Ambitious governors such as Ronald Reagan, Jerry Brown, and Pete Wilson used the office to launch presidential campaigns. Other governors, such as Pat Brown and George Deukmejian, were considered as potential running mates by their parties' presidential nominees. Earl Warren left the governor's office to serve as chief justice of the U.S. Supreme Court. Every governor since World War II has been reelected at least once. Mastery of the office entails the effective use of three kinds of authority: explicit powers, independent powers, and informal powers.

EXPLICIT POWERS.   The governor is expected to be the electorate's leader and a check on the power wielded by the other branches of government. Explicit powers—constitutional powers explicitly delegated to the governor—provide the basic tools governors use to fulfill these responsibilities. One such tool is the line-item veto. This permits the governor to remove, or "blue-pencil," single line-item appropriations and initiatives from legislation without vetoing the entire bill. The governor may also employ a full veto of any legislative bill, with vetoes subject to override by two-thirds vote of both the assembly and the senate. In practice, only about 8 percent of all laws are vetoed, and overrides are extremely rare. Normally the governor's office gets involved well before the final passage of a bill, thereby reducing the probability of a veto at the end of the process. The governor has 12 days to sign a bill into law or to use the veto, thereby sending it back to the legislature. If the governor does nothing, the bill becomes law without his or her signature.

Other explicit powers of the governorship include acting as the head of state and as the commander-in-chief of the California National Guard. The California National Guard is activated at the discretion of the governor, typically in response to natural disasters and emergencies and in large-scale civil disturbances.[4] The governor also has the authority to call a special session of the legislature to address issues of critical importance should they occur while the legislature is out of session. Further, under the exercise of executive clemency the governor may unilaterally grant reprieves (postponement of sentences), pardons (a full release from custody), or commutations (reductions of sentences) to convicts within state jurisdiction. Executive clemency, however, is checked by the will of the majority on the supreme court when it comes to those convicts with past felon records whom the governor wishes to pardon or commutate.

Explicit powers of the governorship may also be shared with other branches of government. For example, the governor has the prime responsibility to watch over the "fiscal ship of state," submitting to the legislature a state budget spending plan on or before January 10 of each year. The legislature has until June 15 to alter, modify, or confirm the state budget, though this deadline is rarely met in practice. Another significant power that the governor must share is naming appointees to prominent positions in state government and to part-time citizen-panels spanning over 300 state boards, commissions, and councils. Of these gubernatorial appointees, 600–700 require confirmation by a majority of the state senate. Judicial appointees, usually experienced lawyers who share a similar judicial philosophy as the governor, must be approved by the Commission on Judicial Appointments.

INDEPENDENT POWERS. The governor's independent powers are most visible in his obligatory role to enforce state law through a sprawling 200,000-person administrative bureaucracy consisting of more than 60 departments, most of which are grouped within six mega-agencies: Business, Transportation and Housing, Natural Resources, Health and Human Services, State and Consumer Services, Corrections and Rehabilitations, and Environmental Protection. The executive heads of these agencies are appointed by the governor (subject to senate confirmation) and play a key strategic role in determining how legislative policy should be implemented.

There is wide policy discretion that cabinet officials may choose to follow as implementation orders from the governor filter down through the respective bureaucracy. The ultimate "will" of the sitting governor through these independent entities is felt throughout the governance of the state. For example, Governor Arnold Schwarzenegger signaled a strong commitment to the environment by naming Terry Tamminen, a Santa Monica environmental activist, to head the California Environmental Protection Agency. Governor Jerry Brown's appointment of Adriana Gianturco to head the State Department of Transportation (Caltrans) irritated the highway lobby and the legislature because Gianturco articulated a pro-environmental, mass-transit administrative vision, much like Brown's "small-is-better" orientation. In much the same manner, the senate's veto against the confirmation of Victor Veysey as Governor George "Duke" Deukmejian's head of the Department of Industrial Relations was in large part due to Veysey's noted "pro-business bias" and fear by a Democratic-controlled senate that worker safety, among other issues, might get short shrift. The governor's independent powers are also reflected in various independent boards and commissions that cover a range of issues affecting a wide arena of state policy—from education policy to ethics to agricultural relations. Among the most important of these are the following:

- The five-person Public Utilities Commission, appointed by the governor for six-year terms, which regulates public and private utilities ranging from gas, water, electricity, and telephone service.
- The Fair Political Practices Commission (FPPC). The FPPC was created by voters in June 1974 to police ethical reforms of the State's Political Reform Act, covering in part campaign disclosures, lobbying activities, and legislators' election spending.
- The Board of Governors of the California Community Colleges. It oversees 71 locally controlled community college districts. The 16-member board is appointed for four-year terms by the governor.
- The University of California Board of Regents, which governs the 10 campuses of the University of California. The Board of Regents consists of 18 members appointed by the governor for 12-year terms; 1 University of California student representative, who serves a one-year term; plus 7 *ex officio* members, including the governor, the lieutenant governor, the assembly speaker, the superintendent

of public instruction, the University of California president, and the president and vice presidents of the University of California alumni association.

- The Trustees of California State University, which governs the 23 campuses of California State University. There are 24 voting trustees, including 16 trustees appointed by the governor, who serve eight-year terms; an alumni trustee, a faculty trustee, and a student trustee, each of whom serve two-year terms; and five *ex officio* members, including the governor, the lieutenant governor, the speaker of the assembly, the state superintendent of public instruction, and the chancellor.

The affirmative action debate launched by Governor Pete Wilson and some of his appointed regents is demonstrative of the governor's capacity to use independent powers to shape public policy discourse and direction.[5]

INFORMAL POWERS. Perhaps the most intangible assets, given the legacy of anti-governor feelings that date back as far as the colonial period, are the informal powers the governor wields. California governors have found that the informal powers associated with the office afford them a wide range of influence and control beyond their formal powers. For instance, the governor is the symbolic head of his or her party and, with allies in the state legislature, can move legislation through the process consistent with the prevailing ideology that defines the party. The governor traditionally plays a critical role during elections in helping to raise campaign funds to assist the party faithful and in shaping the party platform. In this role, some governors have come up against strong intra-party rivalries. Jerry Brown, a Progressive, clashed with the more "moderate" segment of the Democratic party. Moderates felt that Brown's "new spirit" campaign—based in part on his pro-consumerism, his opposition to nuclear power, his empathy for farm workers—would alienate the middle-class and corporate supporters of the party. Pete Wilson was tested in holding off conservative challenges to keep the California Republican party from adopting a "pro-life" platform. The need to balance personal conviction with party politics remains the greatest challenge a governor can face.

The most significant of the governor's informal powers is the ability to use the "bully pulpit" of the office to move policy in a particular direction. Governors have immediate access to the state and national media and have used this leverage to manipulate public opinion. This power, however, is a double-edged sword: Governors also serve as lightning rods for frustrations in the state. Lackluster economic conditions, riots, even natural disasters are often laid at the feet of governors, reflected in poor job ratings and popularity polls. In spring 1981, for example, Jerry Brown's perceived mishandling of the medfly crisis in the rich Central Valley region cost him dearly in votes and earned him the nickname "Lord of the Flies."

The combination of explicit, independent, and informal powers enhances and limits gubernatorial authority in California. Gubernatorial style varies from governor to governor, with some more successful than others. Ronald Reagan leveraged his folksy style from the governor's office to the White House. Jerry Brown tried and failed to use his progressive platform to win the Democratic nomination for president in three different attempts. Still, he reinvented himself as the mayor of Oakland, one of California's most progressive cities in terms of race relations and economic development—and later as attorney general. Pete Wilson, an extremely successful governor, fell flat in each of his two unsuccessful attempts at national office. To paraphrase presidential scholar Richard Neustadt, a governor's most important power may be his or her power to persuade.[6]

The Lieutenant Governor

Like the vice president on the national level, the lieutenant governor is next in line for succession should the governor become incapacitated, but the actual powers of the office are few. Eight states have no such constitutional office. The lieutenant governor casts tie-breaking votes in the state senate, as the vice president must do in the U.S. Senate. The state constitution places the lieutenant governor as an *ex officio* member of several powerful state boards and commissions, including the state Lands Commission, the California State University Board of Trustees, the Regents of the University of California, and chair of the California Economic Development Commission.

Unlike the vice president, however, the lieutenant governor is able to exercise executive power by sitting in as the acting governor when the governor travels outside state boundaries. Candidates for governor and lieutenant governor do not run together on the same ticket in California, as they do in many other states. And because the lieutenant governor is independently elected, winners are frequently from different parties. This can hamstring a governor who has presidential aspirations. Republican Lieutenant Governor Mike Curb was a thorn in Democrat Jerry Brown's side during Brown's fundraising and campaign trips for his 1980 primary challenge to President Carter. During his short-lived run for the White House, Republican Pete Wilson had to contend with the prospect of then-Lieutenant Governor Gray Davis, a Democrat, taking charge. Governor Schwarzenegger is constitutionally prohibited from seeking the presidency because he was not born in the United States. Still, he had to contend with the prospect of handing over executive authority to a Democrat whenever he left the state, first with Cruz Bustamante as lieutenant governor, and later with John Garamendi, a former state insurance commissioner with his own aspirations for the top job.

The Attorney General

The attorney general is the head of the Department of Justice and the state's chief law enforcement official. Under Article V, Section 13 of the Constitution of the State of California, the attorney general must ensure that all state laws are "uniformly and adequately enforced." As chief legal advisor, the attorney general represents the state in lawsuits, offers legal opinions to the legislature on pending bills, and prepares titles and summaries for circulated propositions. In rare cases, the attorney general may step in as a district attorney in any of California's 58 counties if it becomes necessary for the state to enforce a legal mandate.

In government, it is often said that "A.G." stands not for *attorney general* but for *aspiring governor*. California is no exception. Pat Brown and George Deukmejian both held the office of attorney general before they were elected governor. Other attorneys general who tried unsuccessfully to make the move to the top spot include Republicans Evelle Younger and Dan Lungren, as well as Democrat John Van de Kamp. For the first time in 2006, a former governor sought and won the office of attorney general. After two terms as mayor of Oakland, the 68-year-old former Governor Jerry Brown was elected by a 19-point margin over his Republican rival, winning the office that launched his father's political career. Brown campaigned on a platform of aiding local law enforcement and enforcing limits on greenhouse gas emissions.[7]

The Controller

The controller is the state's chief fiscal officer and the overseer of government finance. In that role, the controller chairs the Franchise Tax Board (which collects state income tax), is a member of the Board of Equalization (which collects state sales tax), and is a member of the state Lands Commission. The controller oversees the state payroll and has wide latitude in making sure state expenditures meet state law requirements. This once-sleepy outpost of the executive branch has recently been turned around as an electoral staging area for other offices. Democrat Gray Davis used the office as a stepping stone on his way to the governorship, much as Alan Cranston moved from controller to the U.S. Senate in 1974. John Chiang was elected controller in 2006, becoming the highest-ranking Asian American official elected statewide.

The Secretary of State

When former State Senator Debra Bowen was elected secretary of state in 2006, she became the chief election officer and the state's guardian of documents and records. The office grants charters to corporations, incorporates nonprofit organizations, maintains the state archives, and is the keeper of the Great Seal of the State of California, which is affixed to all documents requiring the governor's signature. Much of the responsibility of the secretary of state's office revolves around its duties as chief elections officer. Not only does the secretary of state verify qualified voters' signatures on petitions for ballot measures, but he or she oversees all state election laws throughout the counties of California. From the printing of ballot arguments to the counting and centralization of election results, this office holds a prominent place within the plural executive.

The State Treasurer

The treasurer is the state's investment banker and the official in charge of maintaining the state's high credit rating. With an annual portfolio of more than $3 billion in state bonds, the treasurer is a major force on Wall Street, although he or she remains relatively obscure to the citizens of California. The treasurer prepares the selling and redemption of state bonds (mainly to finance large infrastructure projects, such as dams, roads, and bridges) and also oversees the investment of securities and stock investments of public employee pension funds. Essentially, what the controller collects the treasurer invests. Jesse Unruh raised the profile of the office during his 13 years as state treasurer, a tenure of service that ended with his death from cancer in 1987. In recent years, the job has been used as a staging area to campaign for higher office. Democrat Kathleen Brown left the office after a single term to launch an unsuccessful campaign for governor in 1994. She was succeeded by Republican Matt Fong, who left after one term in 1998 and then lost his bid for the U.S. Senate. Fong was followed in that office by Democrat Phil Angelides, who challenged Schwarzenegger for governor and lost. In 2006, former Democratic State Senate Leader and Attorney General Bill Lockyer was elected treasurer.

The Superintendent of Public Instruction

The superintendent of public instruction heads up the State Department of Education. In this role the superintendent is both an independently elected official and an administrator who implements the policies of the 10-member appointed board of education. Although most decisions about education rest at the local level, the State Department of Education is often involved in such areas as teacher credentialing, text approval, curriculum adoption, and state fiscal assistance to local school districts. The superintendent sits *ex officio* on the Board of Regents of the University of California, the California State University Board of Trustees, and the Board of Governors of the Community College System.

While technically nonpartisan, the superintendent's office is at times swept up in politics. California public schools languished during the 1980s as a bitter political feud between Republican Governor George Deukmejian and Democratic-leaning Superintendent Bill Honig prevented the two offices from cooperating on education policy. In 1994, former Assembly Education Committee Chair Delaine Eastin, a liberal Democrat, became superintendent. In the election, Eastin defeated Maureen DiMarco, a protégé of Republican Governor Pete Wilson. Over the next four years, Wilson seized the initiative on education policy and worked with his own appointed secretary of education and the legislature to increase funding and push for reduced class size in primary grades. Finding herself shut out of the process, Eastin used the office mainly as a bully pulpit. Governor Gray Davis built a stronger working relationship between the administration and the superintendent's office by appointing former State Senator Gary K. Hart as his secretary of education. In that capacity, Hart helped steer several key education bills through the legislature, but the relationship between the state's two top education officials has been more often adversarial. Democratic State Senator Jack O'Connell was elected to the superintendent's office in 2006, even as Republican Arnold Schwarzenegger was reelected.

The Insurance Commissioner

Unlike other statewide offices, which are provided by the constitution, the insurance commissioner's position was created with the 1988 passage of Proposition 103. Voters added this office to oversee the operations, rate setting, and regulatory functioning of the state Department of Insurance. Prior to the passage of Proposition 103, the commissioner was appointed by the governor. Consumer advocates had for years complained that the relationship between the insurance companies doing business in the state and the commissioner, who usually came from the insurance industry, was "too cozy." Two years following the passage of Proposition 103, Democrat John Garamendi ran as a pro-consumer advocate and became the state's first elected insurance commissioner. His successor, Republican Chuck Quackenbush, was elected with heavy support from the insurance industry, until Quackenbush eventually resigned amid accusations of financial misappropriations. Garamendi returned in 2002, after serving in the Clinton administration, serving another term before he was elected lieutenant governor in 2006. Steve Poizner was elected insurance commissioner in 2006.

The Board of Equalization

In addition to its eight constitutional officers, California voters elect the five members of the state Board of Equalization. The state controller has a seat on the board, and the others are elected from four districts, each consisting of roughly one-fourth of the state's population. Two of the districts—one in coastal Northern California and the other in Los Angeles County—have a majority of Democratic voters. The other two are majority-Republican: one consisting of the Central Coast, Central Valley, and Sierra Nevada region, and the other consisting of Orange, San Diego, Riverside, and Imperial Counties. Despite the low political profile of this board, members wield a great amount of power in collecting state and local sales taxes as well as use taxes and excise taxes from the sale of gasoline, beverages, alcohol, and cigarettes. Another important function is to review and harmonize the tax assessments of California's 58 counties.

THE BUREAUCRACY

Working under the direction of the executive officers are the civil servants who do the work of government, from the clerks processing driver's licenses to Caltrans crews repairing freeways to the officers of the California Highway Patrol. This is the "face" of California government, embodied in the dedicated public employees comprising the state's civil service. By the beginning of Gray Davis' tenure as governor, the number of state employees had grown to 277,903. Figure 6.1 outlines the various agencies within the executive bureaucracy. Most of these positions have civil service protection, a reform designed to limit political patronage. In order to ensure that an incoming administration can be effective, agency heads and members of boards are exempt from this rule and serve at the will of the governor. The number of exempt positions has long been a point of contention between elected officials and agency staff. In his two terms as governor, Pete Wilson more than doubled the number of exempt positions, from 550 when he took office to 1,351 in 1996.[8]

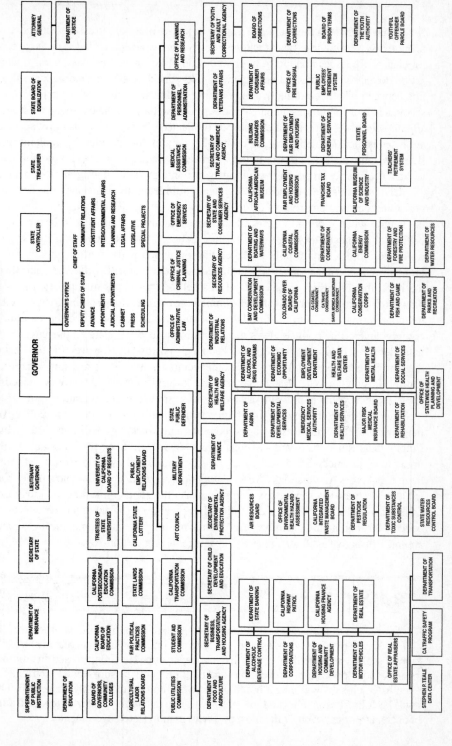

FIGURE 6.1 THE EXECUTIVE BUREAUCRACY

Today's civil servants are addressing broad institutional pressures designed to make the system more efficient and less costly for taxpayers. Included in the agenda for change are issues ranging from privatization of key state industries, to affirmative action, to the right for collective bargaining. The state's public servants walk a delicate line between what we normally term as being "political" and being "technical." Civil servants hold an enormous amount of power because they are the ones who must actually implement the rules and dictates made by elected officials. Administrative agencies are responsible for rulemaking, or developing the day-to-day rules for implementing state law. Only the legislature or initiative process can create laws, but statutes are written in a necessarily broad way, requiring agency interpretation during implementation.

Civil servants are foremost professionally minded individuals operating within a prevailing partisan environment. Ideally, they are neither Republican nor Democrat but neutral when serving in their official capacities, using their technical expertise to achieve the goals set by legal statute. In practice, however, there is some "wiggle room" to mold a certain policy: Depending on which party controls the executive branch, we sometimes see a partisan-tinged outcome (yet still within the mandate of the law). In California, we see less of this behind-the-scenes manipulation than in other high-patronage states. Through competitive civil service examinations, the ethical constraints of a public administration career, and a workforce that is almost entirely covered by civil service's merit system protections, state employees are not beholden to elected officials to gain or keep their positions.[9] However, the old dictum that "politicians come and go, but the bureaucrats last forever" rings somewhat true: California's civil service system has served Californians well since it was created in 1934. Explicit political pressure or favoritism is rare within the bureaucracy.

In 1977 state employees won the constitutional right to enter into collective-bargaining agreements to set wages, benefits, and working conditions. The Public Employment Relations Board was created to oversee collective bargaining and prevent unfair labor practices. State workers are mostly represented by the powerful California State Employees Association (CSEA), a major player in state politics and a major contributor to statewide Democrats' campaigns. As the state employees' political arm, CSEA has battled over such issues as closed-agency shops (meaning union dues can be collected from nonunion members) and the dismantling of state employment programs around affirmative action with the 1996 passage of Proposition 209.

The Un-California   *Daniel Weintraub*

Walk along the pedestrian plaza near the state Capitol some afternoon in the spring or summer, and you're likely to run into an aging man seated at a cheap metal table, eating frozen yogurt from a paper cup. He'll be dressed in rumpled slacks and a loud, short-sleeved shirt and he'll probably be surrounded by friends. If you listen closely, you'll hear him muttering profanities and talking basketball. This will be John Burton, a legend in California politics and the leader of the California Senate, after the governor the most powerful man in state government.

Burton will have no security guard with him, no cops or aides to brush people away. His only defense is his famously foul mouth and what can be, on bad days, a menacing growl. Reporters or citizens alike are equally free to approach him, and chances are, the citizen will get the warmer reception.

Burton's casual bearing is not unusual here, and in fact the people who govern the nation's largest state are surprisingly accessible. Even Gov. Arnold Schwarzenegger, the megastar and multimillionaire, has taken to doing lunch on the town, with security unobtrusive enough to allow the occasional visitor to approach for a handshake or a brief chat.

That air of informality is at the heart of Sacramento's charm, although the city's leaders don't seem to recognize it. The mayor and local business honchos are forever pining for "major league status," whatever that means, hoping to be recognized far and wide as some sort of world-class city. They sense, correctly, that to the rest of California, Sacramento is the afterthought capital, the place you stop on the way to someplace else. When I left my native San Diego seventeen years ago to move here to write about state government and politics, friends and family looked at me blankly. Sacramento?

But that's exactly what I like about it. With its two gorgeous rivers—the Sacramento flowing from the north state and the American gurgling down from the Sierra—the city feels more Midwest than California. Huge shade trees line downtown boulevards, creating canopies above the streets of the prewar neighborhoods of brick and stucco homes that surround downtown to the south and east. Its central city, with the exception of a few faded blocks here and there, is vibrant and growing more so, with a mix of business and housing that makes living near where you work more affordable, and more desirable, than in the state's major urban centers.

The climate also is not what most people associate with California, and it has a noticeable effect on the local psyche. The weather is just uneven enough to give residents a sense of the changing seasons and the rhythms they can bring to life, the shared discomfort of dealing with the damp winter cold and the blazing hot summers. Storms that bring snow to the nearby mountains and fill the region's reservoirs are not shunned as unruly intruders but welcomed like old friends. People here realize that water falling from the sky is not an irritant but part of the cycle of life. My children, growing up in Sacramento, have learned that fresh produce doesn't just show up on the grocery shelves but comes from the nearby fields, the result of the risk and hard work of farmers and laborers alike.

The city's distinguishing geographic characteristic—its flatness—is usually considered a negative. Indeed, the long stretch to the distant horizon can make you feel lonely. But the level terrain also seems to have flattened the social strata, which is far more welcoming than what you find in California's coastal communities. There are few of the super-rich here, and while Sacramento has its share of poor people, there is no great expanse of grinding poverty, no slum to speak of. Lacking hills on which the wealthy can perch and look down on the rest of the town, Sacramento has neighborhoods where the well-to-do live in close proximity to the up-and-coming. The only coastal property is on the river banks, which, while lined with sprawling ranch-style mansions, are not everyone's idea of luxury living. Any sense of exclusivity is pierced by the existence of a publicly owned and accessible parkway that stretches along the American River from near the foothill town of

Folsom all the way to Sacramento, where it connects with a bike trail that sits atop the east bank of the city's namesake river.

California's capital, in other words, is about as un-Californian as you can get. Its defining trait might be an almost total lack of pretense. There is plenty of puffery inside the Capitol building, of course, but ninety-nine percent of Sacramentans never go there, even though one in four in the workforce toil for one level of government or another. Get out from under the dome and this is still a very real place—even for the politicos.

Sure, the glitz is coming. The downtown is increasingly dotted with high-end restaurants, where valet parking is becoming the norm. High-rise condo towers with rents north of two thousand dollars a month are on the drawing board. And Schwarzenegger's crowd is packing the bars and bistros, giving off not just as aroma of expensive cigars but the slight whiff of a Southern California state of mind.

But so far we have taken his arrival in stride. It's not as if the city's streets are now crowded with Hummers. And those you do see tend to be spattered with mud, just back from a trip to the mountains. Around these parts, people actually drive them there.

Source: "The Un-California" by Daniel Weintraub. In *My California*, Donna Wares, ed. (Angel City Press: Santa Monica, 2004) pp.175–178.

SUMMARY

California's political institutions are in need of repair. California's plural executive is functionally responsible for implementing programs and enforcing laws. The fragmentation of the executive branch makes political control of the vast state bureaucracy daunting. Blue-ribbon panels have issued numerous proposals to reform the system, ranging from a unicameral legislature to reducing the number of constitutional offices. Proponents of reform argue that these reforms would reduce the fragmentation of power, cut legislative gridlock, strengthen the governorship, and simplify the ballot. However, the state's elected officials have not embraced these ideas.

NOTES

1. Quoted in *California Journal* 21 (January 1990): 8.
2. Since the second constitution was adopted in 1878, the voters have called for a constitutional convention only once—in the 1930s—and the state legislature refused.
3. See Roger Noll, "Executive Organization: Responsiveness vs. Expertise and Flexibility," in *Constitutional Reform in California*, Bruce Cain and Roger Noll, eds. (Berkeley, CA: Institute for Governmental Studies, 1995).
4. The Guard was called out, for example, during the Northridge Earthquake in 1994, as well as in the civil unrest in Berkeley during the 1960s and in Los Angeles during 1965 and 1992.

5. Kit Lively, "A Jolt from Sacramento," *The Chronicle of Higher Education* (June 9, 1995): 25.
6. Richard Neustadt, *Presidential Power* (New York: John Wiley and Sons, Inc., 1980).
7. Jim Herron Zamora, "Attorney General: Brown Makes a Bit of History." *San Francisco Chronicle* (November 9, 2006): A19.
8. A. J. Block and Claudia Buck, eds., *California Political Almanac* (Sacramento, CA: State Net Services & Publications, 1999), p. 80.
9. Ninety-eight percent of the state's civil servants are protected.

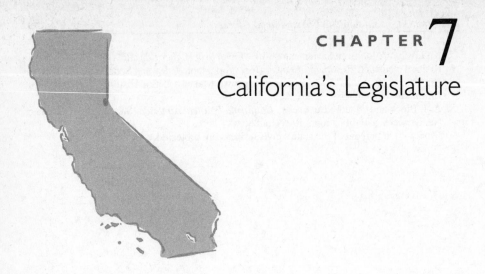

CHAPTER 7

California's Legislature

The California state legislature is comprised of two bodies: the assembly and the senate. This bicameral arrangement is typical of every state in the union except Nebraska. The 80 members of the assembly are elected for two-year terms, and the 40 members of the senate are elected for four-year terms. Under Proposition 140, assembly members may serve a maximum of three terms (six years), and senators are limited to a maximum of two terms (eight years). Half of the senate and the entire assembly are elected in November of every even-numbered year.

The size and representation of each assembly and senate district is extremely important in the balance of democratization. Between 1923 and 1965 California's legislature was fashioned much like the congressional model: Representation in the assembly was based on population (like the House of Representatives) and in the senate on counties (like geographic area in the U.S. Senate). The result was that rural central and northern counties dominated the legislature. For example, under the "federal plan" adopted in 1926, 21 senators from small northern and central counties represented less than 10 percent of the population; Los Angeles County, at the time with 35 percent of the state's population, had only one senator. The U.S. Supreme Court decision in *Reynolds* v. *Sims* (1964), and the subsequent decisions mandating "one-person/one-vote" in legislative districting, had a profound effect on the California legislature.[1] California's 1966 elections ushered in a younger, better-educated, urban-based, more diverse cast of legislators, breaking the northern and central state's rural veto power over southern urban interests.

Legislative mapping is critical in defining power relations in the legislature. Every 10 years, following the national census, the legislature must reapportion itself, drawing new district boundaries to equalize the shifting demographic changes. The intense political competition in California has made redistricting a hardball sport, pushing more mundane legislative business aside during reapportionment battles.[2] Typically, the majority party in the legislature will manipulate the district boundaries to increase its number of "safe" (noncompetitive) seats. The legislature adjusts all

120 districts in the state and realigns California's 53 congressional districts, so the stakes are quite high. The results are like abstract art, with some districts having very unusual patterns—one senate district ran from a section of the California coast clear across the mountains and deserts to the Arizona border. More importantly, the process gives an unfair advantage to the majority party in open-seat races.

So gridlocked and distasteful have the last few reapportionment battles in California been that the battle has spilled from the legislature to the courts and the initiative process. In 1991, after Governor Wilson vetoed the legislature's redistricting plan, the state supreme court appointed three retired judges ("special masters") to draw up a more "objective" plan, which remained in place through 2000, when a Democratic legislature and governor redrew the map. After Schwarzenegger became governor, a Republican plan to hand redistricting authority to another panel of three retired judges was placed on the ballot for a special election in 2005. Schwarzenegger campaigned hard for Proposition 77, but it was voted down, 59 percent to 41 percent, in the special election, along with a few other ballot measures designed to advance his agenda through the initiative process.

THE STATE OF THE LEGISLATURE

In November 1966 California voters overwhelmingly approved Proposition 1A, which sought to professionalize the part-time legislature.[3] Staff consultants were added, as were specialized adjunct offices including the senate and assembly offices of Research, Legislative Counsel, the Audit General, and the Legislative Analyst office. The California legislature was *the* model for other states to emulate. It was efficient, orderly, modern, and, most essentially, corruption free. In the early 1970s it was rated by most experts of state governance as the nation's best state legislature. By the 1990s, however, California's legislature had lost much of its luster. Corruption, ideological and institutional gridlock, and budgetary politicking gave momentum to government reform efforts, though the results have been underwhelming.[4] While legislators collect annual paychecks of $99,000, plus generous expense accounts, the multi-billion-dollar state budget still languishes each year past its constitutional deadlines. While partisan gridlock continues to dominate both houses, special interests have been amassing war chests to circulate confusing, often self-serving, propositions onto the California ballot through the initiative process. Reforming the legislature has proven to be a massive undertaking. Many argue that campaign finance reform heads the list of necessary changes. To be competitive in a typical state legislative race, a candidate must raise between $500,000 and $750,000. Proposition 112 cut down on potential payola scenarios by outlawing the practice of giving large honoraria to legislators.

In 1990, voters expressed their frustration with the legislature's scandals and gridlock—not by voting incumbents out of office but by passing term limits. Proposition 140 limited state senators to two four-year terms and members of the assembly to three two-year terms. Supporters of the initiative argued that term limits would limit corruption and lead to a new generation of "citizen-legislators," whose interests would be closer to those of their constituents.

During the late 1990s, both chambers suffered from the loss of experienced members. The brain drain was most severe in the assembly because two-year terms coupled with the limitations of Proposition 140 ensured that at least one-third of the chamber would be rookie lawmakers. (Termed-out members of the assembly could still serve eight years in the senate, where their lawmaking experience would be an asset.) Critics of term limits feared that the reform would undo the benefits accrued by professionalizing the legislature in the first place because inexperienced lawmakers would have to rely on bureaucrats, lobbyists, and staffers for information, and that it might weaken the institution relative to the governor. The voters were unimpressed by these arguments in 2008, when they rejected a measure to reform the term limits law. Proposition 93 would have reduced the maximum number of years in the legislature from 14 to 12 but would have allowed legislators to serve the entire time in a single chamber instead of skipping from the assembly to the senate. One provision of Proposition 93 would have "grandfathered" incumbent legislators, so that the time already served would not have applied to their new 12-year limits. Essentially, the measure allowed them to start their term limit clocks over again. Opponents of Proposition 93, including the state Republican party, seized on this provision. Ads featuring Assembly Speaker Fabian Nunez and Senate Pro Tem Don Perata (both Democrats) reminded voters that the reform would allow each of them to stay in their posts 12 more years. "The law," said one ad, "would let termed-out politicians stay in office and preserve their opulent lifestyles." California's term limit law remains unchanged, but institutional reform will continue to be a major issue.

The Human Side of the Legislature

The composition of the legislature's membership does not mirror the state's diversity. Asian legislators are grossly underrepresented, given their proportion in the general public—as are Latino legislators (although Latinos are the fastest-growing group of legislators, reflecting the statewide increase in Latino politicization). About one-quarter of the legislators are female—although women comprise over half of the state's population. African American legislators comprise around 8 percent of the total legislature—about equal to their percentage in the overall public. There are currently three open lesbians who serve in both houses. White male legislators make up around 75 percent of the California legislature. The predominant occupation of most who enter the legislature is attorney, followed by businessperson. Critics argue that the lack of diversity represented by sitting legislators is a problem, especially when scarce resources are carved up. Others argue that representative democracy was never meant to be a pure looking-glass at ourselves. Indeed, it is the political parties that need to create an inclusive "big-tent" perspective, reflecting the concerns of all constituencies, if the legislature is to be successful.

The work of the legislature goes beyond introducing and voting on individual pieces of legislation. Beyond pure lawmaking, legislators do the following: They provide constituent services, act as monitors to oversee and check executive agencies, function as budget negotiators during annual appropriations process which sets the state's budget, and—for those who sit in the state senate—they have responsibilities in confirming or rejecting hundreds of gubernatorial appointments to state boards, agencies, and commissions. Little of this could be accomplished without the professional assistance of personal member and institutional legislative staff. Personal staff helps the member in a number of ways: They are his or her eyes and ears in the district—helping constituents and looking after state issues as they impact the district; capitol personal staff help draft speeches, prepare and analyze bills for the member, and work with other party caucus staff to coordinate joint efforts. Institutional staff assist the entire membership of the legislative branch. For example, the legislative analyst office prepares an analysis of the governor's annual budget as well as assessing the fiscal implications of other legislative proposals and ballot measures. The legislative counsel office drafts the actual pieces of legislation introduced by every member of the legislature and offers legal opinions to members on state matters. Finally, the audit general office conducts both management and fiscal audits on behalf of the oversight function the legislature constitutionally possesses.

Legislative Organization and Procedures

The assembly and senate each have unique internal rules regarding leadership structure, committee formation, and constitutional responsibilities. The senate serves under the state constitution as a confirming or ratifying body for gubernatorial appointments. And while the "power of the purse" is a joint legislative responsibility, the annual state budget bill traditionally starts in the assembly, which is closer to the electorate. A member of either house may introduce a bill, and a majority—21 votes in the senate and 41 in the assembly—is needed for passage. A two-thirds majority is needed for "urgency" measures, constitutional amendments, and to pass the state budget. As in the U.S. Congress, most legislative work gets done in standing or select committees. Assembly members generally serve on at least three committees, while senators, due to their smaller numbers, serve on four or five committees.

As on the federal level, leadership differs in each house. The lieutenant governor is technically the senate's presiding officer, yet he or she is rarely present and votes only to break a tie. The presiding officer of the senate is the president pro tempore, who also sits as *ex officio* chair of the powerful Senate Rules Committee. The Rules Committee assigns all senators to their respective committees and assigns all bills to committees.[5] The senate president pro tempore is third in line of succession should the governor and lieutenant governor be unable to administer their offices or are absent from the state.

The speaker of the assembly has long been regarded as the second most important office in the state.[6] Other than the governor, no one commands more centralized power, visibility, and control over legislation as the office once dubbed the "Imperial Speakership." At one time, such speakers as Jesse Unruh and Willie Brown enjoyed the power to preside over the chamber and dominate all assembly floor action, the power to select all chairs and vice chairs of the assembly's committees, and the power to distribute all resources of the chamber—including such perks as prime capitol office space, additional staff, and larger district budgets for sympathetic allies. The speaker can also influence the nomination of other majority leadership positions—including the speaker pro tempore, majority floor leader, and caucus chair. Successful speakers have maintained party discipline by centralizing campaign contributions from influential special interests who wish to curry favor with the majority party. During assembly elections, the speaker has traditionally used his or her campaign war chest and consultants on behalf of his or her party faithful in order to win or retain legislative seats. Once a member was elected—aided in large part by the speaker's generosity—the member was expected to be loyal to the speaker's leadership and agenda. While many of the absolute powers of the Imperial Speakership have been eroded or chipped away through the passage of term limits and restrictions on the transfer of campaign funds, the speaker still retains a central role in California's legislature and governance.[7] Speakers in the post-Willie Brown era have had to quickly advance their agendas and seek new governing coalitions to cement their leadership.[8]

The Legislative Process

There are three types of legislation. A *bill* is a proposed statute that, if passed, becomes a codified law. A *constitutional amendment* is a change to the state constitution, requiring a two-thirds vote of each house to be placed in front of the voters in the next election. *Resolutions* are legislative expressions or opinions; they may range from an expression honoring a single constituent to a demand that another tier of government do something or take a particular action. Resolutions have no legal force, only that of moral suasion. They are normally passed on a voice vote and are not subject to a gubernatorial veto. All legislation is signified by a set of initials, denoting its type and origin, as well as a unique identification number. For example, the number of a bill originating in the assembly is designated with an "AB," while a bill that originates in the senate begins with an "SB." The 3,000 bills introduced each year in the legislature come from every sector of California. While they must be carried and authored by a member of either chamber, the ideas for bills may come from the suggestions of average constituents or from any of the other actors in California politics, such as the governor, the judiciary, state constitutional officers, lobbyists and special interests, media, local and county governments, or from bureaucrats.

 Figure 7.1 outlines the life cycle of a bill. When a bill is submitted, the member asks legislative counsel to do a legal "mock-up" of the bill and then delivers a signed copy to the "hopper" of the clerk of the assembly or the secretary of the senate. Its title is read, given a number, and printed. The state constitution requires that each bill receive three readings. After its first reading, the Rules Committee assigns it to a specific committee. After listening to testimony on both sides, the committee can act in several ways: It can pass it on by a majority vote; it can pass it with certain amendments; it can reconsider the bill at some future time; it can refer the bill to another committee; or it can effectively kill the measure by holding it in committee or sending it for interim study. Bills that have significant fiscal implications must not only be heard in a "policy committee," but also in a "fiscal committee," such as Assembly

FIGURE 7.1 THE LIFE CYCLE OF LEGISLATION

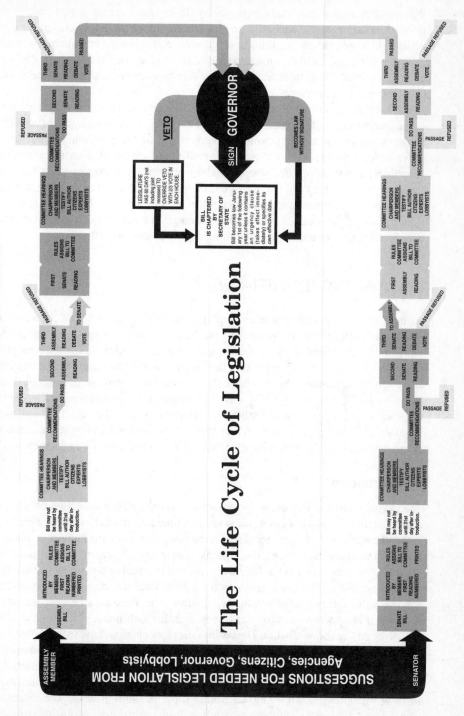

The Life Cycle of Legislation

Ways and Means. If the bill is approved by the committee(s) it is sent back to the floor of its originating chamber to be read a second time and is scheduled for floor debate. Bills are read for the third time, debated, and followed up with an electronically recorded roll-call vote in the assembly or a voice vote in the senate. Only by unanimous vote of the entire chamber can a vote be switched, and only if the change does not recast the outcome.

If a bill passes one chamber, it is sent on to the other, and the process is replicated. If amendments are added in the second house, it must go back to the house of origin for a vote on the changes. If the changes are approved, the bill goes immediately to the governor for signature or veto. If changes are not approved the bill goes to a conference committee composed of three senators and three members of the assembly. The conference committee may kill the measure if there is no agreement or amend it still further and issue a conference report, which is then sent back to both houses for approval. If both approve, the measure goes to the governor. If one house rejects the report, additional conference committees may be formed to try to iron out differences.

LAWMAKING BY INITIATIVE

Aside from the legislature, another important source of law is the electorate itself. Progressive era reformers wanted the public to be able to bypass the legislature through the instruments of direct democracy. Because of their belief in the corrupting influence of big business over politics, the Progressives were convinced that an active and attentive electorate should check their elected representatives through direct ballot measures. By 1911 the Progressives succeeded in adding three instruments to the state constitution, the initiative, the referendum and the recall. These tools empowered Californians to make policy themselves—and even to reverse the actions of government—while preserving the framework of representative democracy.

The Initiative

The initiative is a tool that citizens can use to amend the state constitution or establish a state statute. To place a constitutional amendment on the ballot, petitioners must gather the signatures of 8 percent of registered voters (based on the number of voters in the last gubernatorial election). For a simple statute, only 5 percent is needed. In real numbers, this means that in the 150 days permitted to circulate a petition, one needs to collect over 690,000 valid signatures for a constitutional change and more than 430,000 valid signatures for a statutory initiative. This is no easy task for grassroots activists. It has become relatively easy, however, for well-financed interests to place initiatives on California's ballot. The business of proposing initiatives, circulating petitions, and campaigning for the measures has become a major industry in California.

The use of paid signature-gatherers to qualify ballot proposals increased dramatically in the 1960s and 1970s. An attempt to restrict spending on ballot initiatives in 1974 was struck down by the California supreme court after the U.S. Supreme Court ruled that most campaign spending limits were unconstitutional on the grounds that they violate free speech.[9] It has become common for political consulting firms to initiate ballot measure drives simply to generate business. It is not unusual for a single company to gather the signatures, raise money, and produce ads in favor of an initiative that it initiated in the first place. In the 1980s, a Georgia manufacturer of lottery tickets, working with the Irvine-based firm Butcher-Forde, spent $2.3 million to qualify and campaign for Proposition 37, which resulted in the California state lottery.[10] In 1992, all seven of the initiatives that appeared on the general election ballot were qualified with the help of just two firms: Westlake Village-based Kimball Petition Management and Sacramento-based American Petition Consultants.[11] Ironically, the initiative process, which originated in a reform movement meant to limit the influence of special interests, has empowered those interests at the expense of representative democracy. Table 7.1 reveals the broad range of subject matter and the increasing frequency of proposed initiatives and statewide referenda in the decades since 1912.

Of the 23 states that allow statewide initiatives, only 17 allow constitutional amendments through this process, and California places the fewest restrictions on the content of these initiatives.[12] The only check to the citizen initiative constitutional amendment is final judicial review by the courts. For example, in 1964 the U.S. Supreme Court ruled unconstitutional Proposition 14, which was intended to repeal the Rumford Fair Housing Act, which prevented racial discrimination in the sale of homes. The constitutional amendment passed with over two-thirds of the statewide vote, yet was ruled null and void.[13] A more recent constitutional amendment, Proposition 187 (see Chapter 13), suffered a similar fate when parts of the law were overturned in the courts.

The Referendum

There are two types of referenda. The first is the "protest" referendum, which gives voters the power to cancel a piece of legislation approved by the legislature and the governor before it actually goes into effect. Typical legislation (except for urgency measures) have a time delay of 90 days after passage before the law is enacted. A petition of at least 5 percent of the votes cast for all candidates for governor in last gubernatorial election can suspend this legislation until the next statewide election, giving the voters an opportunity to register their preferences. The referendum has rarely been used at the state level because of the difficulties of gathering so many signatures within a 90-day window. In one recent exception, voters overwhelmingly approved Proposition 163, overturning the state "snack tax" in 1992.[14]

Referenda have been more common at the local level to halt unpopular municipal acts. The second type of referendum, which is used more frequently, follows the state constitutional requirements that all legislatively based efforts to sell state bonds, as well as all legislatively sponsored constitutional amendments, be put before the voters. Thus, it is by legislative action rather than by petition that this type of referendum appears on the ballot. If the legislature wants to amend a proposal previously passed through the initiative process, such action must first pass both houses of the legislature and then appear on the ballot for popular vote.

TABLE 7.1 INITIATIVES AND REFERENDA BY SUBJECT, BY DECADE: Number on Ballot (Number Approved)

DECADE	BOND ACTS*	ELECTIONS	TAXATION	ECONOMIC REGULATION	EDUCATION	HEALTH	MORALS	ENVIRONMENT	CIVIL RIGHTS & LIBERTIES
1912–1919	2 (1)	6 (0)	6 (1)	5 (2)	1 (1)	2 (0)	10 (2)	0	0
1920–1929	1 (1)	5 (2)	8 (1)	12 (2)	3 (1)	7 (3)	6 (2)	1 (1)	0
1930–1939	1 (0)	2 (1)	7 (0)	11 (4)	3 (0)	3 (0)	8 (3)	7 (1)	0
1940–1949	0	0	3 (1)	3 (0)	3 (2)	1 (0)	3 (0)	1 (0)	1 (0)
1950–1959	0	1 (0)	4 (1)	1 (0)	3 (2)	0	1 (0)	1 (0)	0
1960–1969	0	0	1 (0)	1 (1)	0	0	1 (0)	0	2 (1)
1970–1979	1 (1)	1 (1)	5 (3)	1 (0)	3 (1)	1 (0)	4 (0)	4 (2)	4 (2)
1980–1989	1 (1)	4 (3)	11 (5)	8 (3)	2 (2)	10 (5)	0	7 (4)	8 (4)
1990–1996	19 (7)	8 (5)	21 (8)	18 (5)	7 (4)	7 (1)	3 (1)	13 (4)	14 (13)
1997–1999	4 (2)	3 (2)	2 (2)	0	4 (2)	1 (1)	2 (2)	2 (1)	3 (2)
2000–2006	19 (14)	11 (4)	13 (4)	5 (1)	6 (3)	5 (1)	11 (8)	3 (3)	9 (4)
TOTAL	48 (27)	41 (18)	81 (26)	65 (18)	35 (18)	37 (11)	49 (18)	39 (16)	41 (26)

*General category. Bond acts are broken down into specific categories, such as education.

The Recall

The recall is a special election held to remove an elected official before his or her term expires. The recall had never been used successfully against a statewide-elected official before Governor Gray Davis was removed from office in 2003. That recall (discussed in Chapter 12) eclipsed a significant event in the 1990s, when voters recalled two state legislative leaders, including the assembly speaker.

In order to mount a recall, petitioners must gather signatures of 12–20 percent of those who voted in the last election. If this effort is successful, a special election is held to decide whether to remove the official before the end of his or her term. A recall is not the same as impeachment, which is available to the legislature if it seeks to remove a sitting official for malfeasance. It became easier to launch a recall in 1974, when voters approved a statewide initiative that streamlined the requirements to qualify a recall election for the ballot. Proposition 9 removed the waiting period to begin gathering signatures for a recall petition and made all elected officials subject to recall before the end of their term, even if they had not violated any law.

Because there are no longer any specified grounds needed to remove an official, recall petition drives have been increasingly used to punish politicians for unpopular policy positions and performance. The first successful recall was used against Los Angeles–area Republican Assemblyman Paul Horcher by constituents outraged at his support for Democratic Speaker Willie Brown in 1994. The following year, voters in Orange County recalled Republican Assembly Speaker Doris Allen over her power-sharing agreement with assembly Democrats. The gun lobby tried and failed to recall Senate Pro Tem David Roberti in 1994 over his support of an assault weapon ban. These types of recalls against state representatives have escalated not because of concern over corruption, as the Progressives had envisioned, but purely for revenge by highly mobilized interest groups.[15]

SUMMARY

The legislative process seldom produces tidy or clear outputs. The courts become active players in the policy process when new laws are subject to judicial review. Even relatively uncontroversial state laws are products of multiple compromises. Vague and general laws are enacted, reflecting the unresolved tensions that were present in the debates over their formulation. Judicial interpretation is often required to break the political and policy deadlocks.

Direct democracy, an innovative reform of the Progressive era, has become problematic in the setting of modern-day California. Frustrated voters have preferred to use the initiative process to lash out at the system through term limits and other initiatives, which undermine the effectiveness and discretionary power of elected representatives by heaping new amendments onto the constitution. Term limits may only serve to enhance the power of the bureaucracy, as legislative and constitutional "short-timers" lacking experience in government are forced to rely on agency expertise. At the same time, special interests have learned to effectively exploit the initiative process by running big-budget campaigns and inducing policy changes at the ballot box, effectively bypassing the opportunity for meaningful debate within a democratically elected legislature.

Columnist David Broder expressed this sentiment when he commented that California policy suffered from "Californocracy."[16] By allowing non-elected citizens to place measures on the statewide ballot and to approve or disapprove specific policies, he argued, representative democracy suffers. The legislature is too often encouraged to pass difficult decisions on to the public—a public that is too often apathetic and uninformed. On the other hand, there is a valid reason for the endurance of direct democracy. Californians demand input and participation, even if the result is often less than desirable. A process that grants citizens the *potential* to participate is perhaps more important to Californians than the outcome.

NOTES

1. See *Baker v. Carr*, 369 U.S. 186 (1962); *Wesberry v. Sanders*, 376 U.S. 1 (1964); *Reynolds v. Sims*, 377 U.S. 533 (1964); *Mahan v. Howell*, 410 U.S. 315 (1973); *City of Mobile v. Bolden*, 446 U.S. 55 (1980).
2. See A. G. Block, "The Reapportionment Failure," *California Journal* 22 (November 1991): 503–505.
3. Proposition 1A was a product of legendary Assembly Speaker Jesse Unruh.
4. Between 1986 and 1994, for example, Shrimpgate, an FBI sting focused on the shrimp market, netted several legislators, staff, and lobbyists in extortion, racketeering, and conspiracy charges.
5. Much of the power of the Rules Committee is in its ability to "kill" a bill simply by sending it to an unsympathetic committee.
6. Dan Morain, "Assessment of Brown's Speakership Is a Mixed Bag," *Los Angeles Times* (June 8, 1995): A1.
7. As demonstrated in Propositions 68 and 73.
8. John Borland, "Fade from Brown," *California Journal* 22 (April 1996): 8–13.
9. See *Hardie v. Eu*, 18 Cal. 3rd 371 (1976); *Buckley v. Valejo*, 424 U.S. 1 (1976).
10. For a discussion of the unintended consequences of direct democracy, see Peter Schrag, *Paradise Lost: California's Experience, America's Future* (New York: The New Press, 1997), pp. 188–256.
11. Charlene Wear Simmons, "California's Statewide Initiative Process" (Sacramento: California Research Bureau, 1997).
12. Some critics have called the state constitution "hyper-amendable." For example, 27 constitutional amendments appeared on the ballot in the form of initiatives between 1980 and 1994, and 10 of them were approved by the voters. See Bruce Cain, Sara Ferejohn, Margarita Najar, and Mary Walther, "Constitutional Change: Is It Too Easy to Amend Our State Constitution?" in *Constitutional Reform in California*, Bruce Cain and Roger Noll, eds. (Berkeley, CA: Institute of Governmental Studies, 1995).
13. See discussion in Raphael J. Sonenshein, *Politics in Black and White* (Princeton, NJ: Princeton University Press, 1993), pp. 68–73.
14. Amy Chance, "Welfare Measure Loses: Snack Tax Repeal Wins," *Sacramento Bee* (November 4, 1994): A1.
15. Eric Bailey and Dan Morian, "Capitol Game: Revenge of a Spurned Politician," *Los Angeles Times* (June 7, 1995): A1. Also see A. G. Block, "A Twisted Tale of Revenge," *California Journal* 27 (January 1996): 34–41.
16. David Broder, "Californocracy in Action," *Washington Post* (August 13, 1997): A21.

CHAPTER 8

California Justice

Featured Reading / Pages 99–100
Lori Cox Han
Women on the California High Court:
Ideological Diversity in Action

We're here . . . to carry out the will of the people. If the people and the State want three strikes, then we say that's fine, but they have to realize that we need . . . resources. . . . What worries me is when people begin to feel [that] they don't have access to the courts, that they have to go to [private alternatives]. If you're rich, fine; if not, tough, go to the streets.

—Los Angeles Superior Court Judge Gary Klausner

The judiciary is often held up as insulated from the daily machinations of politics. In reality, the judiciary and the entire justice system are political institutions, and judicial outputs (e.g., legal decisions, court resource allocation, police oversight) are political variables that render a specific judicial philosophy. Politics permeates the justice system from every corner: Governors select like-minded jurists to sit on the benches of California courts; the legislature sets and approves court budgets, prison construction and judicial laws; California's multiple law enforcement chiefs—from the attorney general to each county's district attorney—are elected officials responding to political pressures from their respective constituencies; judges must face the electorate in judicial elections and are subject to recall, sometimes falling prey to public opinion and special interests. Judicial outputs therefore are politically tinged but have a great amount of power in molding public policy and the political process.

From the 1940s through the 1960s California's system of justice was held up as a model for other state judiciaries. It won praise for its independence and judicial decision making. Under the guidance of forceful leadership, demonstrated by chief justices such as Donald Wright, Roger Traynor, and Phil Gibson, the California supreme court often influenced the path that the U.S. Supreme Court would follow. The California court became a national leader because it pioneered the "independent-state-grounds" doctrine to provide expanded individual rights beyond those mandated under the U.S. Constitution. Justice Stanley Mosk (an Edmund G. "Pat"

Brown appointee) argued that while the U.S. Supreme Court sets the constitutional rulings for the nation, those constitutional grounds should be regarded as the basic floor, or minimum, not the ceiling. Thus individual states are always free to provide more expanded constitutional guarantees than the more restrictive ones interpreted from the U.S. Constitution. This doctrine has, at times, encouraged the California supreme court to follow a more liberal interpretation. With the conservative turn of the California supreme court by the mid-1980s, this doctrine has fallen from favor, with the court deferring more often to the U.S. Supreme Court for judicial direction.[1]

CALIFORNIA'S COURTS

The state and local courts are the backbone of the nation's justice system. Nine out of every 10 court cases in the United States are conducted in state courts. Each year state court systems throughout the United States process approximately 80 million civil, criminal, and traffic cases.[2] It is also on the state judicial level that most citizens interact with the state—either in the form of settling conflicts or in the manifest of state law, ranging from wills and probate, to contracts and torts, to marriage, divorce, and adoption. The structure of California's judicial system is outlined in Article VI of the state constitution. The courts are divided into two distinct levels: trial courts and appellate courts. Trial courts are the initial points of access to the judiciary. Trial courts have original jurisdiction because the cases originate there. Superior courts make up this lower level. Appellate courts are designed to hear appeals from the lower courts and have no original jurisdiction. The appellate level includes the court of appeals and the California supreme court. In addition to the courts, four important institutions assist the judiciary. They include the Commission on Judicial Appointments, the Commission on Judicial Performance, the Judicial Council, and the Commission on Judicial Nominees Evaluation.

Superior Courts

The California state constitution requires that at least one superior court reside in each county of the state. These are essentially the state's trial courts, with jurisdiction in both civil and criminal law cases. Superior court judges are elected in non-partisan races; however, many superior court judges reach the bench initially through gubernatorial appointment. If a vacancy occurs, the governor may appoint a replacement to sit on the bench until the next election. Given the power of judicial incumbency, these gubernatorial appointments are typically retained during the following election cycle, guaranteeing long-term employment as a jurist.

In 1998, voters approved Proposition 220, which allowed counties to voluntarily consolidate municipal courts with their superior courts. Eliminating the two-tiered system allowed courts to streamline their operations and reduce their backlog of cases. By 2001, all 58 counties had voted to consolidate their court systems. Prior to the consolidation movement, municipal courts were processing over 90 percent of

FIGURE 8.1 CALIFORNIA COURT SYSTEM

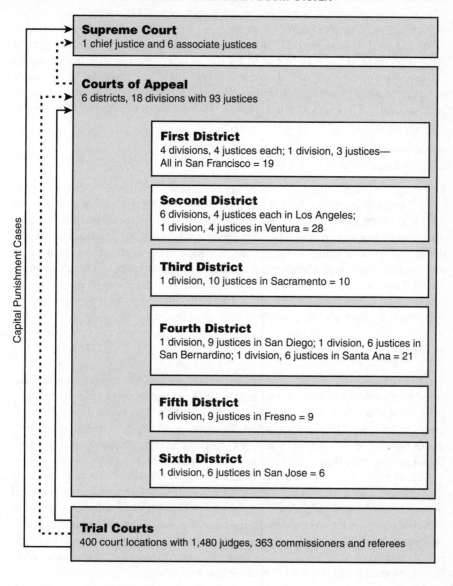

Capital Punishment Cases

Supreme Court
1 chief justice and 6 associate justices

Courts of Appeal
6 districts, 18 divisions with 93 justices

First District
4 divisions, 4 justices each; 1 division, 3 justices—
All in San Francisco = 19

Second District
6 divisions, 4 justices each in Los Angeles;
1 division, 4 justices in Ventura = 28

Third District
1 division, 10 justices in Sacramento = 10

Fourth District
1 division, 9 justices in San Diego; 1 division, 6 justices in
San Bernardino; 1 division, 6 justices in Santa Ana = 21

Fifth District
1 division, 9 justices in Fresno = 9

Sixth District
1 division, 6 justices in San Jose = 6

Trial Courts
400 court locations with 1,480 judges, 363 commissioners and referees

———— Line of Appeal   •••••••••• Line of Discretionary Review

Note: Death penalty cases are automatically appealed from the Superior Court directly to
the Supreme Court.

Source: Judicial Council of California/Administrative Office of the Courts.

the state's judicial business. These cases included civil lawsuits involving less than $25,000, small-claims actions, and preliminary hearings on some felony charges were heard in municipal courts.[3] Previously, superior courts heard felony criminal cases and civil matters over $25,000 and acted as courts of appeal for municipal court renderings.[4] Due in large part to the rise of juvenile crime and the mandatory "three strikes, you're out" initiative, criminal felonies (crimes that carry a penalty of one year or more) have been jamming the court caseload in urban and suburban superior courts. The average time to hear a civil law case in Los Angeles County, for example, is between five and seven years.

District Courts of Appeal

The state is divided into six court of appeal districts, with more than 88 jurists elected for 12-year terms. These courts serve as a screening mechanism to reduce the workload of the state supreme court. They usually grant appeals considering only questions of law, not questions of fact. There are no juries, no introductions of evidence, and no interrogations of witnesses. Normally three jurists sit as a full panel in the appellate court, considering transcripts from the lower court and brief oral arguments. The court of appeals also has jurisdiction over decisions of quasi-judicial state boards. While most lower-court verdicts are upheld by the appellate court, an appeal is still possible directly to the state supreme court.

California Supreme Court

The California supreme court is composed of one chief justice and six associate justices. As the highest court in the state, it has been an active participant in the major public policy debates, from civil rights to the death penalty to the status of immigrants in the state. The court has broad discretionary authority to decide which civil and criminal cases it will hear, with cases involving capital punishment receiving pro forma review. The state supreme court has original jurisdiction to issue writs (or orders) over the following areas: (1) *habeas corpus* ("produce the body"), which requires that a state-detained person must be brought before a judge so that legal detention can be determined; (2) *prohibition*, which prevents a lower court from exercising jurisdiction over a certain case; and (3) *mandamus* (or mandate), which commands a public servant to perform a specific duty under their domain. An example of mandamus would be the state supreme court ordering a county district attorney to enforce provisions of the "three strikes" initiative.

In its role as the state's final court of appeals, the state supreme court considers approximately 150 of the 3,000–4,000 cases appealed each year. In the cases that are decided, written majority and minority opinions are rendered, based on a legal analysis of state statutes and the state constitution. As a symbol of its separation from the political world, the supreme court makes its home not in Sacramento but in San Francisco. Supreme court judges are confirmed for 12-year terms in the same manner as district court judges.

The supreme court begins by first determining whether it wants to review a lower court's decision, based primarily on the constitutional grounds of the California constitution. This first stage is largely how we come to define the "tone and character" of a particular sitting supreme court. A "judicial activist court" will lean in favor of pursuing broad policy and political debates, reaching, if necessary, into the lower courts to pull cases that best reflect a ripeness for judicial review. A less activist court, following what judicial scholars term a "court of judicial restraint," would tend to rule very narrowly on cases it accepts, shying away from overturning legislative decisions or inserting itself in the political battles around the controversial policy battles of the moment.

Starting with the court clerks who prepare and research a conference memorandum, the court at its weekly conference meeting decides which cases shall be reviewed and which decisions "shall be left standing" (meaning that the decision rendered from the lower courts shall be final). The granting of a case to move forward requires four affirmative votes. One of the justices voting for review of a particular case is assigned the task of preparing a calendar memorandum (closely resembling a draft legal opinion) for his or her judicial colleagues to review. At this stage, there is some legal horse-trading back and forth, as each individual jurist renders his or her own deletions/additions and approval/dissenting positions on the draft. When four or more jurists approve with the outline of resolving the case, the chief justice then moves forward in scheduling it for oral arguments.

Hearing oral arguments from attorneys from both sides of a case takes place for one week of every month, except July and August. The oral argument phase of determining a case is not an opportunity to retry the matter at hand. Rather, it is an opportunity for the court to inquire about the fine points of the law and for individual justices to reexamine their initial position on the pending case. After oral arguments, the justices reconvene, and if there is still a majority of the court (four or more members) in favor of resolution of the case, the chief justice assigns one of the members in the majority to draft the final legal decision. After the majority opinion is finished and circulated to all seven justices, dissenting and concurring opinions may be issued as the court publicly hands down its legal rendering.

JUDICIAL SELECTION

Vacancies of judges on a district court of appeals and the supreme court are chosen in the following three-step method: (1) governor's nomination; (2) approval by the Commission on Judicial Appointments (in consultation with the Commission on Judicial Nominees Evaluation; both are discussed later in more detail); (3) a confirmation vote (good for a 12-year term) in the first gubernatorial election after an appointment has been approved. There are no opposing candidates, only a voter's choice between "yes" and "no," with the question: "Shall _____ be elected to the office for the term prescribed by law?"

Voters choose superior court judges for six-year terms in nonpartisan elections. The only requirement for judges who serve at this level is that they must have practiced law for at least five years and be in good standing with the state bar. Because most voters know little about a jurist's temperament or judicial renderings, incumbency plays a major role. Over 95 percent of judges throughout California face no opposition and are automatically reelected. While traditional endorsements for judicial candidates may mean something (especially in the few contested judicial races), little campaign money is raised overall (especially in comparison to, say, state legislative races). Most of the money raised goes to "state mailings" and other direct voter contact.

In the end, the prevailing question on most citizens' minds in California is: "Should we have an elected judiciary at all? Or should judges be 'above electoral politics' and perhaps appointed for life terms?" In which case is democracy better served? Is there a danger in compromising impartiality of the judiciary if unpopular legal decisions come back to haunt a judge during election cycles? Or should judges be accountable to the "will of the people," keeping judges (like every other public servant) responsive to the needs of the governed?

The balancing act between judicial accountability and judicial independence is a sensitive one. Throughout the 1960s and 1970s, the California supreme court was held in high esteem for its professional and progressive decisions that went head-on into the controversies of the day. Some of its decisions equalized school funding formulas across the state, regardless of local tax bases, desegregated school districts by court-ordered busing, intervened to broaden the legal rights of defendants in criminal cases, and ended the quota system in higher education by highlighting "reverse discrimination" yet affirming affirmative action as a lofty goal. The California supreme court is often in the eye of the hurricane, practicing what some call "judicial activism"—an active partner in shaping major public policy debates.

One of the major flashpoints between the state supreme court and the legislature is the death penalty, which the court declared unconstitutional. The death penalty later was restored by legislative mandate, and California had the largest death row in the nation by 2006, with 650 prisoners awaiting execution. In 1986, an unprecedented event occurred: Supreme Court Chief Justice Rose Bird and two associate justices, Cruz Reynoso and Joseph Grodin, were removed from office by the voters. Bird, who had overturned 61 death sentences, had become a lightning rod of the voters' frustration—losing by a landslide of 32 points, the first time this had happened in California's 52 years under its judicial-retention election process. The defeat of the three liberal judges gave Governor George Deukmejian the rare opportunity to stack (or "pack") the court with conservative "judicial restraint" appointees. Governor Pete Wilson followed in this path as well. During the Malcolm Lucas and Ronald George court era, there has been a 180-degree turn in the tendencies of the court. For example, in the area of criminal law, the post-Bird courts have rarely turned down a lower-court-ordered death penalty decision, except in some unusual cases where gross trial errors were made.[5]

THE JUDICIAL BUREAUCRACY

There are four institutions that assist the courts in California and are themselves key actors in the judicial system.

The Judicial Council

The Judicial Council is a 21-member state board that oversees the overall administration of the court system. The Judicial Council consists of 15 judges from all tiers of the court system, plus 4 lawyers from the state bar and 2 members of the state legislature. The chief justice chairs the council. The purpose of the council is to improve the efficiency and workload of the courts, keep records, organize various seminars for trial and appellate court judges, conduct research on the court system, periodically brief the legislature on the "state of the courts," and propose judicial reforms.

One recent blue-ribbon report issued by the Judicial Council is worth noting. California has used the traditional standard jury system. *Grand juries* (19–23 citizens depending on the county) investigate public officials and agencies and can return indictments. *Trial juries* usually consist of 12 registered voters in civil and misdemeanor cases; fewer than 12 may be used if both parties agree.

The Judicial Council has put forth a reform proposal to transform California's jury system by allowing non-unanimous verdicts (11–1 vote) in felony convictions except in the cases of death penalty or life in prison; encouraging jurors to confer during trial; and punishing jurors who shirk their civic responsibility.[6] All eligible citizens of California are required to serve on a trial jury if summoned. Only a few individuals are automatically excused from serving: ex-felons, police officers, and some government employees. Trial juries are composed of citizens whose names are drawn from the state's voter rolls and vehicle registration lists. Being a juror is not glamorous, involving limited court compensation and long delays in getting impaneled on a jury (some describe this as waiting in a "cattle-car" environment or indentured servitude approaching "state slavery"). Despite the hassles, jurors serve as critical participants in the democracy we all treasure via a judicial system we all recognize is a cherished commodity. The controversies surrounding the jury systems are set in historical record. Some, like Alexis de Tocqueville, saw jury service as "one of the most efficacious means for education of people which society can employ."[7] Others viewed the jury system with disdain for its capriciousness of lay citizens unfamiliar with the law.

The Commission on Judicial Performance

Created in 1961, the Commission on Judicial Performance is made up of 11 members, only 3 of whom are judges. This commission investigates complaints about judicial misconduct or malfeasance and can recommend the censure, recall, or removal of a judge ruled unfit to serve. The supreme court may discipline or remove a judge (or a court referee or court commissioner) upon recommendation of the

Commission on Judicial Performance. The supreme court must remove any sitting judge found guilty of a felony or a crime involving "moral turpitude." Finally, the commission can recommend the censure, removal, or retirement of justices who are on the supreme court after the approval of a tribunal of seven court of appeals judges selected by lot.

In 1994, the legislature proposed a constitutional reform measure, Proposition 190, that opened up the commission to greater public scrutiny and review. Monitoring the professional ethics of more than 1,500 judges who sit on California's tribunals at all levels is no easy mandate. Having a "closed system" whereby judges would essentially monitor other judges seemed outdated and fraught with the potential for accusations of cover-ups. Proposition 190, passed overwhelmingly by the voters, established new guidelines for the commission and a "sunshine strategy" to remove these past hearings from secrecy to open exposure. Furthermore, it rearranged the composition of the commission itself, tipping the scales to "citizen non-lawyers" as the controlling majority on the commission in charge of regulating judicial behavior and conduct.

The Commission on Judicial Nominees Evaluation

The Commission on Judicial Nominees Evaluation is a 25-member body of the California Bar Association that rates the judicial nominees of the governor. The governor is required by statute to submit nominees for judgeships to the commission to determine fitness for the position. Confidential recommendations are returned to the governor regarding each name submitted. The rankings are quite simple: "exceptionally well-qualified," "well-qualified," or "not qualified." The commission thus acts as a pre-screening for evaluating gubernatorial appointees and can actually act as a check on the governor should a "not qualified" candidate be moved ahead—perhaps using the public stage to embarrass the governor when this jurist runs for judicial office on the ballot. The checks and balances historically provided by this commission, may itself be up for reinterpretation. Former Governor Pete Wilson for example, tossed aside the "unqualified" rating by the commission for his nominee to the supreme court, Janice Rogers Brown.[8] What normally would have been an embarrassment for Pete Wilson turned out to be "political fodder" for him. Wilson took on the commission, arguing that the individual members were biased against Ms. Brown, who happened not only to be a politically conservative woman but also African American.

The Commission on Judicial Appointments

The Commission on Judicial Appointments must approve a governor's nominee to the court of appeals. A majority must vote in approving the nomination, normally with input from the Commission on Judicial Nominees Evaluation. Only once has the commission officially rejected a governor's nomination, but in the past the commission has also caused the governor to remove a nominee from consideration based on the prevailing votes. Supporters of this commission process insist that this body serves as a "depoliticized" reviewing mechanism against a governor's appointment of unqualified individuals to the appellate bench. They point to the highly politically charged process on the federal level, where a president's judicial nominee must be confirmed by a majority of the U.S. Senate. Critics, however, are still dismayed that the commission may still block nominees—not so much based on their legal qualifications as on their pronounced judicial philosophy. This was clearly evident during the Jerry Brown days, when then Attorney General George Deukmejian threw his weight around to block several liberal (yet highly qualified) Brown judicial nominees. In the case just described, when Pete Wilson pushed ahead with his nomination of Supreme Court Judge Janice Rogers Brown despite her "unqualified" ratings, she was able to muster a unanimous vote of approval from this three-member commission— proving, once again, that politics sometimes does override judicial standards.

Women on the California High Court: Ideological Diversity in Action
Lori Cox Han

As the largest and most diverse state in the nation, and as a state often noted for its progressive brand of politics, it is surprising that California has yet to elect its first woman governor. However, the state's highest court cannot be criticized for having a male-dominated bench. At the start of 2005, three of the seven justices on the California Supreme Court were women. They include: Associate Justice Janice R. Brown (appointed in 1996), Associate Justice Joyce L. Kennard (appointed in 1989), and Associate Justice Kathryn Mickle Werdegar (appointed in 1994). Brown, the only African American justice on the County, was notable more conservative than her other moderate Republican colleagues (six Republicans total), and she clashed often with moderate Chief Justice Ronald M. George. As a result, she gained the attention of the White House and President George W. Bush, who nominated her to a U.S. appellate court position in July 2003. However, Senate Democrats had successfully blocked her nomination along with certain other conservative Bush appointees to the federal bench during the first Bush term, but Brown was eventually confirmed to the U.S. Circuit Court of Appeals for the District of Columbia in June 2005.

The most notable woman jurist in California's history, however, would have to be the state's former Supreme Court Chief Justice Rose Elizabeth Bird. As the first woman ever to serve on California's highest court upon her appointment in 1977, she served on the bench until January 1987. From the start, Bird had a distinguished career in both the law and public service. She received her law degree in 1965 from Boalt Hall School of Law at the University of California, Berkeley (a time when only a handful of women were accepted to top law schools). She clerked for the chief justice of the Nevada Supreme Court after graduation and in 1966, she became the first woman hired as a deputy public defender in Santa Clara County. She taught at Stanford Law School from 1972 to 1974, and then in 1975, Governor Jerry Brown appointed her as the first woman to serve as a cabinet member in California. As secretary of the Agriculture and Services Agency, she had administrative responsibility over 12 different state agencies.

Under Bird's leadership, the Supreme Court strengthened environmental laws, consumer rights, and the rights of women and minorities. Her accomplishments also included the 1984 adoption of the first rule to permit television and photographic coverage of court proceedings in trial and appellate courts with the consent of the presiding judge. Bird also introduced the first use of word and data processing to the Supreme Court and courts of appeal. In 1987, she appointed the Committee on Gender Bias in the courts, which began the trend for more studies in the years to follow on state courts' treatment of people based on gender, race and ethnicity, sexual preferences, and disabilities.

But more important, Bird received national attention for her opposition to the death penalty, becoming a lightning rod on the issue by invalidating every one of the 58 death penalty cases that she heard on appeal. Supporters of Bird claimed that she had been "appropriately circumspect, cautious, and thorough" in her review of all 58 death penalty cases, and she was joined by at least one other justice in overturning each sentence. Opponents of Bird and her death penalty decisions claimed that she used a "series of minute legal technicalities . . . to prevent the implementation of California's death penalty" as the only California Supreme Court jurist between 1978 (when California's death penalty statute went into effect) and 1986 who had not voted to affirm a single death penalty case. Bird's opponents were eventually victorious, as California voters removed Bird and two of her liberal colleagues from the Court in a 2 to 1 vote in 1986. The election marked the first time that Californians had voted not to retain a Supreme Court justice. Bird died at the age of 63 from complications of breast cancer in 1999. Since leaving the high court, she had remained completely out of the public spotlight. However, regardless of one's opinion on the death penalty, perhaps Bird's legacy can be found in the fact that California continues to have the largest backlog of death row inmates in the nation.

Source: "Women on the California High Court: Ideological Diversity in Action." From Lori Cox Han, *Women and American Politics: The Challenges of Political Leadership* (McGraw-Hill, 2007) pp.140–141.

SUMMARY

Judicial policymaking is laden with political undertones. The criminal justice system is directly affected by the priorities set by the courts, judges, and politicians. California's prison system is one of the state's largest growth sectors—consuming almost 10 percent of the state's general fund revenues. This is not surprising, given the current "tough-on-crime" attitudes of the populace and the judicial system. Critics and supporters are still arguing over the end results of California's criminal policies: Has crime gone down because of stricter punishment, longer determined sentences, and capital punishment? Or are other less tangible issues, like a thriving economy, low unemployment rates, and a general aging of the population, driving the spiral downwards? However we cut the deck, Californians will continue to tinker with their judicial apparatus, which in turn will affect the criminal justice and civil law system.

NOTES

1. In fact, in many controversial areas (such as police searches, busing, and the death penalty), the voters of the state used the initiative process to overturn several unpopular judicial mandates.
2. Bureau of Justice Statistics, *State Court Caseload Statistics* (Washington, DC: U.S. Printing Office, 1983).
3. In 1994, all justice courts in California were converted to municipal courts. They were essentially holdovers from an earlier period when "justices of the peace"—mostly in rural counties—functioned in the same jurisdictional arena as did the municipal court structure.
4. With the rise in civil litigation and the mandatory sentencing of the "three strikes initiative," urban courts are severely overloaded. It currently takes between five and seven years to hear a civil lawsuit in Los Angeles County.
5. The future of the death penalty in California was called into question once again when a U.S. District Court ruled that the way the state administers its lethal injections violates the Eighth Amendment ban on cruel and unusual punishment (*New York Times*, December 16, 2006): A10.
6. Stephanie Wilson, "Major Reforms Proposed for California Juries," *Los Angeles Times* (April 30, 1996): A3.
7. Alexis de Tocqueville, *Democracy in America* (New York: Vintage Books, 1945), p. 296.
8. Charles L. Linder, "Will Wilson Defy State Supreme Court History?" *Los Angeles Times* (April 28, 1996): M3.

CHAPTER 9

Intergovernmental Relations

Featured Reading / Pages 111–112
Gar Alperovitz
California Split

The federalist model of U.S. politics allows power to remain as close to the state as possible. The U.S. Constitution states that all powers not explicitly identified by the federal constitution, federal courts, or federal statute reside with the state. In general, issues that affect only the local jurisdiction are best left to the city, with issues that affect a regional area left to the county, those that affect several counties left to the state, and issues that affect two or more states left to the federal government. Beyond that, any issue that has constitutional implications can be regulated by the federal government. Clearly, with 50 states and some 85,000 local governments, intergovernmental relations are extremely important. Within California alone, there are 58 counties, 478 municipalities, and 3,400 special districts.

Relations between levels of government have been both good and bad for California. The state has been the beneficiary of billions of federal dollars since World War II. This spending has delivered great defense and infrastructure projects to the state. California receives over $230 billion a year in federal largesse—in the form of programs for education, welfare, housing, or infrastructural assistance for mass transit and highway construction. However, Californians pay over $240 billion each year in federal taxes.[1] This chapter explores the different levels of California governments, as well as the way they interact with each other. To illustrate the intergovernmental relationships, the chapter concludes with a policy case study on welfare reform. Although all policies require effective intergovernmental relationships, welfare reform impacted governments at all levels in an extremely deep way. And because welfare reform is, in many ways, a redistribution of service responsibilities and fiscal authority, the chapter concludes with an assessment of how different levels of government experience differential benefits.

CALIFORNIA IN NATIONAL POLITICS

California has figured prominently in national politics in part because of the many Californians who have become national leaders. Governor Earl Warren went on to be chief justice of the U.S. Supreme Court from 1953 to 1969. Richard Nixon and Ronald Reagan used their California base to seek and win the presidency and then appointed Californians to prominent White House posts. Nixon brought fellow Californians Casper Weinberger and David Packard. The Californians serving in the Reagan administration included Ed Meese, William French Smith, Michael Deaver, James Watt, and George Schultz. Bill Clinton, who claimed to be a "special friend to California," brought out many highly visible native sons and daughters, including Secretary of State Warren Christopher and White House Chief of Staff Leon Panetta, Defense Secretary William Perry, Commerce Secretary Mickey Kantor, and Economic Advisor Laura D'Andrea Tyson. Upon his election in 2008, Barack Obama tapped a number of Californians for key posts in his administration. Among them were Los Angeles Congresswoman Hilda Solis, selected as labor secretary, Lawrence Berkeley Laboratory Director Steven Chu as energy secretary, and Los Angeles Deputy Mayor Nancy Sutley as chair of Obama's Council on Environmental Quality.

No presidential campaign can afford to ignore California. California controls 54 electoral votes—the largest of any state—almost as many as the 15 smallest states combined. The state played a key role in the contest between Democrat Bill Clinton and Republican Bob Dole for the presidency in 1996. With the South becoming solidly Republican, California had become a critical state to Clinton's reelection prospects. Because California has one-fifth of all the electoral votes, Clinton could not have won reelection without carrying California. It is clear why Bill Clinton was a "special friend," based on this electoral scenario. As part of his reelection strategy, Clinton maintained a constant positive presence in California, made easier by a series of natural and other disasters, which helped the president look more presidential and sympathetic to the average Californian. Floods, earthquakes, fires, and even the 1992 Los Angeles riots kept Federal Emergency Management Agency (FEMA) dollars flowing into the state. In September 1995, Clinton promised and delivered $329 million to bail out the health system in Los Angeles County, keeping the county from going bankrupt. The state's influence in presidential elections will only increase now that the state's primary elections have been moved from June to February, making California one of the early deciders.

CALIFORNIA'S CONGRESSIONAL DELEGATION

Representative Nancy Pelosi's ascent to the speakership of the House of Representatives in 2007 is certainly the best example of California's rising clout in Congress. Subsequently, some other members from the state have achieved positions of status and influence, including Senate Intelligence Committee Chair Dianne

Feinstein and Representative Henry Waxman, who took over the powerful Energy and Commerce Committee after the ouster of its longtime chair, John Dingell of Michigan. Beyond these high-profile leadership posts, California has been something of a "sleeping giant" in Congress, with an unrealized potential to mobilize a voting bloc consisting of 12 percent of the House of Representatives. The consensus that had unified the California delegation in the 1940s and 1950s broke apart as early as the 1960s. Since that time, the delegation has been divided by ideological, geographic, and ethnic differences. These divisions are somewhat understandable, given the complex and competing interests in a state as large and diverse as California. In the absence of a cohesive congressional delegation, an army of lobbyists has instead been employed by California's various interests. Thus, most major California cities have their own paid lobbyists in Washington, as do the state legislature, the state's two public university systems (the University of California and California State University), and a myriad of private and public organizations.

When important state issues are at stake, however, California's House members have rallied and voted together. Rare examples of cooperation can be observed in votes on some critical issues, including funding for the space station, water restoration, the Bay Delta Accord, Medicaid reimbursement, intellectual-property protection, funding for the cleanup of military bases, and transportation projects such as the Alameda Corridor Project. One observer noted that if California's House delegation could only get its "bipartisan act together," then with 53 House seats, the state "is uniquely positioned to control the game. Of course, other state delegations will be thinking the same thing. But none have the numbers that California does—almost half again as many as runner-ups New York and Texas."[2]

California's Representatives: Bringing Home the Bacon?

Between 1981 and 1985 the federal government spent nearly $25 billion more in California than it took back in federal taxes. California won between 18 percent and 22 percent of all federal procurement spending in the 1980s. But with the slowing of the defense boom, federal procurement spending peaked in 1986 at $187 billion. California's share of the federal procurement has slipped from its high of nearly 22 percent in 1986 to under 15 percent today. As a result, California has been a "donor state" to the federal treasury over the past several years. The state's taxpayers paid $10 billion more in federal taxes than they got back in federal services and spending. California's share of federal spending fell from a peak of 13 percent in 1984, to a stable 12 percent during the late 1980s and early 1990s, to a 20-year low of 11 percent in 2004.[3] In addition, California was hit harder than any other state by the first four military base closure rounds in 1988, 1991, 1993, and 1995.[4] During this period, 40 of California's military installations were either shut down or realigned. And, in its Quadrennial Defense Review (QDR), the Defense Department announced continued base closures. The California congressional delegation is attempting to protect the state's 34 remaining major installations.[5] By 2004, California received 79 cents in federal spending for every dollar paid in taxes.

LOCAL GOVERNMENTS

Only Pennsylvania and Illinois have more sanctioned local government entities than does California. Because the constitution makes no explicit reference to local governments, they are "creatures of the states," created under state authority, and designed to enable the state to perform its functions throughout its territorial boundaries. It is through California's counties, cities, special districts, and regional agencies that residents come into contact with government authority—be it in public safety, education, rent control, air pollution, or land use.

Counties

California's 58 counties are extremely diverse; they range from tiny Alpine County, with some 1,000 residents, to sprawling Los Angeles County, with its 11 million residents—larger than 42 states of the union. San Bernardino County is the largest in terms of area—covering over 20,000 square miles. San Francisco comprises one of the smallest areas—only 49 square miles. Nearly every California county is administered by a five-member board of supervisors elected in a nonpartisan race every four years. The lone exception is San Francisco, a combined city and county, which is governed by 11 board members and a mayor. Supervisors have legislative, executive, and quasi-judicial duties. In most cases, supervisors govern with the assistance of an appointed chief administrative officer. Other county officials may be independently elected, including the sheriff, the district attorney, the assessor, and the county superintendent of schools.

County governments were created as geographic subdivisions of state government in order to deliver administrative services. The county's role as an agent of the state has made it the major administrator of funds, which come from a combination of local taxes, the state, and the national government. Currently, more than half of county revenues come from the state, while 90 percent of their budget commitments are determined by state mandates.[6] On average, California counties spend approximately 26 percent of their annual budget on public safety, 13 percent on public health, and 40 percent on public assistance and welfare. Counties provide all-purpose services to unincorporated areas in their jurisdiction, as well as contracted services that smaller cities cannot provide. For example, the County of Los Angeles contracts with several cities to provide such services as policing, fire protection, ambulance services, jail facilities, tax assessment, and elections. Because the suburban city of Lakewood was the first municipality to contract with the county for these services, this model has become known as the "Lakewood Plan."

Cities

There are 478 cities in California. Cities may incorporate for a variety of reasons, including local pride, the retention of housing values, control of land-use and zoning decisions, or access to tax revenues. The two types of cities are *general law*, which derive their powers from statutes set by the state legislature, and *charter*, which have greater flexibility of home-rule because of locally crafted and implemented city charters. There are two basic forms of city government operating in California: the *council-manager* form and the *mayor-council* form. Most California cities use the council-manager form. Under the council-manager form of government, legislative authority rests with the city council, but the council appoints a city manager to administer city operations and administration. These governments may have an elected mayor, but the office is largely ceremonial. Because the city manager is a full-time professional executive who does not face the voters, the council-manager form is believed to be less political and less corruptible than the mayor-council form, though critics point to the fact that a city manager's job security depends upon pleasing a majority of city council members. In cities with the mayor-council form of government, voters elect a mayor, who wields executive power, as well as the city council, which is the legislative body of the city. In "strong" mayor systems, the executive branch has the power to set the budget, appoint city heads, veto legislation, and control policy debate. In systems with "weak" mayors, the balance of power favors the legislative branch. Thus, the city council has not only policy oversight, but administrative oversight in running city agencies. The mayor may be independently elected or may be one of the city council members who periodically rotate into the mayor's position. The major exception to these two basic forms of city government is the city-county of San Francisco, which is governed by an elected board of supervisors and an elected mayor.

As William Fulton points out in *The Reluctant Metropolis*, cities compete with one another to attract new sources of revenue.[7] In the post-Proposition 13 world, sales and business taxes are the primary sources of revenue for city governments to deliver the services city residents are increasingly demanding. Proposition 13 capped state property taxes, allowing an annual increase of only 1 percent, and reduced the cities' share of property tax revenue. The impact on California's cities was immediate. In 1978, for example, just before Proposition 13 became law, the three major cities in Ventura County's Oxnard Plain collected $8 million in property tax and $10 million in sales tax. In 1979, after Proposition 13 became effective, the cities collected only $3.7 million in property tax and $12 million in sales tax.[8] It was clear where future revenues would be sought. To this end, local governments try, whenever possible, to attract affluent residents and to provide economic incentives for commercial or industrial growth—be it big-box retail, shopping malls, car dealerships, or light (non-polluting) industries.[9]

Special Districts

There are more than 3,400 special districts in California providing specialized services that no other local government provides within a defined area. Special districts include agencies that monitor, regulate, and tax for such services as water, street construction, pest control, flood control, public schools, community colleges, transportation, mosquito abatement, waste disposal, land reclamation, and air quality control. In the post-Proposition 13 era, they also serve as a mechanism to provide public services by sidestepping existing constitutional limits on taxation. Even though two-thirds of special districts are governed by elected boards of directors, most of these bodies are little understood by the average citizen. Critics have argued that special districts are problematic because of their lack of overall coordination and planning, as well as the number of staff and personnel each employ at a direct cost to the taxpayer. Because of a popular belief that special districts are unaccountable and inefficient, state law has limited their growth since the 1960s.

Regional Governments and Agencies

Most regional governments in California exist to aid local governments in planning, coordination, and data generation. Municipalities join regional governments voluntarily, hence these agencies have little or no real power other than the "bully pulpit" to press for corrective policy changes that cross jurisdictional boundaries. Examples are the Southern California Association of Governments (SCAG) and the San Diego Association of Governments (SANDAG). There are also several regional agencies that deliver a specific service. For example, the Bay Area Rapid Transit District (BART) or the Los Angeles County Metropolitan Transit Authority (MTA) are agencies designed to deliver mass transit to regions that include more than a single county. The California Coastal Commission governs land use in coastal areas. The Bay Area Air Pollution Control District and the South Coast Air Quality Management District (SCAQMD) are entrusted with considerable political power to regulate air pollution over vast regions (see Chapter 13). Regional governments and agencies serve the broader goals of multijurisdictional (regional) governance, through cooperative data collection, resource sharing, and state-mandated regulation implementation.

The Future of State–Local Relations

In 1995, a blue-ribbon panel concluded that political power in California—with its myriad of government agencies—is fragmented, unaccountable, confusing, and, in many areas, redundant. As part of its package of suggested reforms, the California Constitution Revision Commission sent to the state legislature a proposal suggesting a radical restructuring of local government. If placed on the ballot and approved by the voters, the plan would have authorized local "charter governments," allowing residents to combine existing agencies—including cities, counties, as well as school districts, water boards, sewer districts, and other types of agencies. It also would have redefined the relationship between the state and local governments by forcing the state to reconsider its unfunded mandates. The legislature has yet to act on this proposal, to the dismay of the financially strapped counties.

FEDERALISM TODAY: WELFARE REFORM AS A CASE STUDY

The United States is now engaged in a national experiment in the decentralization of social programs. These measures will significantly alter the major federal–state–county relationships pertaining to a myriad of social programs in all 50 states. In its simplest form, the experiment would unravel the fundamental principles that were shaped in the New Deal legislation of the 1930s and repeal major segments of the Great Society legislation of the 1960s.

Historically speaking, this "New Federalism" is the latest wave in a long succession of measures to shift more power and authority from the federal government to the states. In the 1970s, President Nixon proposed revenue sharing and simplification of government operations by transferring planning and management functions to state and local governments. The thrust of his New Federalism policy was to consolidate grant programs in an effort to reduce the complexity of national programs into a manageable handful of block grants—and ultimately to save taxpayers money.[10] In the early 1980s, President Reagan won a major concession to realign the federal government's categorical grant program. His administration consolidated some 57 categorical grants into nine block grants.[11] The Nixon and Reagan block grant initiatives were designed to prune the federal bureaucracy, restrict paperwork, and enhance decision making and control at the local level.

New Federalism has long been a contested terrain, however, because increasing state authority over programs allows states to fund some programs at a lower level and to terminate other support programs altogether. Republicans have favored reducing the federal role, while Democrats have argued for greater security and oversight in program delivery. President Clinton was able to bring about bipartisan support for one area of reform with the Personal Responsibility and Work Opportunity Reconciliation Act (PRWORA) in 1996. This 500-page document was the cornerstone of Clinton's initiative to "end welfare as we know it." The proposal was not without controversy, however. One side of the debate contends that given sufficient discretion, the states can devise more innovative, cost-effective services, that are better able to reduce welfare dependency. On the other side of the debate are critics such as Peter Edelman, who resigned his post as the assistant secretary for planning and evaluation at the Department of Health and Human Services to protest the new welfare law. According to Edelman:

> [Welfare reform] does not promote work effectively and it will hurt millions of poor children by the time it's fully implemented. What's more it bars hundreds of thousands of legal immigrants from receiving disability and old-age assistance and food stamps, and reduced food-stamp assistance for millions of children in working families. . . . [Under block grants] there will be no federal definition of who is eligible and therefore no guarantee of assistance to anyone: each state can decide whom to exclude any way it wants, as long as it doesn't violate the constitution (not much of a limitation when one reads the Supreme Court decisions on this subject). And

second, that each state will get a fixed sum of federal money each year even if a recession or a local calamity causes a state to run out of federal funds before the end of the year.[12]

The effects of welfare reform will be felt everywhere in the state. Welfare recipients are not concentrated in any one county or region. To assess the impacts in California, it is appropriate to review the major elements of the new law.

Title I: Block Grants for Temporary Assistance for Needy Families (TANF)

- Eliminates Aid to Families with Dependent Children (AFDC) and consolidates federal funding for AFDC and related programs (such as job training) into a TANF block grant.
- The state was required to implement the block grant by July 1, 1997. The date is important because it triggered the beginning of the five-year time limit for assistance.
- Prohibits use of block grant funds for teen parents under age 18 unless they are (1) attending school and (2) living in an adult-supervised setting.
- Establishes five-year lifetime limit on family use of block grant funds. States may exempt up to 20 percent for hardship.
- Requires at least one adult in a family that has been receiving aid for more than two years to participate in "work activities," including employment, on-the-job and vocational training, and up to six weeks of job searching.
- By 2004, TANF required 90 percent of two-parent families to participate in work activities. Single parents must work 30 hours each week, or 20 hours for families with a child under age six.
- Imposes penalties on states for noncompliance.
- States must place at least 50 percent of cash welfare recipients in jobs or work programs.
- Federal funds cannot be used to provide cash benefits to adults who fail to find work within two years.
- Cash aid is reduced by 25 percent for recipients who do not cooperate with child-support enforcement agencies or in establishing paternity.
- States have the option to deny additional cash aid to welfare recipients who have additional children.
- States that have received federal waivers to conduct reform programs may continue to operate under those waivers.

Title II: Supplemental Security Income (SSI)

- Eliminates benefits to children who are "relatively less disabled." Currently, children may be eligible if an impairment exists that precludes them from "age-appropriate" activities.
- Eliminates SSI payments to prison inmates incarcerated for more than 30 days.
- Children no longer qualify for SSI benefits unless they have a medically proven disability that causes "marked and severe functional limitations."
- Most elderly immigrants are denied SSI benefits unless they obtain citizenship or work in the United States for 10 years.

Titles III, VI, VII, and VIII: Child Care, Support and Nutrition, Food Stamps

- Individual food stamp allotments were reduced across the board by 3 percent.
- The standard deduction applied to food stamp applications to determine eligibility will no longer rise with inflation.
- The deduction for housing costs was frozen at $300 per month, beginning in 2001.
- Able-bodied adults with no dependents lose food stamps after three months (six months if laid off) unless they work at least 20 hours per week.

Whether or not such self-reliance is achieved, the five-year lifetime limit means that the federal government would no longer be obligated to share the cost of public support of children and other members of families with adults who, though able-bodied, have long-term dependency needs. Many of these families would be transferred to general assistance, the residual welfare program for those who do not fit into AFDC or other welfare categories. Because general assistance receives no federal funds, the cost burden would shift to state and local governments. A shift from AFDC to block grants may thus create serious risks for the welfare population; the largest risk is the complete end of entitlements. Although general assistance provides a secondary safety net, its benefit levels are often considerably lower. Children, in particular, may be severely disadvantaged. Nor is there any requirement that states and localities fully fund general assistance. If they cannot or do not, it is not clear what resources will be available to needy families. Since counties are service providers of last resort—for health care, housing, and general assistance—it is likely that services once provided for by the federal government will now fall to states and counties. This is particularly challenging for large urban counties like San Diego, Los Angeles, Alameda, San Francisco, and Sacramento.[13]

In 2003, the adult recipients of TANF cash grants who had exceeded their 60-month limits began to lose their benefits. In compliance with PRWORA, the state had created the California Work Opportunity and Responsibility to Kids (CALWORKS) program, which continued to fund benefits for children after their parents were cut off. Fortunately, the robust economy of the late 1990s made it possible for California to move families off the welfare rolls with greater success than the nation as a whole. By 1999 the number of families on public assistance had dropped 31 percent from the peak in 1995, and 90 percent of this decline was attributed to job creation, the expansion of the Earned Income Tax Credit, and an increase in the minimum wage.[14] California has more than 10 percent of the nation's population but more than 20 percent of the nation's welfare caseload. Whether the experiment with welfare reform will succeed remains to be seen. One thing we know for certain: The federal government stands to gain the most because much of the proposed projected savings from welfare reform will come from California alone.

California Split
Gar Alperovitz

Something interesting is happening in California. Gov. Arnold Schwarzenegger seems to have grasped the essential truth that no nation—not even the United States—can be managed successfully from the center once it reaches a certain scale. Moreover, the bold proposals that Mr. Schwarzenegger is now making for everything from universal health care to global warming point to the kind of decentralization of power which, once started, could easily shake up America's fundamental political structure.

Governor Schwarzenegger is quite clear that California is not simply another state. "We are the modern equivalent of the ancient city-states of Athens and Sparta," he recently declared. "We have the economic strength, we have the population and the technological force of a nation-state." In his inaugural address, Mr. Schwarzenegger proclaimed, "We are a good and global commonwealth."

Political rhetoric? Maybe. But California's governor has also put his finger on a little discussed flaw in America's constitutional formula. The United States is almost certainly too big to be a meaningful democracy. What does "participatory democracy" mean in a continent? Sooner or later, a profound, probably regional, decentralization of the federal system may be all but inevitable.

A recent study by the economists Alberto Alesina of Harvard and Enrico Spolaore of Tufts demonstrates that the bigger the nation, the harder it becomes for the government to meet the needs of its dispersed population. Regions that don't feel well served by the government's distribution of goods and services then have an incentive to take independent action, the economists note.

Scale also determines who has privileged access to the country's news media and who can shape its political discourse. In very large nations, television and other forms of political communication are extremely costly. President Bush alone spent $345 million in his 2004 election campaign. This gives added leverage to elites, who have better corporate connections and greater resources than non-elites. The priorities of those elites often differ from state and regional priorities.

James Madison, the architect of the United States Constitution, understood these problems all too well. Madison is usually viewed as favoring constructing the nation on a large scale. What he urged, in fact, was that a nation of reasonable size had advantages over a very small one. But writing to Jefferson at a time when the population of the United States was a mere four million, Madison expressed concern that if the nation grew too big, elites at the center would divide and conquer a widely dispersed population, producing "tyranny."

Few Americans realize just how huge this nation is. Germany could fit within the borders of Montana. France is smaller than Texas. Leaving aside three nations with large, unpopulated land masses (Russia, Canada and Australia), the United States is geographically larger than all the other advanced industrial countries taken together. Critically, the American population, now roughly 300 million, is projected to reach more than 400 million by the middle of this century. A high Census Bureau estimate suggests it could reach 1.2 billion by 2100.

If the scale of a country renders it unmanageable, there are two possible responses. One is a breakup of the nation; the other is a radical decentralization of power. More than half of the world's 200 nations formed as breakaways after 1946. These days, many nations—including Brazil, Britain, Canada, China, France, Italy and Spain, just to name a few—are devolving power to regions in various ways.

Decades before President Bush decided to teach Iraq a lesson, George F. Kennan worried that what he called our "monster country" would, through the "hubris of inordinate size," inevitably become a menace, intervening all too often in other nations' affairs: "There is a real question as to whether 'bigness' in a body politic is not an evil in itself, quite aside from the policies pursued in its name."

Kennan proposed that devolution, "while retaining certain of the rudiments of a federal government," might yield a "dozen constituent republics, absorbing not only the powers of the existing states but a considerable part of those of the present federal establishment."

Regional devolution would most likely be initiated by a very large state with a distinct sense of itself and aspirations greater than Washington can handle. The obvious candidate is California, a state that has the eighth-largest economy in the world.

If such a state decided to get serious about determining its own fate, other states would have little choice but to act, too. One response might be for an area like New England, which already has many regional interstate arrangements, to follow California's initiative—as it already has on some environmental measures. And if one or two large regions began to take action, other state groupings in the Northwest, Southwest and elsewhere would be likely to follow.

A new wave of regional devolution could also build on the more than 200 compacts that now allow groups of states to cooperate on environmental, economic, transportation and other problems. Most likely, regional empowerment would be popular: when the Appalachian Regional Commission was established in 1965, senators from across the country rushed to demand commissions to help the economies and constituencies of their regions, too.

Governor Schwarzenegger may not have thought through the implications of continuing to assert forcefully his "nation-state" ambitions. But he appears to have an expansive sense of the possibilities: this is the governor, after all, who brought Prime Minister Tony Blair of Britain to the Port of Long Beach last year to sign an accord between California and Britain on global warming. And he may be closer to the mark than he knows with his dream that "California, the nation-state, the harmonious state, the prosperous state, the cutting-edge state, becomes a model, not just for the 21st-century American society, but for the larger world."

Source: "California Split" by Gar Alperovitz, *New York Times*, February 10, 2007.

SUMMARY

Ever since California was officially admitted to statehood in 1850 as the first non-contiguous American territory to become part of the Union, it has had to build its psychic and pragmatic bridges to protect its interests in Washington. The ongoing debate over where California stands in the federal system, and whether it can use its numeric clout to tip the balance of power in its favor, is really part of its historic legacy. This chapter has examined the complex structural and personal relationship the Golden State has developed over the years with the key centers of national power. In the federal system, states and their representatives must compete for their share of federal dollars without losing sight of the national agenda or the overall development of the United States.

NOTES

1. Tax Foundation, Special Report No. 139 (March 2006) *Federal Tax Burdens and Expenditures by State* (www.taxfoundation.org/files/sr139.pdf)
2. Tim Ransdell, "California's Prospects in Washington," *San Diego Union-Tribune* (November 2, 1996): 12.
3. California Institute for Federal Policy Research, "California Balance of Payments Background Data," 1991–2004 (www.calinst.org/pubs/CalShare2004-tables.pdf).
4. Herbert Sample, "Downsizing California's Military-Industrial Complex," *California Journal* (September 1995): 39–42.
5. Faye Fiore, "State Delegation Braces for Base Closure Battle," *Los Angeles Times* (May 23, 1997): A1.
6. See Laureen Lazarovici, "Counties in Crisis," *California Journal* (November 1995): 32–34.
7. William Fulton, *The Reluctant Metropolis: The Politics of Urban Growth in Los Angeles* (Point Arena, CA: Solano Books, 1997).
8. Ibid., pp. 260–261.
9. Paul Kantor, *The Dependent City Revisited* (San Francisco: Westview Press, 1995).
10. See Richard E. Thompson, *Revenue Sharing: A New Era in Federalism* (Washington, DC: Revenue Sharing Advisory Service, 1973).
11. George Peterson, et al., *The Reagan Block Grants: What Have We Learned?* (Washington, DC: The Urban Institute Press, 1986).
12. Peter Edelman, "The Worst Thing Bill Clinton Has Done," *The Atlantic Monthly* (March 1997): 43–44.
13. The preferred outcome of achieving self-reliance through employment—the goal of the new programs—raises further tough questions: Will additional education and training sufficiently increase skills and instill better work habits? Will child care and transportation be available? Will child care, Medicaid, and food stamps extend beyond welfare? Wisconsin, for instance, has determined that in its own welfare reform experiment, child care and Medicaid must be extended to all working poor, in part to maintain the incentive of welfare family heads to transition to work. Many other states have not yet developed an integrated perspective, leaving welfare recipients to wonder about interim support. Further, child care funding will be reduced under block grants, but AFDC work requirements will increase the demand for child care. This leads some to wonder whether the quality of child care will diminish—and with it, the positive effects of child care on child development. Funding for family protective services will also be reduced under block grants, raising the possibility that cases of child abuse and neglect will more often be handled by removing the children from families and placing them in foster care, which remains an entitlement.
14. Steven Haider, Jacob Klerman, and Elizabeth Roth, *The Relationship Between Welfare Caseload and the Economy*, Labor and Population Program Working Paper Series (Santa Monica, CA: RAND, 2002).

Featured Reading / Pages 121–123
Gary Delsohn and Margaret Talev
Travels with Arnold

Public policy can be described as a public response to public problems. Governmental legislation, programs, and controls are all mechanisms that public bodies utilize in an effort to improve the public welfare. *Public policy* has been defined in different ways by different observers. Peters defines *policy* as "the sum of government activities . . . [that have] an influence on the lives of citizens."[1] Lasswell points out that public policy determines "who gets what, when, and how."[2] Contemporary policy analysts might also include "why?" In a real-world context, public policy can be understood as public responses to perceived public problems.[3] Policy actors are those individuals and groups, both formal and informal, who seek to influence the creation and implementation of these public responses.

Using the metaphor of game strategies, this chapter explores the function and influence of public policy in California. Beginning with an overview of the rules and strategies of the policy "game," the chapter moves on to explore how entrepreneurial policy "players" exploit the points of vulnerability in that process. In doing so, the chapter reviews the policy actors, including the institutional actors—the governor and executive bureaucracy, the state legislature, and the courts—and the non-institutional actors—the media, parties, interest groups, and political consultants. Finally, the chapter explores California's budget as a case study of policymaking in the state.

RULES OF THE POLICY GAME

Several observers have described the public policy process as a game. The game metaphor is not intended to trivialize the process but rather to suggest that policy actors must utilize rational strategies to maximize their interests. Players will increase their chances of winning to the extent that they have knowledge of the policy bureaucracy (bureaucratic knowledge), access to individuals within the bureaucracy (network), citizen backing (size of constituency), money for political contributions, and resources to mount an effective public relations campaign (media). But these resources are only part of winning the policy game. It is also necessary to understand the rules and culture of the policy environment. The following discussion explores the context and environment of the policy game in California.

Maximizing Policy Strategies

In *The Prince*[4] Machiavelli presents a blueprint for the effective development and maintenance of power. Machiavelli's notion of *virtù*—the ability to control political destiny—is based on the successful manipulation of human circumstances. The virtuous prince is good, merciful, and honest, as long as expediency dictates, yet he must be prepared to be cruel and deceptive. Control is the primary consideration, both of one's populace and of one's neighboring states. Ultimately, *virtù* requires successful strategies to maximize policy interests.

Murray Edelman[5] similarly argues that those who seek to maximize their policy interests will use deceit and symbolism to manipulate the policy discourse. No one person can possibly experience the entire world. Yet everyone has an image or "picture" of the world. Burke suggests that however important that "sliver of reality each of us has experienced firsthand," the overall picture is a "construct of symbolic systems."[6] This construct is based on political cognitions that Edelman suggests are "ambivalent and highly susceptible to symbolic cues."[7] Government, Edelman argues, influences behavior by shaping the cognitions of people in ambiguous situations. In this way, government, or policy, elites help engineer beliefs about what is "fact" and what is "proper."

Maximizing policy strategies is critical for winning the policy game. Each player, regardless of his or her position in the policy environment, seeks to influence policy outcomes. The degree to which players utilize rational strategies—however creative, however slippery—will determine the degree to which policy success can be achieved. This is not to suggest that there are no ethical constraints on players; there are. Rather, the Machiavellian legacy in our political environment recognizes that strategy and cunning are acceptable and necessary components of the policy game.

Some suggest that democratic processes are dominated by the influence of economic elites—specifically, corporate elites. Domhoff argues that there is a social upper class that effectively operates as a ruling class by virtue of its dominance of economic resources. While there are other political resources—for example, expertise and bureaucratic knowledge—these other resources can and are purchased. Thus, as Domhoff[8] points out, financial power is often the basis of policy influence. If it is true that policy influence requires requisite political resources, inequality in resource distribution is tantamount to inequality in political representation. Maximizing policy strategy, therefore, includes maximizing the ability to raise funds.

POLICY ACTORS

The policy process is significantly more subtle than many realize. While the state constitution provides for a legislature that makes laws, an executive that enforces laws, and a judiciary that interprets laws, the policy process has evolved into a confusing web of state departments, agencies, and committees that make up the institutional policy bureaucracy. And, unlike the federal level, California's constitution requires that governmental authority be shared with voters through the initiative process, the recall, and the referendum. In addition, the vast network of organized citizen groups (parties, interest groups, and political action committees), as well as the rise of the electronic media, political consultants, and other image-making professionals, further complicates the process. The role each actor plays, in combination with the relationship between actors in policy bureaucracies, is ultimately what determines policy outcomes.

Institutional Policy Actors

THE STATE LEGISLATURE.   The legislature is the central institution in the policy process because of the powers given to it by the state constitution. Within the legislature, power is centralized in the committees. Committee chairs have a disproportionate influence over policy as a consequence of their power to determine committee agendas. Similarly, certain committees have more policy influence than others. The Assembly Rules Committee, for example, is responsible for determining which bills will be heard and in what order. The appropriation committees in both the assembly and senate are responsible for reviewing any legislation that requires funding. The power that members of such committees hold and the powers of committee chairs make them key players in the policy process.

Legislative staffers are another source of influence that is often overlooked. In *The Power Game*,[9] Hedrick Smith describes staffers as "policy entrepreneurs." Staffers are important in two areas. First, the increasing use of staff to service constituents in district offices strengthens the legislator's stature among local voters, perhaps explaining in part the strength of incumbency. Second, staffers are the real expertise behind the legislator. With hundreds of bills introduced in an average session, legislators rely more and more on staff to analyze legislation, negotiate compromises, research issues, and meet with lobbyists. In their roles as legislative analysts and policy negotiators, as well as their role as political confidants and counselors, senior staffers have significant policy influence. And, with term limits now state law, staffers will have more experience than legislators, giving them even more power to influence.

THE GOVERNOR AND EXECUTIVE BUREAUCRACY.   The governor is mandated by the California constitution as a partner in the policy process. But, unlike the legislature, the governor can only approve or disapprove legislation, he or she has no power to amend legislation. As we saw in Chapter 6, California's constitution requires that the seven nongubernatorial executive officers be directly elected, an arrangement that dilutes the governor's power further. Thus, the policy priorities of the governor cannot be directly imposed. Rather, governors must rely on legislative partners in both houses, and on, what Richard Neustadt calls the "power to persuade."[10] This persuasion comes as a result of several factors. Paul Light suggests that executive policy is a result of the "stream of people and ideas" that flow through the executive office.[11] If public policy is a process of identifying problems, identifying solutions, and implementing those solutions, the identification of problems and solutions, Light argues, is tied to the assumptions held by players in that stream. The policy stream must accommodate the issues that percolate up through the systemic agenda, as well as those issues that may be on the executive agenda.

The implementation of gubernatorial policy objectives involves a different set of problems than those of the legislature. While the legislature makes laws, the governor can only recommend laws. Effective governors use the powers and perks of their office to maximize their policy agendas. Appointments are a major source of policy influence. By appointing individuals who share his or her political perspective and agenda, a governor is able to extend influence throughout the executive and judicial bureaucracies. Cabinet officers and heads of regulatory agencies establish policy priorities within their agencies. And, since most legislation allows for a significant measure of discretion among implementing and enforcement agencies, the cabinet officers and agency heads have wide latitude in defining, implementing, and enforcing policy.

The policy influence of regulatory agencies within the executive bureaucracy is substantial. Meier[12] describes the regulatory process as a combination of regulatory bureaucracies (values, expertise, agency subculture, bureaucratic entrepreneurs) and public interaction (interest groups, economic issues, legislative committees and subcommittees). Regulatory outcomes are a consequence of subsystem interaction between all of these influences. Those who are best able to influence these subsystems are best able to maximize their interests. As a result, policy subsystems are major points of access for policy influence.

THE COURTS. The influence of judges in interpreting laws has a significant impact on policy. And this impact is not free of political influence. Unlike the federal system, state judges are vulnerable to political scrutiny. This was most dramatically demonstrated in the expulsion of Chief Justice Rose Bird and two of her colleagues in 1984. The policy role of the judiciary is not universally appreciated. The current debate over judicial activism and judicial restraint is only the most recent in a long discourse. In "Towards an Imperial Judiciary?"[13] Nathan Glazer argues that judicial activism infringes on democratic policy institutions and that an activist court erodes the respect and trust people hold for the judiciary. Still, whether a court is active or passive, there are significant policy implications. Non-action is in itself a policy decision with substantial policy implications.

Non-Institutional Actors

Public policy is not merely the result of independent policymaking institutions. Non-institutional actors also play a significant role: The public elects legislators and executives; the media influences policy through its inherent agenda-setting function; parties influence policy through their role of drafting and electing candidates; and organized interest groups lobby elected officials and non-elected policymakers (e.g., agency staff). Policy, then, is a result of institutional processes influenced by non-institutional actors.

THE MEDIA. The media are influential to policy outcomes because they help define social reality. The work of McCombs and Shaw[14] suggests that the media influence the salience of issues. As Lippmann[15] observed in 1922, perceptions of reality are based on a tiny sampling of the world around us. No one can be everywhere, no one can experience everything. Thus, to a greater or lesser extent, all of us rely on media portrayals of reality. Graber[16] argues that the way people process information makes them especially vulnerable to media influence. First, people tend to pare down the scope of information they confront. Second, people tend to think schematically. When confronted with information, individuals will fit that information into pre-existing schema. Since news stories tend to lack background and context, schemata allow the individual to give the information meaning. In such a way, individuals re-create reality in their minds.

The data collected by Iyengar and Kinder[17] show that television news, to a great extent, defines which problems the public considers most serious. Iyengar and Kinder refine the agenda-setting dynamic to include what they call "priming"—the selective coverage of only certain events and the selective way in which those events are covered. Because there is no way to cover all events or cover any event completely, selective decisions must be made. But, there are consequences:

> By priming certain aspects of national life while ignoring others, television news sets the terms by which political judgements are rendered and political choices made.[18]

The implications for public policy are serious. If policy is a result of a problem-recognition model, then the problems that gain media recognition are much more likely to be addressed.

California politics relies on the media to distribute political messages. With 36 million people, it is not possible for policy advocates in California to truly meet the voters as they might in New Hampshire or Iowa. Television, radio, and newspapers allow politicians, candidates, and interest groups to cover more ground with less money. In the Los Angeles television market alone, for example, policy advocates can reach 10 million people at once. As we will see in Chapter 11, political parties and interest groups can translate their financial resources into air time to get their messages across.

POLITICAL PARTIES. Political parties are distinct from other citizen organizations. Rather than attempt to influence existing policymakers, parties seek to get their own members elected to policymaking positions. While interest groups seek influence on specific policy issues, parties seek influence on a wide spectrum of policy issues. Parties develop issue platforms, draft candidates, campaign on behalf of candidates, and mobilize voters. In short, parties work to bring citizens together under a common banner.

While most people may think of parties only during election cycles, party policy influence extends beyond campaigns. While the rise of the media over the past 40 years has deemphasized the power of parties in electoral politics, parties continue to play a dominant role in policy outcomes. Due to the institutional role parties play in the legislature and the grassroots role that parties play at the local and county level, the party that emerges dominant often determines the direction policy will take. The governor is responsible to the party that got him or her elected, and therefore must pursue at least some of the policy objectives articulated at the party convention. The legislature continues to distribute committee membership and chairmanships according to party affiliation. While negotiation and compromise are typically necessary, the general direction of legislative policy is directly tied to the ideology of the majority party. The strength of political parties has waned over the past three decades (see Chapter 11), but parties maintain policy influence in critical areas. Elections, patronage appointments, legislative committees, and policy discourses all reflect the influence of parties. In the 1920s Republicans outnumbered Democrats, but by 1934 the majority of Californians were registered Democrats. The Democratic Party has maintained its numeric advantage ever since. While the governor's office has shifted between both parties, Democrats have maintained a legislative majority since 1970, with the exception of a Republican majority in the assembly from 1995 to 1996. As a consequence, California Democrats have defined the state's legislative agenda for a generation.

INTEREST GROUPS. Interest groups are a fundamental partner in policymaking. Citizens participate in the policy process through communication with policymakers. Such communication takes place individually (e.g., letters to elected representatives) and collectively. Interest groups facilitate collective communication. James Madison recognized the propensity for individuals to factionalize in an effort to maximize political influence.[19] Robert Dahl further refined the analysis of Madisonian democracy, arguing that in an open society all persons have the right to press their interests. To the extent others share these interests, collective pressure may allow greater policy influence. Indeed, Dahl argued, those issues that have greater salience have greater interest group representation.[20]

The interest group dynamic, however, is not so simple. While it may be true that many salient issues have interest group representation, the strength of that representation is not tied to the strength of the issue salience. Further, the salience itself may be a consequence of interest group action. When studying policy outcomes it is necessary to identify the policy actors and the political resources they use. Maximizing policy interests—winning the policy game—requires specific political resources. The most common resources include bureaucratic knowledge, a network of contacts, citizen backing (size of constituency), an ability to make political contributions, and an ability to mount a public relations (media) campaign. Clearly, no group utilizes all these resources. But the ability of an organized group to utilize one or more of these resources is critical for policy influence. Interest groups have been major players in the state's election cycle through their independent expenditures on behalf of legislative candidates. While California voters elected to limit direct contributions to candidates to $3,600 per election in 2000's Proposition 34, interest groups spent $100 million between 2000 and 2008 communicating directly with voters in their efforts to influence elections. Teachers' unions, trial lawyers, prison guards, environmentalists, energy companies, and many other special interests actively work to influence the state's political institutions.[21]

POLITICAL CONSULTANTS.   Increasingly, political expertise is purchased by those who have the need and the resources. In reviewing the rise and structure of the political consulting industry, Sabato[22] exposes the fragile relationship between articulating ideas in a political marketplace and manipulating public opinion. It is virtually impossible to win at the policy game without the marketing skills held by consultants and strategists. Like many other policy resources, political consultants are costly. As a consequence, those with greater economic resources enjoy a policy advantage.

The extremely competitive nature of California's political environment has made political consulting a growth industry in the state. There are 14 major political consulting firms in the state, representing candidates at all levels of government.[23] In addition, there are thousands of additional firms offering media consulting, public relations, survey research, direct mail, and fund raising. Critics argue that the selling of politics has become just as slick and self-interested as the selling of cars. Public policy has become just another commodity in a market environment. The implication, of course, is that the policy process may be less democratic as a consequence. It is often political consultants, rather than public-interested candidates, who are defining the political discourse in the state. Whether or not one perceives this as a problem might be related to an individual's access to the financial resources needed to purchase these services.

POLICY OUTPUTS: CALIFORNIA'S BUDGET AS A CASE STUDY

The California state budget provides a good case study on the policy process. Because the budget defines fiscal allocations, it serves to define the state's policy priorities for the following year. As such, the budget process brings both institutional and non-institutional actors into passionate political battle. Legally, the formal budget process plays out as follows:

*   January 10: Governor submits his or her budget to both houses of the legislature.
*   February: Legislative analyst publishes *Analysis of the Governor's Budget*.

- March and April: Senate and assembly budget subcommittees hold hearings on each budget item.
- May: Governor submits the "May revision," a revised estimate of revenues and expenditures. Subcommittee hearings end. Senate and assembly budget committees send bills to their full houses.
- June: Conference committee of both houses meets to reconcile differences between senate and assembly version of budget bills and ultimately sends recommendation to both houses for final vote.
- June 15: Budget goes to the governor for signature.[24]

While the process at first glance appears to include only the institutional policy actors, there are several points at which non-institutional actors become involved. Long before the governor's budget is submitted in June, citizens, interest groups, corporations, and legislators lobby the governor's office and each other in order to maximize the chances of receiving funding for policies they favor and for cutting funding for policies they are against. Once the governor's budget is made public, these groups direct their attention to the senate and assembly budget committees and subcommittees, lobbying and testifying at budget hearings.

Simultaneously, those groups with the economic resources will begin to lobby the public through both paid and non-paid media. Political advertising can be used to cue public concern, which may cue public budgetary demands. Similarly, policy advocates may seek media coverage through news or public affairs programming. Not only is this type of publicity free, it places a mantle of objectivity on the policy objective. As opposed to a paid political advertisement, news coverage of an event held by an interest group will carry more weight with the public if the messenger is a reporter or commentator.

Travels with Arnold   *Gary Delsohn and Margaret Talev*

A t 4 o'clock one autumn afternoon in the throes of Gov. Arnold Schwarzenegger's first bill-signing season, Gary Delsohn, a *Sacramento Bee* political reporter and coauthor of this article, answered the phone. The thick accent on the other end of the line was unmistakable.

It was Schwarzenegger, eager to chat at a time when he should have been too busy. Delsohn was working on a profile of Legislative Affairs Secretary Richard Costigan, Schwarzenegger's point man on the hundreds of bills the state Legislature was sending his way in a last-minute crush. The profile could go in any number of directions. Costigan's work ethic and intellect were respected across party lines, but Democrats were troubled by his background as a Chamber of Commerce lobbyist. The governor had decided the best way to influence the story's tone was to step in himself—and turn on his trademark Hollywood charm.

Delsohn asked Schwarzenegger how he was doing. "Fantastic, now that I hear your voice," Schwarzenegger said. "You really get me going." Giggles trickled across the other end of the line. The Governor's staff was with him in the room.

"So tell me," Schwarzenegger said. "You guys know the slant you are going to take before you do any of the interviewing. Are you going to build him up or tear him down?" Delsohn played along. "Let's tear him down." "Well," said the Schwarzenegger, "he's a total waste. I can tell you that." Then the governor spent another 15 minutes on the line effusively praising Costigan.

At 57, still one of the most glamorous, recognizable men in the world, still fit from his regular workouts, Schwarzenegger doesn't so much interact with reporters as shadowbox with them. He flirts as easily with male reporters as with the women and revels in head games. We've been doing this dance since the summer of 2003, reading his books, watching his movies, studying lawsuits and financial disclosures and peeking into the parallel universe of bodybuilding. We've watched him with President Bush, interviewed his friends and business partners, his rivals and his admirers. We've also chased him across the globe (he does not take reporters with him on his private jets, so we fly commercial) on trips to Israel, Germany and Japan and back and forth across the United States.

Each trip features the same phenomena: stampedes of autograph-seeking fans and packs of awestruck local media. Would any other politician be chased, as Schwarzenegger was during a trade mission to Tokyo, by more than 100 Japanese reporters shouting at him to flex his muscles and imploring him to yell out movie lines such as "I'll be back!" or "Hasta la vista, baby!"? And when the scrum of cameramen crowded in to record the start of a private meeting with Prime Minister Junichiro Koizumi, Koizumi looked a bit overwhelmed, telling Schwarzenegger, "You're more popular than Bush."

That popularity, which transcends anything enjoyed by any other modern politician, makes Schwarzenegger both a fascinating and frustrating governor to cover. The hard-hitting reporting that would give rise out of any other politician rarely elicits a reaction from the former actor, who is rich and famous enough not to care. So far, Schwarzenegger has done many of the things for which he criticized his bland predecessor, Democrat Gray Davis—taking millions of dollars in special-interest money and dodging tough budget choices—but stories about these contradictions have drawn little interest outside the state Capitol in Sacramento and California's small community of political aficionados.

During Schwarzenegger's first year in office, the California press corps and national reporters who regularly write about him developed a fuller picture of his political and ideological motivations. This immigrant from a small town in Austria, who came to the United States with only a physique and a dream, is one of politics' greatest showmen. A socially liberal capitalist and serial exaggerator, he is an exceptional salesman with boundless energy who long ago traded in steroids for calcium supplements. He taps his persona with the moviegoing masses to leverage the fortunes of other politicians. But he hasn't, at least by the time this story went to press, risked that popularity for any major policy initiatives.

While he often keeps a distance from the California press corps, Schwarzenegger made clear his sense of his relationship with the media in a January 2004 speech to the Sacramento Press Club. "I mean, think about it. When I first came over here, who the hell knew who Arnold Schwarzenschnitzel was, right? I mean, nobody."

His press coverage in the 1970s made bodybuilding a main-stream sport, he said. That attention turned him into the highest paid actor in the business. "That doesn't mean I always got great review. As a matter of fact, I got horrible reviews many times," he said. "But that's OK . . . I got a lot of publicity." The same was true in his run for governor, he said. "It was really the press that helped me to get to the place where I am today."

As he spoke, reporters at the press luncheon fiddled with their rolls, faces flushed, wondering whether he was trying to humiliate them, or was he serious, or what? "Here's a big applause to all of you," he said.

Later, he took questions, starting with one from Mike Montgomery, a public radio reporter. "Let's start right here at the front, with this gentleman right here in the beautiful blue turtleneck sweater." Before Montgomery could begin, Schwarzenegger told the audience that a California state senator had given him some advice: "Always compliment the journalist. Always make them feel like they look good, they look sexy." Those who knew the state senator in question—a wry, somewhat shy conservative—also knew that Schwarzenegger had come up with that advice on his own.

Source: Gary Delsohn and Margaret Talev, "Travels with Arnold", *American Journalism Review,* February/March 2005.

SUMMARY

This chapter has explored the role and influence of actors in the policy process—both institutional (the legislature, the governor and executive bureaucracy, and the courts) and non-institutional (media, parties, interest groups, and political consultants). From the discussion it can be seen that policy outcomes are typically a result of institutional processes and non-institutional influence. As the previous chapters explain, California's political culture and structure is quite complex, representing the diverse interests of 36 million Californians. The policy game, therefore, is important to understand. As Californians pilot the ship of state, there is little consensus as to who is at the helm. While the governor may be the captain, the crew are under little obligation to follow the governor's course. With the multitude of destinations sought, it is little wonder that California politics are contentious and passionate. But that, after all, is what democracy is all about.

NOTES

1. B. Guy Peters, *American Public Policy: Promise and Performance*, 3rd ed. (Chatham, NJ: Chatham House Publishers, 1993), p. 4.
2. Harold Lasswell, *Politics: Who Gets What, When, and How* (New York: St. Martin's Press, 1988).
3. See Stella Theodoulou and Matthew Cahn, *Public Policy: The Essential Readings* (Upper Saddle River, NJ: Prentice Hall, 1995).

4. Niccolo Machiavelli, *The Prince*, in Peter Bondanella and Mark Muse, eds., *The Portable Machiavelli* (New York: Penguin Books, 1983).
5. Murray Edelman, *Constructing the Political Spectacle* (Chicago: The University of Chicago Press, 1988).
6. Kenneth Burke, *Language as Symbolic Action* (Berkeley: University of California Press, 1966), p. 5.
7. Murray Edelman, *Politics as Symbolic Action* (Chicago: Markham Publishing Co., 1971), p. 2.
8. G. William Domhoff, *Who Rules America Now?* (New York: Simon & Schuster, Inc., 1983).
9. Hedrick Smith, *The Power Game: How Washington Works* (New York: Ballantine Books, 1988).
10. Richard Neustadt, *Presidential Power* (New York: John Wiley and Sons, Inc., 1980).
11. Paul Light, "The Presidential Policy Stream," in Michael Nelson, ed., *The Presidency and the Political System* (Washington, DC: CQ Press, 1984).
12. Kenneth J. Meier, *Regulation: Politics, Bureaucracy, and Economics* (New York: St. Martin's Press, 1985).
13. Nathan Glazer, "Towards an Imperial Judiciary?" *Public Interest* 41 (Fall 1975): 104–123.
14. Maxwell E. McCombs and Donald L. Shaw, *The Emergence of American Political Issues: The Agenda Setting Function of the Press* (Boston: West Publishing Company, 1977).
15. Walter Lippmann, *Public Opinion* (New York: The Free Press, 1922).
16. Doris Graber, *Processing the News: How People Tame the Information Tide*, 2nd ed. (New York: Longman, 1988).
17. Shanto Iyengar and Donald Kinder, *News That Matters: Television and American Opinion* (Chicago: The University of Chicago Press, 1987).
18. Ibid., p. 4.
19. James Madison, "Federalist #10," in Alexander Hamilton, James Madison, and John Jay, *The Federalist Papers* (New York: New American Library, 1961).
20. Robert Dahl, *Who Governs?* (New Haven, CT: Yale University Press, 1961).
21. "Special-Interest Spending Takes Off," *Sacramento Bee* (October 16, 2008).
22. Larry J. Sabato, *The Rise of Political Consultants: New Ways of Winning Elections* (New York: Basic Books, 1981).
23. Ibid.
24. Adapted from *California State Budget At-a-Glance*, published by the Senate Budget and Fiscal Review Committee, July 1992.

CHAPTER 11

Non-Institutional Players: The Media, Political Parties, and Interest Groups

Featured Reading / Pages 133–135
Jordan Rau
Term Limits Add Up to Brain Drain

Communication is an essential feature of representative democracy. Citizens and leaders must be linked in order for the political system to function effectively. Leaders need to be aware of citizens' concerns so that they build policy accordingly and so they can mobilize policy support. Citizens must be aware of their representatives' actions so that they can provide policy feedback and so they can hold leaders accountable in elections. Democratic theory suggests that citizens know their local elected leaders, having worked with them at the local level. In some states, that may still be the case. California, however, is so large and complex that communication between elected leaders and the public is a carefully mediated process. The media, political parties, and interest groups are the vehicles through which these communication functions take place.

The role of parties in linking the public to their elected leaders has also changed over time. The influence of parties has declined as a consequence of several reforms—some going back to the Progressives and some more recent—as well as a consequence of the emergence of media power over the past 40 years. Commensurate with the rising power of the electronic media, and the rising costs associated with media politics, interest groups and political actions committees (PACs) have gained power through their ability to channel economic resources to campaign staff.

MEDIA POLITICS

Through political advertising, editorials and commentaries, and news and entertainment programming, media elites—those who exert a disproportionate influence over media content—are effectively able to control access to California's political discourse. The degree to which ordinary Californians and their grassroots organizations are able to compete in this arena frequently determines the extent to which they are able to affect policy outcomes. At the same time, interest groups play a dominant role in applying direct pressure to the policy process and indirect influence through campaign contributions. The linkage between media politics, parties, and interest groups is made clear when correlating the costs of amplifying one's message through broadcast media and the significant role parties and interest groups play in financing campaigns. The media provide the vehicle through which candidates and elected officials communicate with the public: Parties and interest groups are vehicles that citizens use to communicate with elected officials.

Media Effects and the Vulnerability of Political Attitudes

A significant body of research has been compiled on the question of mass media's effect on political attitudes. The initial research found little relationship. The discussion was reframed in the 1960s, when political scientist Philip Converse questioned the dominant notion that citizens are rational actors with fully developed attitudes on a wide variety of issues.[1] Walter Lippmann, after all, warned attitude researchers early in the twentieth century that individuals, like the media, simplify complex reality into a manageable representation. People simply cannot focus on every conceivable issue.[2]

Mass media, however, play a major role in defining the boundaries within which the public debate exists. The specific effect the media have on how individuals feel about specific issues is subtle. Rather than overtly propagandize, the media define the opinion choices citizens have. Over a lifetime, the cumulative effects of media messages are significant. Between 1946 and 1961 the Yale Program of Research on Communication and Attitude Change conducted numerous studies on the effect of communication on political attitudes. Shearon Lowery and Melvin DeFleur summarize the Yale findings:

> In summary, the many separate but related studies of the Yale Communication Research Program can be categorized as focusing on the communicators, the message, the audience, and the audience's responses to persuasive communications. In terms of the communicator, the program found that source credibility was an important factor in obtaining immediate opinion change. Low-credibility sources were seen as more biased and more unfair than were high-credibility sources. The researchers also found that the effects of the communicator's credibility diminish over time, because members of the audience tend to disassociate the message from the communicator. However, these credibility effects can be reinstated simply by reminding the audience who said what. Overall, however, most of the opinion change obtained was short rather than long term. Thus, while it is not difficult to change opinion immediately after a persuasive communication, when the change is measured a month later the audience has often reverted to its original position.[3]

These studies suggest that repeated exposure to a similar message agenda, especially when delivered by sources deemed to be highly credible, results in opinion change to reflect the message agenda.

Observational learning is the most widely cited process through which television affects attitudes. People internalize depictions of reality and form attitudinal responses. This exists both within entertainment programming and news programming. Entertainment programming creates roles that viewers often accept as accurate depictions of social interactions, with which they measure their own social interactions. News programming is much less subtle, in that it overtly articulates an interpretation of reality upon which viewers base political attitudes.

Numerous studies have pointed out the inverse relationship between education levels and opinion influence by televised media. Nonetheless, issue awareness has always remained rather low among the whole population. People are simply too busy living their lives to follow politics closely. It is thus fair to assume that the influence of media on political attitudes is substantial, in that the media are the only access most individuals have to the world around them beyond their immediate community. The ability to determine the agenda and scope of media messages, then, may in fact translate into the ability to influence political attitudes.

The Media and Governmental Politics in California

The ability to amplify one's message is critical in policy debates as well as elections. Electronic and print media, therefore, are necessary tools. In the past, the traditional family-owned newspapers played a major role in California's political history, reflecting the economic and political interests of their publishers. Families used their papers to push policies, candidates, and commerce that they favored. All the large publishing families held an interest in land speculation and industry, and therefore generated extremely favorable—some might say skewed—coverage of the land speculation and development that came to characterize the first half of the twentieth century. The involvement of the Otis family's *Los Angeles Times* in pressing for Owens Valley water to support sprawling residential development in the San Fernando Valley is merely one of the better-known examples.[4] Hearst's *San Francisco Examiner*, the de Young brothers' *San Francisco Chronicle*, and McClatchy's *Sacramento Bee* all followed similar paths. It was not until the 1970s that professional management and public ownership of newspapers forced more professional balance.

The Vietnam War demonstrated the power of broadcast media over print media. Television coverage of the war brought home the gritty reality of combat as never before. Americans increasingly turned to their televisions to get their news. By the war's end in 1974, television had emerged as the primary source of information for Californians: Virtually all California households owned at least one television. The importance of television to politics had been made clear in the Kennedy–Nixon debate in 1960.[5] But there remain serious questions as to the quality of information broadcast. In a state the size of California, statewide coverage is critical for keeping citizens informed. Yet no California station maintains a news bureau in the state capital. State politics receive less than 2 percent of newscast time, most of which is rehashed from newspapers and wire services.[6] Observers suggest that national political coverage, although much less relevant to the everyday life of most people, is much more in demand, as is the typical scandal, crime, and fire coverage of local news.

The Media and Electoral Politics in California

Since 1960 political advertising has emerged as a major determinant of outcomes in the electoral arena. It is also a major factor in the abstract area of attitude acquisition, defining for many voters who is more "presidential" or more "electable." Political advertising is successful in establishing an agenda both for the immediate election at hand, as well as the ongoing political climate. Several studies have found that political advertising can cause substantial change in voter attitudes.[7]

The need to advertise on television has increased the already colossal cost of mounting a statewide campaign in California. The 2006 gubernatorial race provides a case in point. The primary campaigns collectively spent over $29 million. The general election campaign between Democrat Phil Angelides and Republican Arnold Schwarzenegger was one of the most expensive governor's races ever to date, with the two campaigns spending $32 million.[8] Driving these figures is the high cost of advertising on television. To run a credible campaign for statewide office and to reach the voters from Alpine County to San Diego County, candidates must purchase massive amounts of paid TV ads to blanket the state.

Paid Media

Broadcast media markets are defined by areas of dominant influence (ADI). ADIs are the geographic boundaries that encircle a common audience. California is divided into 15 ADIs. Due to the concentration of population in four urban centers, however, 85 percent of the state can be covered in four ADIs: Los Angeles, San Francisco, San Diego, and Sacramento.[9] The cost of advertising is dependent on an ADI's size and the Nielsen rating of a particular show, in addition to ad length. Los Angeles currently is the nation's most expensive ADI, at $1,150 per rating point. A 30-second spot on a show with 10 rating points would cost $11,500. In the 1994 gubernatorial race, political spots in Los Angeles ranged between $12,000 and $30,000. The enormous costs of political advertising on television may be prohibitive for smaller races or challengers with small campaign war chests. The high prices charged for California ADIs encourage all candidates to seek free media.[10]

Free Media

Free media includes any news coverage a candidate might acquire through press conferences, photo opportunities, and staged spectacles. During campaign cycles, staged events tend to dominate political news coverage. Between cycles, elected officials hold news conferences to maximize visibility. Since candidates for office require extensive visibility, there often is a sense of spectacle to such events. The O. J. Simpson case provided ample opportunity for Los Angeles District Attorney Gil Garcetti to acquire statewide, and even nationwide, visibility. In the same way, elected officials are often tempted to pursue sensational policies in an effort to stimulate coverage. Within days of the death of Princess Diana, State Senator Tom Hayden was on the radio talk show circuit, pushing for anti-paparazzi legislation. Certainly some elected officials will pursue symbolic policies that may attract political support but may be extremely difficult to implement. Many observers suggest that Pete Wilson's support of Propositions 187 and 209 was targeted at maximizing free media coverage in an effort to gain national visibility for a possible second run for president.

Arnold Schwarzenegger is, perhaps, the best example of successfully using free media. His entry into politics was made possible by his celebrity as a film actor and frequent guest on television. He announced his campaign for governor on *The Tonight Show with Jay Leno*, and he continues to appear as a frequent guest to make his case for various policies or to talk his way out of political trouble. Unlike Gray Davis, his immediate predecessor, Schwarzenegger has been able to leverage his personal charisma through friendly free media environments. Similarly, Maria Shriver, Schwarzenegger's wife, has been able to use her background as a network journalist with many years of public visibility to successfully establish the California first lady's office as a major center of political influence.

POLITICAL PARTIES IN CALIFORNIA

One reason for the media's significant role in state politics is California's weak party system. Early in the twentieth century, Progressive reformers practically dismantled the parties in their zeal to fight corruption and the influence of special interests. California Progressives were concerned about the power of party machines, such as Boss Ruef's rule over San Francisco, and the domination of state government by the Southern Pacific Railroad. The introduction of nonpartisan local elections, cross-filing, the construction of a civil service system, and the end of patronage are all reforms that weakened the influence of state parties in government and in elections. Public loyalty to the two major parties has also been in decline, both in California and nationwide.

The California State Election Code provides detailed rules and structures that both the Democratic and Republican parties must follow. These guidelines, however, were created by elected legislators—Democrats and Republicans—and thus the parties themselves enjoyed great latitude in scripting the guidelines. Registered voters of both parties elect representatives to the county central committees in the primary elections. County central committees are the primary managers of local party activities. The workhorses of California's 58 county central committees are the assembly district committees, which are responsible for campaigns in the 80 assembly districts statewide. While these committees may appear to be independent, party affairs tend to be dominated by existing officeholders in each county who control the power, money, and resources locally. The state central committees have about 2,500 to 3,000 members on the Democratic party side and about 1,400 members on the Republican side. They coordinate state party affairs, orchestrate political campaigns for party designates, draft the state party platform (an agenda of major ideological principles and goals reflective of the party's stance), and select presidential electors.

In addition, the state central committees, along with their executive board, nominate delegates to the national convention and serve as the state's party representatives on the national committee of each party.

The Role of Parties in California Politics

For many years, parties in the legislature maintained discipline by redistributing campaign money among members. This practice began under Assembly Speaker Jesse Unruh, who coined the overused phrase "money is the mother's milk of politics."[11] It continued under subsequent speakers, from Democrat Willie Brown to Republican Curt Pringle, whose domination of party campaign funds allowed them to maintain control of the institution and its agenda. However, the passage of Proposition 208 in 1996 limited the practice of redistributing campaign money, making the maintenance of party discipline more difficult.

The once-dominant role of the parties in campaigns and elections has been diminished since the Progressive era, and recent reforms have further weakened the parties. In 1974, in the aftermath of Watergate, California voters adopted Proposition 9, which was sponsored by Common Cause and Secretary of State Jerry Brown (then a candidate for governor). The initiative required politicians to disclose campaign contributions and expenditures of $100 or more as well as donations that could be potential conflicts of interest. It also established the California Fair Political Practices Commission (FPPC), an enforcement agency with the power to launch its own investigations into campaign finance abuse and to issue fines when violations occur.

In 1988, voters approved Proposition 73, which limited individual contributions to $1,000 and organizational and PAC contributions to between $2,500 and $5,000. The California supreme court struck down the measure in 1990. Voters approved Proposition 208 in 1996, which limits individual donors and groups to a maximum of $250 per candidate in an election, although they are allowed to donate more if the candidate agrees to a voluntary spending limit. It also imposes spending limits on parties and prohibits the transfer of funds between candidates. In short, Proposition 208 will severely restrict the role of the parties in state elections if it is allowed to stand. Currently, the measure is being held up in court. The waning influence of parties may have begun during the Progressive era, but voters continue to view party influence as suspect.

INTEREST GROUP POLITICS

If broadcast and print media are used by elected officials and those seeking office to communicate with the public, interest groups are vehicles through which the public communicates with elected officials. Interest group politics is vilified by many, but it in fact represents a critical aspect of political participation. Interest groups participate in the governmental process by lobbying elected officials. They are also active in electoral politics by donating money and resources to candidates, and even by waging their own political campaigns.

All Californians are represented by several single-issue interest groups. Whether it is the local, county, school district, or favorite grassroots organization, all Californians benefit from the representation these groups provide. However, that representation is not equal, and some organizations benefit from much greater access than others. Interest group politics is a founding principle in American politics. We all recognize the problems of unequal access. James Madison argued 200 years ago that while factionalism represents a threat to democracy, the option to disallow such groups represents an even greater threat. Rather than outlaw interest groups, Madison argued persuasively that interest groups should be encouraged. In so doing, more groups will emerge, creating counterbalance to each other. If 1 group is bad, then 2 groups are better, and 2,000 groups are better yet. Problems emerge when powerful groups have coalescing interests.

The pluralist model of counterbalancing elites' mediating interests is inadequate. The theoretical work done by Mills, and empirical work done by Dye, Domhoff, and Presthus, among others, suggest that rather than competing, the interests of economic elites tend to cohere in key policy areas.[12] Lowi's *The End of Liberalism*[13] argues that this interest group influence threatens the democratic basis of government. If interest groups provide the framework for government–citizen interaction, and these groups are based on individual self-interest, there may be little opportunity for pursuing a meaningful public interest.

In 2005, 344 registered lobbying firms, representing 2,639 paying interests throughout the state and beyond, spent almost $228 million lobbying California state government. The top ten lobbying organizations during this period included the California Teachers Association ($9,456,813), AT&T and its affiliates ($4,065,146), Western States Petroleum Association ($3,130,034), the California Chamber of Commerce ($2,570,516), the California State Council of Service Employees ($2,014,715), Edison International & Subsidiaries ($1,873,265), BHP Billiton LNG International ($1,765,541), the California School Employees Association ($1,570,845), Blue Cross of California (Wellpoint Health Networks) ($1,566,508), and the Consumer Attorneys of California ($1,549,113).[14]

Interest groups have long influenced the California political landscape. The Central Pacific Railroad, for example, dominated California politics from the 1860s through 1910, when the Progressive movement successfully won constitutional amendments and new statutes to limit railroad influence. Today, lobbyists advocate on everything from agriculture, to organized labor, to university student services, to theme parks. When successful, the interest group dynamic allows Madisonian democracy to flourish, allowing the public access to politics and policy in a direct and meaningful way. When unsuccessful, the group dynamic maximizes the power and influence of those interests most able to pay.

Interest groups have learned to exploit the ballot initiative process to circumvent elected representatives altogether. By placing legislative proposals directly before the voters, groups have more control over final policy outcomes. Even when an initiative's chances of victory are slim, interest groups have strong incentives to pursue this type of strategy.[15] These reasons revolve around mobilization and group cohesion. First, a controversial ballot measure can help mobilize group members, whose participation is crucial for the group to be effective. Second, an initiative campaign can invigorate the group itself—regardless of outcome. Even a futile campaign for an unpopular ballot measure is an opportunity to attract and recruit new members. Third, groups have an unparalleled opportunity to influence public opinion in the context of an election. Groups can take advantage of free media to get their message out and possibly influence public opinion in advance of the next legislative session or election. Finally, the issue may entice enough sympathetic voters to go to the polls to influence the outcome of other races on the ballot. The increasing use of the initiative by deep-pocket interests threatens to destabilize the democratic equilibrium Madison was so concerned about.

Interest Groups and Electoral Politics

Stepping into the void that was left by the weakened parties, interest groups are asserting an ever-greater role in the state's political campaigns. Key to their influence are campaign donations from PACs. Much of the money that used to be distributed by parties is now filtered to candidates through PACs which are controlled by interest groups. In contrast to parties, many of these groups are motivated by narrow agendas, to which candidates must cater in order to secure contributions. This reliance on single-issue groups, it is argued, contributes to the fragmentation of politics.[16] Even though individual donors are still the largest source of donations to political campaigns, PACs are growing in significance.

Even without PAC money, the augmented role of interest groups means that in some races, groups can outspend the candidate's own organizations, hijacking the political debate and rendering the parties irrelevant. The influence of interest groups in one recent election gained national attention. A special election was held in 1998 to replace the late U.S. Representative Walter Capps, a Democrat whose 22nd District encompassed San Luis Obispo and Santa Barbara Counties along the central coast. Two Republicans faced the late congressman's widow, Democrat Lois Capps, who was running to succeed her husband. Initially, the campaign revolved around local and state issues, including the future of a nearby Air Force base, HMO reform legislation, and a school construction bond. However, the contest took place in a competitive district, and national interest groups poured hundreds of thousands of dollars into the race in order to influence the outcome. The AFL-CIO, Planned Parenthood, and the Wisconsin-based Americans for Limited Terms spent money on ads and direct mail intended to help Capps. The Republicans competing for the seat benefited from similar activities, financed by the Christian Coalition, the Foundation for Responsible Government (an anti-tax group), and the Campaign for Working Families (a conservative group opposed to late-term abortions).[17] Capps won the election, but only after she and her opponents had lost control of the campaign agenda. They spent most of the campaign debating abortion and term limits, not the issues of primary concern to the voters of the central coast.

Term Limits Add Up to Brain Drain   *Jordan Rau*

Until this year, Margaret Gladstein was chief advisor to the California Assembly's Banking and Finance Committee, which shapes hundreds of laws including those that govern credit cards, identity theft and flood insurance.

But in June, Gladstein appeared before the committee in a different role: representing the California Retailers Assn., a client of her new employer, a Sacramento lobbying firm.

"I've missed all of you," she playfully told the 10 legislators she had worked for.

Gladstein is part of an exodus of experienced legislative staff to California's lobbying corps, known in Sacramento as the Third House. The staff migration—a repercussion of term limits passed in 1990—has strengthened the influence of interest groups in crafting laws but weakened lawmakers' ability to obtain the objective advice and institutional knowledge that once made California's Capitol a model for other states, according to many lawmakers, lobbyists and Sacramento veterans from both parties.

"What we have seen is the empowerment of the Third House at the expense of the Senate and Assembly," said Senate Majority Leader Gloria Romero (D–Los Angeles). "I'm one of the old-timers, but I find myself going to some of the folks who have already left the building to say, 'Hey, can you give me a history lesson?' "

Though all lawmakers hire office staff who often come and go with their bosses, California's Legislature has long been distinguished by policy experts who devoted years and even decades to transportation, agriculture, education or another specific subject.

Paid salaries sometimes topping $100,000, they work as chief consultants in committees or as senior advisors to legislative leadership. In deciding how to vote, legislators routinely rely on the in-depth analyses consultants write for every bill.

But those jobs feel less secure and professionally satisfying, many staffers say, because of the regular changes in committee leadership due to term limits, which cap tenure at six years in the Assembly and eight in the Senate.

"I had the opportunity to work for two very good chairs, but there was a constant uncertainty about who would be the next chair," Gladstein, who earned $105,000 a year in the Assembly, said in an interview. "My current organization is much more stable."

New legislative leaders can push out or reassign staffers and change the office atmosphere from pleasant to oppressive. And committee chairs who once also sought to master policy are now consumed with plotting their next political step.

All this has made it easier for the Third House—which always had the advantage of offering higher salaries—to lure away Capitol experts.

Once there, some former staffers immediately begin work on proposals pending before their former bosses. As in other states, California's former staffers are unencumbered by "cooling off" rules that require former lawmakers and gubernatorial staff to wait a year before lobbying in the areas they worked in.

In the current 2005–06 session, the chief consultants to four major legislative committees—including Andrew Antwih, chief consultant to the Assembly Transportation Committee, and Mark Sektnan, chief consultant to the Assembly Insurance Committee—have moved to the Third House. Not coincidentally, all four left in the year their chairpersons were termed out.

Of course, lobbying has always appealed to staffers enticed by salaries double or more what can be earned on the public payroll. But since 1996, when the first batch of lawmakers was forced out office, annual staff turnover in the state Assembly has increased to 36% from 22% during the four years before the initiative, Proposition 140, passed in 1990, records show.

Forty percent of Assembly aides now have less than two years' experience. Senate turnover has averaged 22% a year since 1996. Comparison figures for the years before the initiative's passage were not available.

"This is one of the subtle effects of term limits that voters probably haven't noticed and may not have wanted," said Thad Kousser, a UC San Diego political science professor who co-wrote a 2004 study on the effects of term limits on the Legislature. "Interest groups play a much more active role in actually drafting the legislation, negotiating the amendments."

The emigration does not disturb many term limits advocates, who view staff as just as interchangeable as their elected bosses.

"It was not, right now, nor was it ever intended to become, a lifetime job to be a staffer in the Capitol," said Ted Costa, one such advocate. "People are always going to go up to bigger and better things. Dick Cheney started as a staffer."

Some other staffers who took their legislative expertise to the Third House in the current two-year session include:

- Nicholas Louizos, who left his job as senior consultant for Assemblyman Hector De La Torre, chairman of a subcommittee overseeing the health and human services portion of the state budget, to become a lobbyist for the California Assn. of Health Plans.

- Patrick Moran, Assembly Speaker Fabian Nunez's advisor on law enforcement issues. He now works for Aaron Read and Associates, whose clients include the state firefighters' union and the Peace Officers Research Assn. of California.

- Robert Giroux, a veteran advisor to former Senate President Pro Tem John Burton and more recently to Nunez. He now works at Lang Hansen O'Malley and Miller Governmental Relations, whose 54 lobbying clients include chemical, alcohol, racing and pharmaceutical concerns.

One former staffer's private sector work exemplifies the type of Capitol influence they can wield. Steven Thompson, a longtime advisor to former Assembly Speaker Willie Brown (whose 14-year tenure galvanized the term limits movement), took a post with the California Medical Assn. after staff cuts required by Proposition 140 eviscerated the Assembly Office of Research, which Thompson had headed.

As head of the government relations office for the influential doctors lobby, Thompson used his knowledge and close relationships with lawmakers to initiate and rewrite dozens of healthcare laws on behalf of physicians. After his death in 2004, the Legislature even renamed a state program he helped create in his honor: The Stephen M. Thompson Physician Corps Loan Repayment Program encourages doctors to work in underserved areas by paying off some of their medical school debt.

Today, former staffers are ubiquitous in the Third House. At the California Chamber of Commerce, seven of 15 employees in the legislative unit previously worked for the Senate or Assembly.

"What better lobbyist could the California Chamber have than one who has served the very Legislature he or she is now working with?" said Vince Sollitto, the chamber's spokesman and a former aide to Gov. Arnold Schwarzenegger.

At Capitol Advocacy, the 7-year-old firm that Gladstein joined when she left the Assembly banking committee, four of the five other lobbyists also spent time in the Legislature.

Capitol Advocacy earned $3.2 million lobbying last year, more than all but four other firms, according to the secretary of state's office. The firm's bigger clients include the Safeway grocery chain, Yahoo, Ameriquest Capital Corp., Apple Computer and Blue Cross of California.

Ron Calderon, chairman of the Assembly banking panel, said the Legislature has raised staff salaries since term limits to try to retain workers. But he said lobbying firms "are looking more than ever at those staff who have the long-term experience" in the Capitol.

To be sure, dozens of well-respected veteran staffers remain in the Capitol, particularly in the Senate, where policy advisors on the environment, public pensions, the judiciary and the regulation of professionals have more than a century of experience combined. Many of the newer ones have also distinguished themselves and are valued by legislators.

And certainly not all those staffers who leave the Capitol would have stayed were it not for term limits.

"It was a career goal of mine to eventually be a lobbyist," said Todd Bloomstine, who left the Senate staff in 2001 and is now a lobbyist for the Southern California Contractors' Assn.

Bloomstine said he had spent five years in the Capitol when a retiring lobbyist with whom he dealt regularly approached him and asked if he had interest in taking over his business. "It just naturally led from my work there," he said.

It is such easy transitions that worry some good-government advocates. They fear that aides' awareness that they may one day end up in the Third House could lead some to compromise the independence of their advice.

"It creates too much of an incentive to shade things while you're working for the Legislature," said Robert M. Stern, president of the Center for Governmental Studies.

"I'm more concerned with the staff leaving than with legislators leaving," Stern said. "When legislative staff goes, the Legislature really has no one to rely on other than the lobbyists or the administration."

Source: Jordan Rau, "Term Limits Add Up to Brain Drain" *Los Angeles Times* (California section), July 23, 2006.

SUMMARY

This chapter has explored the role of the media, political parties, and interest groups in California's political process. In this media age the escalating costs of political campaigns have encouraged interest groups and the media to play an enhanced role in governmental politics and elections, filling the vacuum left behind by weakened political parties. Print and broadcast media—particularly television—have emerged as the dominant tools with which elected officials and those seeking elected office amplify their voices to the public. Interest groups have emerged as the tools of sophisticated citizens who seek to maximize individual participation and influence. However, the major parties still play an important role in the electoral process, as we will see in the next chapter. This chapter began by exploring the impacts and effects of media messages, as well as the markets and costs of political advertising. It then examined the role and impacts of parties and interest groups in California. Ultimately, parties, interest groups, and the media are powerful tools in the policy process. Those individuals and organizations—whether public or private, for profit or non-profit—who can best utilize these tools will enjoy greater influence.

NOTES

1. Philip E. Converse, "The Nature of Belief Systems in Mass Publics," in David Apter, ed., *Ideology and Discontent* (New York: The Free Press, 1964).
2. See Walter Lippmann, *Public Opinion* (New York: The Free Press, 1922).
3. For a full discussion, see Shearon Lowery and Melvin DeFleur, *Milestones in Mass Communication Research: Media Effects* (New York: Longman, 1983).
4. The film *Chinatown* depicts the role of Los Angeles elites, in particular the *Los Angeles Times*, in foisting a false water emergency on Los Angeles residents in order to influence bond measures to fund the Owens Valley water grab.
5. The Kennedy–Nixon debate in 1960 was a turning point for demonstrating the power of television in politics. The debate was both televised and broadcast over radio. Television viewers widely credited Kennedy with "winning" the debate, while radio listeners credited Nixon with "winning." The ability to convey nonverbal cues through a television debate or advertisement has become extremely important—and more so now that most people get most of their information from television.
6. Dan Walters, "Stations Ignore State Capitol," *San Jose Mercury News* (November 22, 1988): B5, in Larry N. Gerston and Terry Christensen, *California Politics and Government*, 10th ed. (San Francisco: Wadsworth, 2008).
7. See Jay Blummler and Denis McQuail, *Television in Politics* (Chicago: University of Chicago Press 1969); Thomas Patterson and Robert D. McClure, *The Unseeing Eye: The Myth of Television Power in Elections*. New York: Putnam, 1976).
8. Thad Beyle and Jennifer M. Jensen, "2006 Aggregate Contribution Information for All States," The Gubernatorial Campaign Finance Database, University of North Carolina at Chapel Hill (www.unc.edu/~beyle/guber.html).
9. Gerston and Christensen, *California Politics and Government*.
10. See Stephen Ansolabehere, Roy Behr, and Shanto Iyengar, *The Media Game: American Politics in the Television Age* (New York: Macmillan, 1993).
11. Unruh's advisors date the earliest use of that phrase in print to the article, "Big Daddy's Big Drive," *Look*, September 25 1962.
12. See C. Wright Mills, *The Power Elite* (Oxford, UK: Oxford University Press, 1956); Thomas Dye, *Who's Running America? The Conservative Years*, 4th ed. (Englewood Cliffs, NJ: Prentice Hall, 1986); G. William Domhoff, *Who Rules America Now?* (New York: Simon & Schuster, 1983); Robert Presthus, *Elites in the Policy Process* (Cambridge, UK: Cambridge University Press, 1974).
13. Theodore Lowi, *The End of Liberalism*, 2nd ed. (New York: W. W. Norton, 1979).
14. Bruce McPherson, *Lobbying California State Government* (Sacramento: California Secretary of State's Office, 2006).
15. See Mark J. Rozell and Clyde Wilcox, *Interest Groups in American Campaigns* (Washington, DC: Congressional Quarterly Press, 1999).
16. See Ross Baker, *The New Fat Cats* (New York: Priority Press, 1989).
17. Todd S. Purdum, "Interest Groups Run Own Race in California," *New York Times* (March 7, 1998): A3.

CHAPTER 12

The Electorate as Players: Elections and Political Participation

California voters have the opportunity to exercise a great deal of power at the ballot box. Every two years, Californians choose the entire state assembly, half of the state senate, and the state's delegation to the U.S. House of Representatives, the largest delegation of any state. In non-presidential election years, Californians must choose candidates to fill the state's executive offices, including the governor and secretary of state. Besides electing candidates for office, the voters are regularly called upon to amend the state's constitution, to reverse legislative acts, and to decide other weighty issues placed on the ballot through the initiative process. This chapter examines the role of the electorate as players in the policy process. It first examines California's election cycle and then goes on to explore the role of declining voter turnout. The chapter considers the implications of voter decline in political participation.

THE ELECTION CYCLE

In California parties have played an increasingly minimal role in the recruitment of candidates, in the selection of nominees, and even in the general election campaign. Consequently, due to the state's candidate-centered politics, candidates must build their own campaign organizations, raise money, and purchase media time, with little or no coordination or support from the state party committees. There are few constitutional restrictions governing who may run for office. One must be a U.S. citizen and a resident of the state. In legislative offices such as the state assembly or senate, the candidate must live in the district that the seat represents. Because there are no explicit regulations as to how district residency must be established, some candidates have been attacked as "carpetbaggers" who move into a district in order to file nomination papers. One must also be a registered voter of the party whose nomination is being sought, although independents can run for partisan offices.

In order to file for candidacy, anyone seeking public office must first file a declaration of intent with the county clerk or register recorder. Nomination papers must be returned within the specified time frame, with a completed petition signed by a specified number of voters and a small filing fee (usually 1 percent of the annual salary for most offices; 2 percent of the annual salary for statewide offices). Upon certification by the elections clerk, the name of the candidate is put on the ballot. Ballots carry with them some inherent biases. The candidate's full name appears, followed by the candidate's party affiliation if the election is partisan. In the absence of other information about candidates, voters look for cues in assessing candidates by their occupational designation. Attorneys and other professionals with impressive titles tend to do well. Another inherent bias is the position of the candidate names. Research has demonstrated that at least some voters simply choose the name on the top of the list. Prior to 1974, all incumbents would be listed first, thus giving them unfair advantage. Today, ballot position is determined by a lottery.

The Primary

Primaries were pushed by Progressive reformers early in the twentieth century to give average people a voice in the nomination of candidates. It was thought that allowing citizens to register their preferences at the polls would reduce the power of party bosses and special interests to wield undue influence at state party nominating conventions. Allowing the voters to choose candidates in a direct primary has become the only legitimate method for the two major parties to decide their candidates for general election in California.

Two recent experiments with California's primary election were expected to have an impact on state and national politics. One was the adoption of an early primary, which was intended to make California a decisive battleground in the presidential pre-nomination campaign. After five decades of holding primaries in June, California experimented with an "early" primary in 2000. The legislature moved the primary date from the end of the nominating season to March, making it one of the earliest in the nation. Holding a March primary—on the heels of the Iowa caucus and New Hampshire primary—was meant to give Californians a greater voice in presidential nominations because of the state's huge share of electoral votes. Unfortunately, the early primaries made no difference in 2000 or 2004 because the nominees for president had already been determined by March. For 2008, Governor Schwarzenegger and the legislature moved the primary up to February 5, making it one of the "Super Tuesday" primaries, helping seal the Republican nomination for Senator John McCain. The early primary failed to play a decisive role in the Democratic contest, however. Despite her win in California, Senator Hillary Clinton ultimately lost the nomination to her rival Senator Barack Obama, who piled up victories in caucus states.

The second experiment was the "open primary," created by voters in 1996 with the passage of Proposition 198. In most states that have open primaries, voters decide which party's ballot to cast in the privacy of the voting booth. California's version of the open primary (also called a "blanket" primary) was modeled after similar systems in Washington and Alaska, where every voter is issued an identical ballot at the polling place on election day. The ballot allowed voters to choose among any of the candidates of every officially recognized party, regardless of the voter's own party affiliation. In June 1998, for example, voters in California's first open primary had the opportunity to choose among 17 candidates (in seven parties) for governor. Under the old system, a voter was issued a ballot only for the party with which he or she had registered.

Proposition 198 passed decisively, with 60 percent of the vote, despite vigorous opposition by both major political parties. The initiative was sponsored by Representative Tom Campbell, a moderate Republican who had lost a bid for his party's nomination for the U.S. Senate to conservative commentator Bruce Herschensohn. In the general election, Herschensohn was defeated by liberal Democrat Barbara Boxer. Ironically, Boxer secured the Democratic nomination after defeating a moderate opponent in a closed primary. Supporters of the open primary argued that the old system of nominations was dominated by the extreme wings of the two parties and that allowing independents and crossover voters to participate would stimulate interest by offering voters more choice and would help moderate consensus-building candidates win nomination.[1] Critics feared that the new rules would create opportunities for tampering with the nomination process—with voters of one party crossing lines to help nominate the weaker candidate of the opposing party. California's major political parties challenged Proposition 198 on this basis, and in 2000, the state supreme court ruled the law unconstitutional. In the end, there was little evidence that the blanket primary led to greater voter participation: Turnout in the blanket primary of 1998 was just 27.4 percent, compared to the 26.2 percent of eligible voters who went to the polls in the closed primary of 1994.[2]

Despite fears of partisan mischief in the blanket primary, there was no evidence of voters of one party crossing lines en masse to nominate a less-electable candidate of an opposing party. In 2002, however, there was some elite-level meddling in the Republican primary for governor. Candidates usually refrain from attacking potential rivals during the primaries, allowing opponents within the rival's own party to do the dirty work while they conserve resources for the general election. Democratic Governor Gray Davis, running for reelection, faced two potential challengers in businessman Bill Simon and former Los Angeles Mayor Richard Riordan. Fearing that the more moderate Riordan would win the nomination, Davis ran ads, attacking the former mayor's moderate positions on social issues in an effort to push conservatives to support Simon in the primary.[3] After a bruising primary campaign and some damaging gaffes by Riordan, Simon won the nomination and was then defeated by Davis.

Of course, not all primary contests are partisan. Nonpartisan elected offices such as judges, local officials, and the superintendent of public instruction also appear on the primary ballot. During the primary, and without the designation of any party label, all the candidates for a particular nonpartisan elected position are placed on the ballot. The one who receives the majority vote (50 percent plus one) wins outright in the primary. If no one receives the majority vote, the top two vote-getters face off in the general election.

The General Election

California holds its general elections on the first Tuesday after the first Monday in the month of November for both state and national offices. The period between the primary and the general election is typically an intense political season in which candidates work to secure their party loyalists and try to attract crossover votes from the ranks of the opposition party and from independent voters. Governor Arnold Schwarzenegger, for example, spent much of the 2006 general election campaign trying to position himself at the political center, attempting to appeal to the "median" voter by splitting the difference between himself and his Democratic rival, Phil Angelides. Schwarzenegger distanced himself from many positions of the national Republican Party and renounced his own support for the illegal immigration measure Proposition 187 in 1994. The Republican governor courted moderates by touting strong environmental initiatives and campaigned in a bus decorated with a panoramic painting of Yosemite Valley. "You don't see that bus saying 'Vote for Arnold Schwarzenegger, Republican,'" he told a reporter, emphasizing his desire to appeal to voters outside his own party.[4]

In a debate prior to the 1998 general election, gubernatorial candidates Gray Davis and Dan Lungren *both* spent time talking about how he was pro-death penalty, against assault weapons, pro-abortion rights, pro-HMO reform, in favor of targeted tax cuts for business, and supportive of public schools while acknowledging that education needed reform. Republican Lungren wanted to eliminate the car tax; Democrat Davis wanted to reduce it. At the same time, each candidate tried repeatedly to show that his opponent held positions on these issues that were out of the mainstream.[5]

Special Elections

A special election is called when there is a vacancy during the term of a member of the state legislature or congressional delegation. These vacancies could be the result of death, retirement, or even resignation, as a term-limited politician leaves to purse more lucrative opportunities in the private sector. When a special election becomes necessary, the governor decides when to schedule the vote. These elections are infrequent, but they come with a hefty price tag: approximately $40 to $50 million. One type of special election is the recall. As we saw in Chapter 7, recall elections were designed by Progressive reformers to remove corrupt politicians from office. In recent years, the recall has been used as a partisan instrument. The most prominent special election by far was the 2003 recall of Governor Gray Davis. Eight years earlier, Assembly Speaker Doris Allen and another Republican assembly member were both removed from office after some of their conservative Orange County constituents, upset over Allen's power-sharing arrangement with assembly Democrats, gathered enough signatures for a recall.[6]

Generally, voters who participate in special elections tend to be highly motivated by partisanship or have passionate feelings about a candidate or an issue at hand.

Turnout in these contests is low, and the electorate tends to be whiter, older, and more ideologically conservative than in the general election. Special elections have characteristics of both primary and general elections. Voters are given a choice of all candidates from all parties on a single ballot. If a candidate gets a simple majority of the vote, he or she is the winner. If no one receives a clear majority, the top two vote-getters face each other four weeks later in a runoff election.

The Recall Election of 2003

The best-known special election was the recall of Governor Gray Davis. Originally created through a statewide initiative in 1911, the recall was designed as a mechanism to remove corrupt politicians from office. A government textbook from that era explained the mechanics of the recall, but its authors were skeptical that it would ever be used, calling the recall "a whimsical notion which both the politicians and serious-minded voters could be trusted to suppress."[7] It would be several decades before this political weapon would be deployed successfully. Recall petitions are easy to initiate, but rarely do they qualify for the ballot. There had been 31 unsuccessful attempts to recall California governors, including Ronald Reagan, Jerry Brown, and Pete Wilson. The Davis recall might have been remembered as another one of these futile efforts had it not been for a cash infusion from millionaire candidate Darrell Issa that funded the petition drive.

Davis began 2003 fresh from his narrow reelection victory against Republican Bill Simon, but the state was facing a host of fresh problems. Davis had several accomplishments in his first term: increasing per-pupil spending, expanding financial aid for college students, raising the minimum wage, and phasing out the problematic gasoline additive MTBE. As the economy boomed during his first term, Davis and the legislature happily spent new revenue and cut taxes. However, a nationwide recession, which had begun around the time of the September 11, 2001, terrorist attacks, hit California especially hard. At the same time, there was a collapse in technology stocks, an important sector in California's economy and a major contributor to its tax base. Finally, there was the devastating energy crisis that began in 2000, after the deregulation of the electricity market. Four years earlier, a compromise between the Wilson Administration and the Democrat-controlled legislature had resulted in a plan that deregulated electricity but imposed price caps on residential customers. The impact of this arrangement was not felt until the summer of 2000, however, when power shortages caused rolling blackouts around the state. Davis was slow to respond to the crisis. He evaded blame by pointing out the criminal actions of the giant energy trading firm Enron and its allies in the Bush administration, but he seemed powerless to act. The governor's approval ratings plummeted from a high of 66 percent (at the start of the energy crisis) to 25 percent in 2003, prior to the recall.

Davis also faced a number of problems of his own making. As the recession slowed the state's revenue stream to a trickle, he downplayed the projected deficit until after his reelection in 2002. Then, in a case of doing too little, too late, he faced a backlash for raising the vehicle registration tax to Wilson-era levels. As the situation worsened, Davis' allies dwindled. The governor's heavy-handed dealings with the state legislature irked Democratic leaders, and he had sparred with Lieutenant Governor Cruz Bustamante, who faulted him for failing to take a firm stand against Proposition 187. By the time the recall qualified for the ballot, there were few willing to rally by his side.

The recall effort was initiated immediately after the reelection of Davis in 2002. Petitions were circulated by Sacramento-area activist Ted Costa, head of the same anti-tax organization founded three decades earlier by Proposition 13 co-author Paul Gann. Costa and his allies used talk radio appearances to mobilize support for the drive, encouraging people to download petitions from the Internet and collect signatures on their own. The movement gathered steam with a cash infusion from Republican Representative Darrell Issa of San Diego. A former car-alarm magnate with his own ambitions of running in the recall election, Issa contributed nearly $2 million of his own money to the petition drive. The money made it possible to collect 1.3 million valid signatures—more than enough to force the special election. Issa had planned to place his own name on the ballot to replace Davis, but he dropped out when Schwarzenegger entered the race.

The recall qualified in July, and by law, the lieutenant governor had to schedule the vote 60 to 80 days later. Bustamante set October 7 as the date and filed papers to run as a replacement candidate. On the fall ballot, voters would be presented with two questions. First, they were asked to decide whether Gray Davis should be recalled. No matter how they answered the first question, they were then asked to choose from a long and confusing list of replacement candidates. Because potential candidates needed to provide only a $3,500 filing fee and the signatures of 65 registered voters, hundreds of people filed papers to run in the recall election. Ultimately, Secretary of State Kevin Shelley certified 135 candidates for the ballot, including some minor celebrities and a number of private citizens who paid the filing fee just to see their names on the ballot.

Californians went to the polls in October, voting to recall the governor by a margin of 55 to 45 percent (see Table 12.1). Regardless of the way they voted on the recall question, voters then had to choose a replacement candidate. Schwarzenegger captured the plurality of the replacement vote (49 percent), beating his closest rivals, conservative Republican State Senator Tom McClintock and Lieutenant Governor Cruz Bustamante, a Democrat who had urged voters to vote "no" on the recall but choose him as their replacement candidate. Unfortunately for Davis, this sent a mixed message to Democrats, and their failure to unite behind their incumbent governor made the recall appear more inevitable.

The Special Election of 2005

Voters registered their fatigue with special elections in 2005, when Governor Schwarzenegger called for a special statewide vote on a proposal to change the way redistricting is conducted. Noting that none of the state senate or assembly seats had

TABLE 12.1   CALIFORNIA GUBERNATORIAL RECALL ELECTION, 2003

	% OF VOTERS	"YES" TO RECALL	"NO" TO RECALL	SCHWARZ-ENEGGER	BUSTAMANTE	MCCLINTOCK
All Voters	100	55	45	49	32	13
Gender						
Male	49	59	41	53	29	12
Female	51	51	49	45	35	14
Age						
18–29	12	54	46	45	35	12
30–44	30	56	44	50	30	12
45–64	40	56	44	50	31	14
65+	18	53	47	47	34	15
Ethnicity						
White	73	60	40	54	26	14
Black	5	21	79	18	67	8
Latino	11	45	55	32	56	9
Asian	6	47	53	46	34	15
Education						
High school or less	15	59	41	48	36	14
Some College	26	63	37	55	25	15
College degree or higher	59	41	49	47	24	12
Party						
Democrat	43	24	76	21	63	8
Independent	12	52	48	46	27	15
Republican	42	88	12	77	4	17
Ideology						
Liberal	34	25	75	21	62	6
Moderate	31	55	45	52	28	13
Conservative	35	85	15	70	7	20
Income						
Less than $20,000	8	53	47	40	39	14
$20,000 to $39,999	15	53	47	42	37	16
$40,000 to $59,999	16	56	44	47	34	14
$60,000 to $74,999	15	53	47	48	32	14
$75,000 and more	46	56	44	54	29	11
Religion						
Non-Catholic Christians	42	68	32	59	20	18
Roman Catholics	25	54	46	48	37	12
Jews	6	31	69	31	52	9
Region						
L.A. County	23	50	50	45	37	11
Orange County	13	70	30	63	22	12

(continued)

TABLE 12.1 (continued)

	% OF VOTERS	"YES"TO RECALL	"NO"TO RECALL	SCHWARZ- ENEGGER	BUSTAMANTE	McCLINTOCK
Rest of Southern Cal.	21	67	33	58	24	14
Bay Area	14	34	66	30	50	10
Rest of Northern Cal.	29	55	45	48	30	16

Note: All other candidates in the 2003 recall election received a combined 6% of the total vote.

Source: *Los Angeles Times* Exit Poll, November 9, 2003. www.latimesinteractive.com/pdfarchive/state/la-100903analysis-b.pdf.

changed party hands in the previous election, Schwarzenegger decried the lack of competition and proposed a plan that would have taken responsibility for redistricting away from the legislature and placed it in the hands of a panel of retired judges. The proposal received a cool reception in the legislature, so Schwarzenegger took his proposal to the arena of direct democracy, which had launched his own political career. He backed Proposition 77, a ballot initiative intended to accomplish the reform he wanted, and campaigned heavily for the measure, along with three other initiatives limiting state spending on public schools, reforming teacher tenure, and restricting the political uses of public employee union dues. However, this was the fourth consecutive year that California voters had been asked to go the polls for a Fall election; fresh in their minds was the recall election of 2003, which fell between regularly scheduled elections of 2002 and 2004. All four initiatives were voted down, and a report concluded that Schwarzenegger's own association with the initiatives damaged them in the mind of the public.[8]

The Business of Direct Democracy

The special elections of 2003 and 2005 illustrate the growing importance of the tools of direct democracy in California. Not surprisingly, an entire industry has emerged to do the work of promoting ballot initiatives. As we saw in Chapter 7, hundreds of initiatives have qualified for the ballot since 1912. Most of them would not have been possible without professional organizations to mount effective campaigns and gather the number of signatures required to qualify initiatives for the ballot. The cost to qualify initiatives allows well-financed interests to set the agenda by placing measures on the ballot. Groups with deep pockets also have an advantage in the campaign because of the cost of direct mail, radio, and television advertising. Tens of millions are spent on advertising campaigns for ballot initiatives in a typical year; in 1998, a total of $92 million was spent on both sides of Proposition 5, the Indian Gaming initiative.

Collecting signatures for initiatives was primarily the work of volunteers for most of the twentieth century. Organizations sometimes relied on paid signature-gatherers to supplement the work of their volunteers, who usually were motivated by a commitment to a cause. What changed was the increased professionalization of the process after the 1970s. For one thing, a larger number of the signatures used to qualify initiatives for the ballot were collected by firms such as American Petition Consultants, which typically paid workers $1 per signature. These firms could be hired by any individual or group willing to pay for their services. In another development, some firms began to test-market issues and propose ballot initiatives on their own. One example is Proposition 37, which created the California Lottery when voters approved it in 1984. Manufacturers of gambling equipment paid for the campaign, but the initiative was conceived and designed by Kimball Petition Management, a consulting firm.[9] Today, the costs to qualify initiatives for the ballot routinely exceed $1 million.

Legislative efforts to limit the money spent on initiative campaigns have been struck down in federal court as unconstitutional limits on free speech. One landmark measure, struck down by the U.S. Supreme Court, was the California Political Reform Act of 1974, which would have restricted a qualification drive to spending no more than 25 cents times the number of signatures needed to place the measure on the ballot. The Court later struck down a 1980 Colorado law that would have banned paid signature-gatherers altogether, and in 1999, the Court struck down a California law that required signature-gatherers to be registered voters of the state. Today, the people who stand outside grocery stores and shopping malls, collecting signatures, are more likely to be mercenaries bused in from another state prior to election season than volunteers committed to a cause.

Direct democracy, which emerged as a mechanism to counter the power big business had at the start of the twentieth century, had itself become big business by the century's end. The extensive power of the tools of direct democracy was not known until decades after their advent, and they have continued to affect the state's politics in the twenty-first century. Legislative attempts to restrict the growth of ballot initiatives and the influence of money in the process have proven futile, and the trends show no sign of abating.

CALIFORNIA'S ELECTORATE

California's electorate is one of the most complex in the nation. While the state has had more registered Democrats than Republicans for most of the postwar era, this partisan balance has not always been reflected in electoral outcomes. Gray Davis was only the third Democrat to be elected governor since the end of World War II. Similarly, in 9 of the last 13 presidential elections, California voted for Republican presidential candidates (the Republican ticket in seven of those contests included either Richard Nixon or Ronald Reagan—both Californians). One reason California has remained competitive is that voters have always been willing to cross party lines. The anti-party attitude of the Progressive era has remained a powerful force in state politics, leading voters to shun party labels in statewide elections and to choose candidates on the basis of multiple criteria. More than one out of five (22 percent) Democratic voters cast their ballots for Schwarzenegger in 2006 (see Table 12.2). This crossover constituency was key to the election of Republican governors in the

TABLE 12.2 PROFILE OF THE 2006 ELECTORATE

| | | GOVERNOR | | | SENATOR | |
	%	SCHWARZENEGGER (R)	ANGELIDES (D)	CAMEJO (G)	MOUNTJOY (R)	FEINSTEIN (D)
Gender						
Male	49	58	37	3	39	55
Female	51	55	41	2	32	63
Age						
18–29	14	44	49	4	29	65
30–44	22	56	39	2	37	59
45–59	35	58	37	3	36	58
60+	29	60	36	1	35	58
Ethnicity						
White	67	63	32	2	41	53
Black	4	27	70	0	87	13
Latino	19	39	56	3	71	22
Asian	6	62	37	1	70	26
Education						
High school	14	55	42	2	36	59
Some college	31	59	36	2	35	58
College grad.	31	58	36	2	40	55
Adv. degree	21	52	45	2	28	66
Party						
Democrat	40	22	74	2	3	94
Independent	25	59	33	5	26	63
Republican	35	93	4	1	79	16
Ideology						
Liberal	25	20	74	5	7	87
Moderate	44	58	38	2	26	69
Conservative	30	86	10	1	74	22
Income						
Less than $15,000	6	45	51	3	19	75
$15–30,000	11	42	54	3	26	66
$30–50,000	15	52	41	4	29	64
$50–75,000	20	60	35	2	43	51
$75–100,000	17	55	41	2	37	58
$100–150,000	18	65	31	2	39	59
$150–200,000	6	62	35	2	39	57
$200,000 or more	8	61	37	1	60	36
Region						
LA County	24	48	48	2	30	65
Other S. Cal.	27	65	30	2	44	50
Cen. Valley	19	66	31	2	63	31
SF Bay Area	20	46	48	3	22	73
Coastal California	11	55	40	4	31	63

Source: CNN Exit Poll of 2,649 respondents, November 9, 2006.

1980s and 1990s. Likewise, 18 percent of Republicans crossed party lines in 1998 and contributed to the landslide victory of Democrat Gray Davis.

Party registration tells only part of the story. The exit poll data in Table 12.2 also reveal that the largest ideological category in the electorate (44 percent) was not "liberal" or "conservative," but "moderate." A clear majority of these self-identified moderates supported Schwarzenegger over his Democratic opponent, Phil Angelides (58 to 38 percent). In contrast, Angelides won a majority of the votes in just a few key Democratic constituencies: African Americans, Latinos, registered Democrats, liberals, and voters earning under $30,000. Senator Dianne Feinstein, a Democrat running for reelection on the same ballot, did much better among "moderates" than Schwarzenegger, winning 60 percent of their vote.

The size and impact of these self-identified moderates may reflect a growing frustration with partisan politics. Nonetheless, California's electorate is growing ever more reluctant to identify with either of the two major political parties. The proportion of the state's electorate registered as Democrats and Republicans has been shrinking over time. While the Democrats and Republicans remain dominant, increasing numbers of independent and minor-party voters have the potential to influence election outcomes, threatening the hegemony of the two major parties. Growing dissatisfaction with the two major parties has fueled the growth of alternative parties in California and nationwide.

Minor Parties

In the 2006 general election, there were four minor parties joining the Republicans and Democrats on the ballot in California. Among these parties were the laissez-faire, anti-tax Libertarian Party and the pro-environment, pro-social justice Green Party. Two minor parties that developed from the social movements of the 1960s were the anti-war Peace and Freedom Party and the conservative, pro-segregationist American Independent Party, which was inspired by the candidacy of former Alabama Governor George Wallace.

A party can qualify for the ballot and field candidates in California if it can gather the signatures of 1 percent of the state's registered voters (158,371 signatures) on petitions seeking official status for the party. Prior to seeking official status, new parties normally hold a party caucus, select party nominees, agree on a party plank, and design a campaign strategy. To remain an official party, a party must get at least 2 percent of the statewide vote for at least one candidate and retain one-fifteenth of 1 percent of registered voters. In some states, minor parties have had a limited impact as "spoilers," skimming enough votes away from one of the two major parties to effectively hand a victory to the other party. So far, minor parties have had little impact on the duopoly of the two major parties in California. As Table 12.3 shows, the Democrats and Republicans accounted for 42.5 percent and 34.3 percent of the state electorate, respectively, in 2006. In comparison, none of the six minor parties could claim more than 4.5 percent of California voters. Voters with no party affiliation, on the other hand, accounted for 18.7 percent of the electorate.

TABLE 12.3   VOTER REGISTRATION BY PARTY, FEBRUARY 2006

PARTY	REGISTERED VOTERS	% OF TOTAL
Democratic	6,727,908	42.5
Republican	5,436,314	34.3
American Independent	315,151	2.0
Green	141,451	0.9
Libertarian	84,093	0.5
Natural Law	22,231	0.1
Peace & Freedom	59,139	0.4
Misc./Non-Qualified	82,332	0.5
Declined to State	2,968,489	18.7

Note: Of the 22,652,190 citizens eligible to register to vote, a total of 15,837,108 (69.9 percent) actually were registered in 2006.

Source: Bruce McPherson, 2006 Statement of the Vote (Sacramento: Secretary of State's Office, 2006).

The Rise of Independent Voters

Despite the proliferation of alternative parties, many voters have shunned party politics altogether. Americans have been less willing to identify themselves as Republicans or Democrats ever since the late 1960s. Mirroring national trends, voters in California have been registering as independents in higher rates. According to the registration figures in Table 12.3, independents comprise nearly 19 percent of California's registered voters—the third largest group after Democrats and Republicans.

Combined, independents and minor-party voters comprise 23 percent of the state electorate. Because no single party can claim a clear majority of the voters, this sizable bloc has significant power to decide the outcome of close elections. This might seem like a big uncommitted group with the potential to challenge the two-party dominance of state politics. In reality, independents tend to be reliable supporters of one of the two major parties at the ballot box. Voting researchers have found that many independents vote for either the Republican or Democratic parties so consistently that they may be considered "closet" Republicans and Democrats.[10] Under California's weak-party system, the benefits of aligning oneself with a party are not always clear. Until recently, independents were effectively disenfranchised from the primary election stage of the process. That obstacle to participation was removed with the elimination of the closed primary in 1996. One possible side effect of the open primary, though, is the further weakening of the two major parties in California.

VOTER TURNOUT

Because of California's (1) weak political parties, (2) system of directly deciding policy through the ballot initiative, and (3) overwhelming numerical significance in presidential elections, the state's voters have considerable power and relevance in comparison to voters in other states. Yet when compared to the national average, California's turnout is quite low. Because of this low turnout, electoral outcomes are often determined by the success a particular campaign has in getting out the vote. That is, the winning side in a campaign is often the one that is more successful at persuading supporters to go to the polls. This rule applies to interest groups as well as candidates. In California's ballot initiative industry, proposition sponsors build strategies around the recognition that they only need a simple majority of voters to approve a measure. Once the paid signature-gatherers have succeeded in placing the measure on the ballot, strategic advertising can mobilize enough potential supporters to make the proposition law. To the firms that sponsor these initiatives, low turnout is actually desirable because a predictable number of voters coupled with targeted advertising is enough to guarantee the success of a ballot measure.[11] Therefore, one consequence of low voter turnout is that California's ballot initiative process is especially vulnerable to manipulation by interest groups.

The Disappearing California Voter

Consistent with national trends, participation in California's elections has been declining in recent years. Only 15.8 million of California's 34 million residents are registered to vote. Still fewer actually exercise that right on election day. In the 1996 presidential election, 52.6 percent of eligible voters in California made it to the polls. In 2000, just 51.9 percent of Californians voted in one of the closest presidential contests ever, but there was a slight upturn in 2004, when 57.7 percent of California's eligible voters went to the polls during an unpopular war in Iraq. Compared to national elections, turnout in gubernatorial elections has been dismal. Since 1982, these statewide contests have attracted little more than half of all eligible voters. The lone exception was 2006, when 56.2 percent of eligible voters turned out for a critical midterm election and reelected Gov. Schwarzenegger. More typical was the 50.1 percent turnout in the previous gubernatorial election of 2002. California now has one of the lowest turnout rates in the nation. Out of all 50 states and the District of Columbia, California ranked 47th in turnout in the 1992 presidential election, despite the unique opportunity that voters had that year to decide two U.S. Senate contests.

One option that has made it easier for many people to vote is the absentee ballot. Any Californian is permitted to register to vote in this manner. Prior to 1978, only voters who had a specific reason—such as illness—were permitted to vote absentee. By the 1993 special statewide election, some 22 percent of the electorate was voting absentee. Modern campaign tactics helped fuel the increase of absentee vote-by-mail. Political parties and candidates routinely try to get their identified loyal constituents to vote by absentee ballot. To the campaigns, absentee votes are analogous to money in the bank, gaining interest. If your absentee voter base is secure, you can expend the rest of your limited campaign resources on mobilizing other sympathetic voters. Although growing in popularity, voting by absentee ballot has not succeeded in increasing participation among traditionally underrepresented groups and classes. Absentee voters tend to be older, more affluent, and conservative than the average voter.

Voter Registration

Chief among the factors that suppress voter turnout are the nation's restrictive voter registration laws. The United States is one of the only democracies that make its citizens register before they can actually vote. In other Western democracies, where there are no registration requirements, turnout rates of 80 to 90 percent are not uncommon. Thus, voter registration is somewhat of an anachronistic impediment to full democratic participation. Supporters of the registration process claim that it reduces potential voting fraud. Critics claim that it is an archaic remnant of earlier colonial America and is a burden that drives some voters away from their electoral right. The two-step nature of the voting process creates an additional obstacle, raising the cost of the act of voting for many individuals who are too busy working and living their lives to meet the registration deadline. As a consequence of this impediment, some states in the United States have begun experimenting with election day registration. This has not yet caught on in California.

In order to be eligible to vote, California residents must register and designate a home address at least 29 days before an election. Once a person registers, he or she stays permanently on the voting rolls until changing party affiliation, changing residence, changing name, or being ruled ineligible to vote by a court decision. Of the 15.8 million registered voters in the state, there are a substantial number of nonvoters whose names remain on the state's voting rolls. These names will remain until the state's election officials orchestrate some procedures to remove this "deadwood." Various efforts have been attempted, such as a "negative purge," whereby nonvoters are contacted by postcards via the U.S. mail. If the cards are returned as undeliverable, then the nonvoter's name is dropped. Needless to say, this is a cumbersome, highly ineffective means of keeping the voting rolls current. There are also political reasons for the deliberately slow pace of this process. Campaign experts believe that Democrats comprise the lion's share of these chronic nonvoters. Thus, the Democrats have not been particularly eager to assist in purging the voter rolls.

Because turnout is key to the outcome of close contests, successful campaigns must mobilize supporters to register to vote well before election day. Thus, voter registration drives are constant fixtures of California politics. The state's two major political parties spend millions of dollars in "soft money" each election cycle to bolster their registration numbers. Professional campaign firms are subcontracted to collect partisan registrations and are paid $3 to $6 per head for a valid completed form. Individual candidates in certain legislative districts have been known to set aside a chunk of money to orchestrate their own voter drive—either solo or in cooperation with an adjoining or overlapping member's jurisdiction. Finally, civic groups, churches, nonprofit organizations, colleges, civil rights groups, and other interest groups also help register voters.

In an attempt to encourage voter participation, in 1995 Congress passed the so-called "motor-voter" law, which allows states to take a more active role in registering voters. State and local service providers at the Department of Motor Vehicles or at the county Department of Social Services may provide registration forms and technical assistance in completing them in order to encourage more registration. This law was highly controversial in a partisan sense because it was assumed that more Democrats than Republicans would be registered in this manner. Even after the law was passed, the Wilson administration dragged its heels for months in implementing the law, until forced by court order to comply. From 1995 and 2006, more than 17.5 million people registered to vote in conjunction with the "motor-voter" law.[12]

Demographics and Voter Turnout

In addition to the registration requirement, socioeconomic factors affect turnout. Not all groups or classes are equally likely to vote. Generally, the socially and economically disadvantaged are less likely to participate in the political process. Hence, these groups are less likely to make their voices heard at the ballot box. One of the key factors that helps predict whether a person is likely to vote is income. Wealthy and middle-class individuals are more likely to vote than working-class individuals. Another factor, which also correlates closely with income, is education. College graduates are significantly more likely to vote than people with no more education than a high school diploma. Paradoxically, increasing rates of education in the general population since the 1950s have not increased turnout overall, although individuals with more education are still more likely to vote than others. Political scientists have grappled for some time with this puzzle.[13]

Partisanship also matters. Republicans are slightly more likely to vote than Democrats, though this may be a function of income more than party affiliation because Republicans have historically been more affluent than Democrats. In addition, people with strong ideological commitment are more likely to vote than those with weak partisan loyalty. Age is another factor: Individuals between the ages of 35 and 55 are considered more likely to vote than younger or older persons. In California, only one-third of people between the ages of 18 and 24 are registered to vote. Men are still slightly more likely to vote than women, although that difference has been shrinking over time.

A final generalization is that ethnicity matters. Whites are more likely to vote than are nonwhites. Of the white population in California, 65 percent are registered to vote, compared with 58 percent of African Americans, 42 percent of the Latino population, and 39 percent of the Asian population. These inequalities in registration rates have consequences at the ballot box. A study of political participation by ethnic groups in Southern California found that African Americans vote in approximately the same rates as whites, while Latinos and Asians vote in significantly lower rates. One reason Latinos and Asians vote in lower rates than whites and African Americans is that immigrants comprise a larger proportion of these communities. Even though voting is their right as U.S. citizens, naturalized immigrants tend to vote in lower rates than native-born citizens.

Much of the difference in turnout rates among these groups can be explained by the factors already discussed. The Latino population, on average, tends to be younger than the white population, with lower levels of income and education. When controlling for

these differences, the gap in voting disappears. As the average age of the Latino population increases, and as the community becomes more affluent and more highly educated
over time, it is projected that the participation gap between Latinos and whites will disappear.[14] At the same time, ethnic identification is believed to increase turnout among
Latinos. The mobilization of young Latinos in support of Antonio Villaraigosa's campaigns for mayor of Los Angeles demonstrates the potential of the emerging Latino
vote. In 2005, Villaraigosa became the city's first Latino mayor in more than 200 years.
While still lagging behind white and African American participation levels, Latino participation grew drastically in the 1990s. This translated directly into benefits for many
Latino politicians, including California's first statewide elected Latino leader,
Lieutenant Governor Cruz Bustamante.

Among Asian Americans turnout has also been low, even though the Asian
community on average is slightly older, with higher rates of income and education. This has been explained by the fact that the Asian community in California
is dispersed around the state. Because they are not as geographically concentrated
as Latino voters, the diverse and diffuse Asian communities are more difficult to
mobilize. But voting is only one form of political participation. As Latinos and
Asians continue to assert political and economic power, their influence and representation will improve. That increase may further drive up levels of voting in
these communities.

Immigration and Participation

California's status as the leading gateway for new immigrants into the United States
has impacts on participation and turnout. Naturalized immigrants, regardless of
national origin, are less likely to participate in politics if they are from nations without
a democratic tradition, although that difference disappears over time. Immigrants who
read newspapers and watch the news on television tend to be more informed and
engaged in local politics. Across the state, numerous foreign-language media outlets
provide the information that helps new immigrants make this transition. For example,
KMEX, one of the Spanish-language television stations in Los Angeles, draws larger
audiences for its local newscasts than any of the English-language alternatives.
Another example is the *Korea Times*. This international newspaper has a circulation
of 50,000 in the Los Angeles area, to which it reports local news as well as news from
Korea. On occasion, minority-language media become advocates for their communities. The Spanish-language newspaper *La Opinion* mobilized readers to oppose
Proposition 187. The newspaper ran stories detailing the ways different communities
would be affected by the initiative, encouraged readers to register to vote, and raised
money for a group working to defeat the initiative.[15]

These media organizations boast a dedication to help their audience become
citizens by educating them about policy issues, particularly those that affect their communities, such as immigration and welfare reform proposals that would have cut benefits to legal immigrants.[16] English-language television also plays an important role in
this process. A study of media use by Korean immigrants in the San Francisco Bay

Area found that exposure to television news was an important predictor of political learning because television is more accessible to non-native speakers than are English-language newspapers.[17] This suggests that television news has the potential to facilitate the assimilation of immigrants, enticing the state's diverse population into becoming more active and involved citizens.

Implications of Unequal Participation

The participation gap has serious implications for a state as diverse as California. It raises questions about the legitimacy of a political system that is based on the principle of majority rule. When 6 out of 10 eligible adults stay away from the polls, it also casts doubt on the ability of a democratically elected legislature to accurately represent public needs, which it must translate into effective policy outputs.[18] If certain subgroups of the electorate are routinely underrepresented at the ballot box, then the bias introduced at the polls may result in inequitable public policies that favor the interests of the majority at the expense of the minority.

Unequal participation is particularly dangerous when there are issues on the public agenda that disproportionately affect minorities. Proposition 187 provides a case in point. In 1994, a sizable majority of California's voters registered their support for the initiative, which was designed to cut off services to undocumented immigrants. While the initiative was approved by a 20-point margin, Californians were clearly divided along ethnic lines. White voters accounted for most of the initiative's support. African Americans and Asian Americans split their votes. In contrast, 77 percent of Latinos were opposed to the measure.[19] This made little difference in the outcome, however. Latinos comprised only 8 percent of the voters on election day in 1994, even though they made up over one-fourth of the state's population. Whites accounted for 80 percent of voters on election day, but they were only 57 percent of the state's population. Given the high turnout among the white majority, it was no surprise which policy preference prevailed on election day.

SUMMARY

There was a slight upturn in voter turnout in 2004 and 2006, when vital national issues of peace and prosperity were at stake, and California had the chance to influence the control of Congress and the White House. Still, declining political participation is the long-term trend in California, as in the rest of the country. There are reasons to be hopeful, however. Thanks to reforms such as the "motor-voter" law and voter registration drives, it has become easier for those who are eligible to register to vote. Most importantly, however, as California's ethnic communities continue to assert their political will, more equitable participation will emerge, with more equitable policy outcomes as a result. California's electorate may prove to be the most important policy player—given greater levels of participation and fewer stumbling blocks.

NOTES

1. Jennifer Warren, "Voters Seem to Enjoy Chance to Shop Around," *Los Angeles Times* (June 3, 1998): A3.
2. For a detailed analysis of the causes and consequences of Proposition 198, see Bruce Cain and Elisabeth Gerber, eds., *Voting at the Political Fault Line: California's Experiment with the Blanket Primary* (Berkeley: University of California Press, 2004).
3. Larry Gerston and Terry Christensen, *Recall! California's Political Earthquake* (Armonk, NY: M.E. Sharpe, 2004).
4. Karen Breslau, "The Mean Green Machine," *Newsweek* (19 June, 2006), 40.
5. Nicholas Lemann, "Government of, by and for the Comfortable," *New York Times Magazine* (November 1, 1998): 37–42.
6. Dan Bernstein, "Allen Recalled by Huge Margin," *Sacramento Bee* (November 29, 1995): A1.
7. Fredrick L. Bird and Frances M. Ryan, *The Recall of Public Officers: A Study of the Operation of the Recall in California* (New York: Macmillan, 1930).
8. *No Side Leads Yes on All Four of the Propositions Backed by Governor Schwarzenegger* (San Francisco: Field Research Corporation, November 1, 2005).
9. Peter Shrag, *Paradise Lost: California's Past, America's Future* (San Francisco: Public Policy Institute, 1998).
10. See Bruce Keith, David Magleby, Candice Nelson, Elizabeth Orr, Mark Westlye, and Raymond Wolfinger, *The Myth of the Independent Voter* (Berkeley: University of California Press, 1992).
11. Peter Shrag, op cit.
12. Bruce McPherson, *Report of Registration* (Sacramento: October 23, 2006).
13. See, for example, Richard Brody, "The Puzzle of Participation," in Anthony King, ed., *The New American Political System* (Washington, DC: American Enterprise Institute, 1978).
14. Carole Uhlaner, Bruce Cain, and D. Roderick Kiewiet, "Political Participation of Ethnic Minorities in the 1980s," *Political Behavior* 11 (1989): 195–231.
15. Victor M. Valle and Rodolpho D. Torres, *Latino Metropolis* (Minneapolis: University of Minnesota Press, 2000).
16. Susan Rasky, "The Media Covers Los Angeles," *California Journal* (July 1997): 42–45.
17. Steven H. Chaffee, Clifford J. Nass, and Seung-Mock Yang, "The Bridging Role of Television in Immigrant Political Socialization," *Human Communication Research* 17 (1990): 266–288.
18. For a classic expression of this argument, see E. E. Schattschneider, *The Semisovereign People* (Philadelphia: Harcourt Brace Jovanovich, 1975).
19. Patrick J. McDonnell, "State's Diversity Doesn't Reach Voting Booth," *Los Angeles Times* (November 10, 1994): A1.

CHAPTER 13

Education Policy

Featured Reading / Pages 164–166
Susan E. Brown
The Zip Code Route into UC

California's goal has been a dramatic one of making higher education available to one and all. The reality, however, reveals a system that favors the rich and the few.

—Susan E. Brown, from *The Zip Code Route into UC*

Not content with traditional answers to public problems, Californians have applied creative and innovative tools to supplement the traditional policy structures. These innovations are both praised and condemned, depending on which communities of interest one resides in. California's willingness to experiment and its reputation as a trend-setter have made the state a leader for the rest of the nation in several key policy areas. Education is one of these policy areas. The 1960 Master Plan for Higher Education, which promised a heavily subsidized public university education to all students, represents California policy innovation at its best.

In statewide polls, Californians continue to identify education as one of the most important issues facing the state.[1] This should come as no surprise, considering that California is home to the nation's largest public school system, serving 5.7 million students. Public schools are the nexus of all community issues and concerns: civic responsibility, cultural literacy, tolerance, job skills, economic growth, and crime are all related to the state's educational system. In addition, schools provide the initial point of access to civic institutions and political bureaucracy. This is true for children, as well as for adults with children. As a consequence, schools have become the battleground for civic discourse. This has been abundantly illustrated over the past several years with school busing in the 1970s, Proposition 13 (1978), and a trio of more recent ballot initiatives: Proposition 187 (1994), Proposition 209 (1996), and Proposition 227 (1998).

Public education provides a critical service to any society. Basic literacy—including the ability to read, write, perform quantitative functions, and critically assess the world around us—is a necessity in any complex society. This is especially true in California. With one of the world's largest economies, California's economic and political success has been based on a skilled workforce. Manufacturing industries and skilled agriculture dominated California's growth years from the 1940s to 1970s. The basic skills taught in California's primary schools, the vocational skills taught in California's secondary schools, and the professional skills taught in California's colleges and universities gave California's industrial sector a highly skilled labor pool at no direct cost.

CALIFORNIA'S PUBLIC K–12 INSTITUTIONS

California's public K–12 institutions are administered in autonomous school districts around the state, with oversight coming through the office of the state superintendent of public instruction. The state superintendent has limited authority to see that individual school districts comply with state and federal mandates. Local districts are charged with administering school policy as well as day-to-day operations. School districts are run by locally elected school boards, thus bringing together local—and often provincial—concerns in conflict with state and federal concerns.

The clash between local and state concerns is often harsh. This is explained, in part, by the relative inexperience of local district boards. School boards are typically the first point of entry to politics. Board members are generally inexperienced but highly motivated. State and federal legislators and staff, on the other hand, tend to be politically well seasoned, but somewhat cynical. This creates serious tension in communicating across institutional lines, and makes partnerships between state agencies and local boards difficult. State agencies tend to view local districts as inefficient, ideological, and marginally competent. Local districts tend to view state agencies as inefficient, coercive, and self-motivated.

The K–12 school boards are autonomous, on the one hand, but remain dependent on state and federal resources on the other. While both the federal and California constitutions recognize the need to respect local control, larger questions have come to dominate federal–state–local relationships. Desegregation, anti-racism and anti-sexism policies, affirmative action, and special education all represent federal interests, while curriculum issues represent state interests. Local issues tend to focus on class size, crime, and cost, and on occasion, provide a forum for ideologically driven reform. Since federal and state agencies maintain the power of the purse, and the state asserts the right of fiscal and managerial oversight, local districts are often in resentful compliance. At best, the policy structure driving K–12 education policy is combative and confusing.

CALIFORNIA'S PUBLIC COLLEGES AND UNIVERSITIES

California's public institutions of higher education are defined by the state's Master Plan for Higher Education (1960). The Master Plan was unique in defining the most comprehensive system of public colleges and universities in the nation. The plan devised a three-tiered system of community colleges, state universities, and research universities. According to the plan, any California resident who desired a college education would have a place in the system. The top 10 percent of California high-school seniors would be eligible for the 10-campus University of California (UC) system; although not necessarily their campus of choice. The top one-third of high-school students would be eligible for the California State University (CSU), and everyone, regardless of GPA, would be eligible to attend their local community college. This system revolutionized higher education by democratizing college attendance. Unlike students at traditional universities around the country, typical CSU students were first in their families to attend a university. The result: Blue-collar workers who built California's industrial economy in the 1940s and 1950s were able to educate their children to compete in the increasingly skilled economy of the 1960s and 1970s, and beyond. California's economic success in the 1990s is directly linked to the three-tiered system of higher education.[2]

THE POLICY QUESTIONS

The challenges facing both K–12 and postsecondary institutions are similar: declining investment in education, overcrowding, an increasing proportion of underprepared students, increasing racial and cultural tensions, increasing violence in communities and schools, declining community support, and—not surprisingly—a consequential drop in student performance. The emerging policy questions focus on these issues. How can schools do more with less? Will higher standards—and testing to those standards—create higher performance? Is violence in the community seeping into schools, or is juvenile crime causing violence in the community? Does community support follow school performance, or does school performance follow community support? Regardless of how people feel about public schools, there is little question that the vexing problems facing the state's school system will only become more severe.

The Funding Infrastructure

The primary tool of educational policy is budgetary allotment. While economic conservatives have long held that "You can't solve a problem by throwing money at it," one can certainly exacerbate problems by withdrawing appropriate financial support. The state's per-student spending is below where it was a generation ago. In 2005, California ranked 29th among the states in per-student expenditure and 8th among the 10 largest states. California spends $739 less per student than the national average.[3] Several factors lead to an even greater disparity among urban districts. Schools are traditionally funded by local communities through property taxes. Since different communities have different property values, tax revenues vary widely. Similarly, supplemental economic support from a local school's community varies according to the neighborhood's median income. This has created systemic inequities in the delivery of education.

California's educational funding woes are impacted by two significant events. First, in *Serrano v. Priest* (1972), the state supreme court held that an educational system financed by disparate property tax revenues was by definition contrary to the equal protection clause. This placed an extra burden on the state legislature to reduce disparities through state funding. Proposition 13 (1978) reduced property tax revenues by 57 percent, forcing counties to deeply cut services. This placed an even greater burden on the state to provide replacement dollars. Whereas the state provided 30 percent of educational funding in 1972, by the mid-1990s the state was responsible for 60 percent.

As a consequence of shrinking property tax revenues and greater reliance on state dollars, K–12 educational funding has become extremely vulnerable. As the state has confronted increasing pressure for scarce resources, school funding has declined. When the state's long boom began to wane in the mid-1970s, educational dollars dropped precipitously. By 1988 the proportion of general fund dollars committed to K–12 education fell to a low of 37 percent. This period of decline paved the way for the success of Proposition 98 (1988), which required a minimum 40 percent general fund commitment.

POLICY RESPONSES

With over 5.7 million students in California's K–12 system, the difficulties facing public education have not gone unnoticed by policymakers. Unfortunately, differing political ideologies and divided government have often kept the state from developing corrective policies. The most significant educational policy to emerge was the Educational Reform Act of 1983 (SB 813). This bill emerged during a brief period of congeniality between then State Superintendent of Public Education Bill Honig—a Democrat with strong support from teachers' unions—and Republican Governor George Deukmejian. SB 813 required increased standards for high-school graduation; more basic subject requirements in math, English, science, and foreign language; and additional hours of instruction over the year. The bill also required increased statewide testing, higher teacher salaries, and the California Basic Educational Skills Test (C-BEST) as a qualifying entrance exam for teachers.

Although these get-tough approaches have achieved some success, the overall quality of public schools continues to decline. The reforms of 1983 were not enough to keep up with decreasing per-student expenditures, overcrowding, and increasing dropout rates. Further reform came in 1991, with the California Learning Assessment System (CLAS), a testing program that asked students to read various literature selections and respond to them. The intent was to get students personally involved in reading and writing by relating the material to events in their personal lives. CLAS sparked contentious debate by conservatives and the religious right. Since CLAS presented students with stories representing the diversity of California families and encouraged independent thought, critics argued that the program was anti-family, pro-homosexuality, intrusive into family privacy, and based on wishy-washy pedagogy. The bill to reauthorize CLAS was vetoed by Governor Wilson in 1994.

By 1993, the school voucher movement succeeded in getting a privatization initiative on the ballot. The voucher plan would have given California parents a set amount of money to spend on their children's education, whether in public or private institutions. The voucher issue added fuel to the contentious education debate by implying that public schools will never improve and that the only rational response was mass exodus. Proponents argued that this competition for public funding would force public schools to improve, while critics argued that vouchers would simply subsidize private schools at the expense of public schools, further eviscerating the public school expenditures.

There is a policy paradox at play. While self-described school reformers continue to call for higher standards, tighter discipline, and more narrow academic curricula, California's emerging demographics suggest that bilingual education, greater remedial instruction, and cultural breadth is, in fact, more appropriate. It is estimated that 1.4 million students in California have limited English skills.[4] Fully one-third of California students speak a primary language other than English, with one-fifth speaking little or no English at all. A recent response to this situation was Proposition 227, sponsored by Silicon Valley businessman Ron Unz, banning bilingual education in public schools. Voters approved the "English for the Children" initiative overwhelmingly in 1998. It is expected that California will continue to diversify and that language minorities will continue to present challenges to educators.

NO CHILD LEFT BEHIND

In recent years, the education reform agenda has been preoccupied with the managerial values of effectiveness and accountability. The federal No Child Left Behind Act of 2002 (NCLB), which set strict accountability standards, is the most prominent example, but that law was not the first effort in California. A state-level accountability initiative was intended to accomplish essentially the same thing: tracking achievement with a new Academic Performance Index beginning in 1999, but the main difference is that it rewarded schools for improvement rather than punishing them for failing to meet standards.[5] NCLB represented the most sweeping change to the federal Elementary and Secondary Education Act of 1965, a law that originally expanded the federal role in education by providing funding to school districts, regardless of location or need. NCLB further expanded the federal role in education by requiring public schools to document outcomes. In order to measure progress, the law defined measures of effort—such as requiring that all teachers be credentialed in the subjects they teach—as well as outcomes, which are measured with scores on standardized tests.

In the year following the law's passage, more than 3,000 California schools were classified as "needing improvement." Many of these schools were located in urban areas (see Table 13.1). This classification caused parents to attempt to transfer their children to other more highly ranked schools. Schools that continued to fall short of the Adequate Yearly Progress (AYP) targets faced sanctions. They were required to provide special tutoring services and tougher corrective actions, including the dismissal of

TABLE 13.1   PERCENTAGE OF SCHOOLS FAILING
TO MEET FEDERAL PHASE I TARGETS, BY DISTRICT

DISTRICT	%
Fresno	73
Santa Ana	69
San Jose	68
Oakland	63
San Francisco	61
Los Angeles	50
Sacramento	49
San Diego	45
Long Beach	24

"poorly performing" staff and lengthening the school year. Schools failing to meet the federal standards after five consecutive years could be shut down, reconstituted as charter schools, or have their management taken over by private firms.

Application of NCLB has been fraught with problems in other states, but California has faced special challenges with the law. Critics complain that the law imposes an unfair burden on California, due to the diversity of the schools in the largest state. Schools are required to divide student populations into subgroups, including ethnic groups numbering 100 or more, and test each of these subgroups. Homogenous schools have an easier time complying with the law because they have fewer targets to meet. Another complication is that federal funds for implementation of required improvements have been held up. Even though NCLB required federal financial assistance to help public schools meet the federal mandates, the federal government has not provided the funding promised for tutoring programs in underperforming schools. In addition, the law requires teachers to pass proficiency tests in every subject they teach, regardless of training and experience. Even teachers with doctorates suddenly were classified as unqualified to teach their subjects under federal guidelines.[6]

At best, public policy can be understood as a public action directed at resolving some public problem. Education policies, however, tend to encompass far more values and ideologies than other policy areas. Since public education provides a structure for social reproduction and basic civic education to all members of society, it is, by definition, an extremely politicized arena. The following examples illustrate the tensions inherent in education policy.

CASE STUDIES

Different school districts around the state confront different types of problems and have provided different types of responses. The following case studies explore the rise of the religious right in the Vista Unified School District in northern San Diego

County, the economic collapse of a school district in the northeast San Francisco Bay Area, and the movement to reform the huge Los Angeles Unified School District.

Vista Unified School District

Vista, in suburban San Diego County, is 35 miles north of San Diego and 90 miles south of Los Angeles. Its web page boasts:

> . . . Vista has a perfect mild Mediterranean climate. Over 92,192 residents enjoy a wide range of year-round outdoor activities in a setting of gentle rolling hills and pleasant rural surroundings. With more than 25 educational institutions for Vista youth, and a business park home to over 800 companies, it is no wonder Vista has been named one of the "50 Fabulous Places to Raise Your Family."[7]

Vista's population of 92,000 is 64 percent white, 39 percent Latino, 4 percent black, and just under 4 percent Asian. The median house value is $443,000, and the median family income is $49,200.[8] Incorporated in 1963, Vista is an archetypal bedroom suburb.

Controversy arose in January 1992, when this sleepy town elected a school board with a three-member conservative Christian majority. The new board enacted several policies that many feared would inject a conservative Christian agenda into the classroom. In May the board sent to committee a policy that would allow the discussion of "scientific evidence" that would challenge dominant scientific theories of evolution and encourage "appropriate discussions of divine creation, ultimate purposes, or ultimate causes (the 'why')" in social studies and English classes.[9] Later that summer, in a 2–3 vote, the board passed a policy stating that "scientific evidence that challenges any theory in science should be presented" in science classes and that "no theory of science shall be taught dogmatically and no student shall be compelled to believe or accept any theory presented in the curriculum."[10] This policy was widely seen as an attack on the statewide curriculum on evolution and an attempt to open the door to the teaching of creationism.

The Vista debate exacerbated tensions between local ideologues and the state Board of Education. Since the state tends to avoid these kinds of conflicts, state officials left it to community members and the ACLU to file suit should the Vista Unified School District actually put creationism on the curriculum. Because Vista is a bedroom suburb with 86 percent of the working population leaving town daily for work, few residents follow school board decisions closely. Ultimately, it became a contest between the Christian right, led by the Institute for Creation Research, and concerned parents mobilized by Larry Lovell, a local marine biologist. As the fundamentalist flavor of the debate emerged, many Vista parents became involved, effectively ending the fight. The conservatives lost the board in the following election.

The Vista case is important in illustrating the complex relationship between the various levels of government. The local district has autonomy, up to a point. But state and local governments are loath to intervene in local political skirmishes. Ultimately, the Vista experience worked just the way democratic theory suggests it should: robust discourse at the local level, culminating with open elections.

Richmond Unified School District

The Richmond case illustrates a fundamentally different aspect of education policy and state–local relations. Richmond is an extremely diverse urban city in the east San Francisco Bay Area, 10 miles north of Oakland. Chartered in 1909, Richmond's population of 103,400 is 29 percent black, 35 percent white, 15 percent Asian, and 34 percent Latino. The median household income is $44,210, median age of residents is 33.9, and median housing unit value is $171,900.[11] The West Contra Costa Unified School District (as the Richmond District is now called) serves some 35,000 students, speaking 70 different languages in 5 north East Bay cities.[12] In the 1990s Richmond Unified School District experienced severe financial distress after years of continuing financial problems. This case is of interest not because of the fiscal crisis but because of the state–local relationship that emerged.

In the late 1980s and early 1990s, at least 20 school districts in California were facing financial collapse. It was common for the state to bail out ailing districts. But by 1991 Governor Wilson refused to sign any legislation bailing out Richmond unless the district granted the state broad managerial authority.[13] Without state assistance, the district would have to close schools for summer vacation six weeks early. The Richmond district was an interesting choice for a showdown. First, the district is predominantly black. Second, although Richmond had a history of financial trouble, its innovative enrichment programs had achieved national acclaim for resolving many of the problems that plague urban districts. As the standoff between the governor and the state dragged on, Contra Costa County's Superior Court ordered the state to do whatever was necessary to ensure that the Richmond Unified School District remain open. In the end the state loaned the Richmond district $19 million.[14]

In its oversight role, the state maintains the right to audit school district finances. In auditing Richmond, the state controller's office uncovered serious problems, including an inability to properly track debts and payments. The audit found that 7 of the 12 district accounting department employees were working in substitute roles, with little or no training. In summarizing the Richmond situation, a spokesman for the controller's office commented, "Richmond is a worst-case example of what happens when a school board does not meet its fiscal responsibility. There is no remedy for deficit financing in a district of finite means than to go broke eventually."[15] The district ultimately went into receivership, with a court-appointed trustee. In 1993, the Richmond Unified School District was reorganized into the West Contra Costa Unified School District.

The relationship between the state and Richmond illustrates the fiscal responsibility the state asserts over local districts. Unlike the ideological and curricular issues involved in the Vista case, when financial questions emerge the state is likely to act quickly and affirmatively. While the state allowed Vista to resolve its own programmatic and constitutional dilemmas, the leash was tightened around Richmond much more quickly. Different areas of education policy rely on different types of partnerships among local, state, and federal agencies. In this way, there may be fundamentally different levels of autonomy and control simultaneously present in state–local relations.

Los Angeles Unified School District

Los Angeles Unified School District (LAUSD) is the second largest school district in the nation. Its 727,000 K–12 students and 138,000 adult students are drawn from 708 square miles in Los Angeles County. LAUSD now employs a total of 77,754 people including 37,026 teachers.[16] Clearly, the district has exploded since it was originally chartered in 1853 and covered only 28 square miles. LAUSD is one of the nation's most diverse districts: 72 percent Latino, 12 percent black, 9 percent white, 4 percent Asian, 2 percent Filipino, and less than 1 percent Pacific Islander and Native American.[17] The district has serious problems: Only 45 percent of high school freshmen graduate after four years. For Latinos, who constitute the majority of LAUSD students, the completion rate is just 39 percent. This staggering dropout rate caused Los Angeles Mayor Antonio Villaraigosa to announce, "We can't be a great global city if we lose half of our workforce before they graduate from high school."[18]

Over the last two decades there have been several movements to reform LAUSD, either by breaking it up or by centralizing power. These initiatives have pulled the district in opposite directions. The shear vastness of the bureaucracy makes the district cumbersome and slow to respond. Some critics, including recent mayoral candidates Steve Soboroff and Bob Hertzberg, have argued that the district is too large to properly serve students and that the central administration is nonresponsive to parents. Further, these critics argue that smaller districts would allow students to attend classes closer to home. Between 1995 and the present, movements to break up the district have emerged in vastly different areas of the city, from core city neighborhoods to the suburbs.[19] The most salient demands for breaking up the district have emerged from the largely white, affluent corridor between Encino and Woodland Hills in the San Fernando Valley. Not surprisingly, this was precisely the same area that was also calling for secession from the City of Los Angeles.

Angelenos, particularly affluent suburban Angelenos, are dissatisfied and angry. Many feel that they are not getting their fair share from downtown, that their concerns are not taken seriously, and that the education of their children—correctly seen as a local issue—has been hijacked by bureaucrats sitting in gray buildings an hour's drive away. High visibility mishaps—such as the development of the ill-fated $200 million Belmont High site and the school board's attempt to dislodge then Superintendent Ruben Zacarias—highlight the problems facing the district. The Belmont High School site was to be the LAUSD's signature school site. Costing upwards of $200 million, the construction was plagued by mismanagement, not the least of which was approval of the site itself, which is contaminated with toxic pollution, making the school uninhabitable without significant mitigation. Zacarias was hired to resolve many of these problems but was pushed out by a new school board majority—backed by the mayor. The board could not fire Zacarias, so instead it hired a district CEO, who would have direct control of the district. This essentially removed any day-to-day authority from the superintendent. The move to undermine Zacarias was also seen as an insult to the district's Latino majority. Critics argued that Zacarias was not given sufficient time to fix the problems he was hired to fix, and they argued that if he were white rather than Latino he would have been replaced in a much more low-profile, respectful way. Zacarias eventually was replaced as Superintendent by former Colorado Governor Roy Romer, who served until after Antonio Villaraigosa was elected mayor in 2005.

Villaraigosa took office with school reform high on his agenda, following a campaign in which poorly performing schools topped the list of voters' concerns.[20] Following the lead of such mayors as Chicago's Richard Daley and New York's Michael Bloomberg, Villaraigosa tried to take control of his city's public schools. Using his resources as a former speaker of the assembly, he bypassed the voters and the local school board and accomplished his goal through legislation. His Sacramento allies, including new Speaker Fabian Nunez and Governor Schwarzenegger, enacted legislation to create a Council of Mayors, representing all 28 cities served by LAUSD. The school board's power is weakened under the plan, while more accountability rests with the superintendent, whose office is strengthened. The Council of Mayors has budgetary authority over the district and has the power to review the board's choice of Superintendent, although that did not stop the Board of Education from appointing its own choice for the new superintendent, David Brewer, while Villaraigosa was away on a trade mission in Asia.[21] Voting in the Council of Mayors is proportional to the size of the cities, so the Mayor of Los Angeles dominates with 80 percent of the vote. Villaraigosa's plan began a six-year trial period in 2006.

The LAUSD conflict is fundamentally an issue of control. Will schools be controlled locally, by city hall, or by a large regional district? If LAUSD is broken up into smaller districts, will parents have more control or will the smaller districts simply be more vulnerable to ideological meddling? Will breaking up the district break the back of the 32,000-member United Teachers of Los Angeles (UTLA)? Will it make teachers more accountable to local parents? These questions reflect the classic concerns of local politics. Unlike both the Vista case and the Richmond case, the LAUSD issue is exclusively local. Because day-to-day education policy is necessarily a local issue, the structure of the local district is beyond the direct reach of the state.

The Zip Code Route into UC   *Susan E. Brown*

California's system of higher education has been celebrated as the nation's model system, providing equal access to the American dream. But a look at who's admitted to the prestigious University of California campuses shows that ZIP code may be as critical as grade point averages in determining who gets in and who stays out.

This is how the system works. The top 12.5 percent of the state's high school graduates are eligible for the University of California; the top 33.5 percent are eligible for the state universities; for everyone else there is open access to community colleges with the option, after two years, of transferring into a four-year institution.

California's goal has been a dramatic one of making higher education available to one and all. The reality, however, reveals a system that favors the rich and the few. The list of the feeder high schools that send more than one hundred students each to UC reads like a social register. It includes Beverly Hills, Palos Verdes, Santa Monica, Rolling Hills, Palisades, and in the San Fernando Valley, Granada Hills, Birmingham, and Taft. With the exception of San Francisco's Lowell and University High Schools, the UC feeders are in predominately, if not exclusively, white, affluent, enclaves. Not surprisingly, the mean family income for freshman at UC Berkeley last fall was nearly sixty thousand dollars, well above the national average.

Both the California Master Plan and Education Code are structured in such a way that students not ordinarily eligible for a state university may be able to transfer after two years at a community college. But, to the extent that transfer from a community college to UC works at all, it works primarily for the select, the affluent—and principally the white—community college. The top ten community college feeder campuses to UC for Fall 1986 were mainly in affluent residential communities: Santa Monica (252 transfers), Diablo Valley (241), Santa Barbara (227), Orange Coast (207), Cabrillo (151), El Camino (143), De Anza (139), San Diego Mesa (138), American River (132), and Saddleback (132).

By contrast, consider Fresno City College, which serves large numbers of minority students from a predominately agricultural region. Only one black and four Latinos (out of a student body of thirteen thousand) transferred to UC in 1986. Imperial Valley Community College, serving a similar student body, sent only three Latinos to UC campuses out of a freshman class of 1,341 that year. At predominately black Compton College, only two blacks transferred to UC campuses in 1986.

Statewide, the 106 community colleges in California sent a total of 189 blacks and 485 Latinos to the eight UC campuses, an average of six minority students from each college. Yet approximately 80 percent of underrepresented minorities who enter college in the state begin their studies in a community college.

While it is surely important to maintain high standards, the goal of a tax-based state educational system should be the development of talents and skills from all socio-economic groups. Public education by its very nature must reflect the entire population that supports it. What California has, instead, is a perfectly correlated system of family income to educational benefits—that is, the wealthiest are rewarded with access to the University of California; middle-income students end up at the California State University; low-income students begin and end their higher education at community colleges.

One possible solution to the perpetuation of a hereditary elite is to expand eligibility to UC and CSU to the top 12.5 percent and top 33.5 percent of students at every high school. There is nothing in state law or the California Master Plan to prevent this more egalitarian approach. Without such a remedy, California will merely continue to favor students from those schools with honors courses, enriched curriculums, well-equipped science laboratories, and optimal learning conditions.

Shouldn't a serious student at an inner-city school who graduates in the top 10 percent of his or her class have the same access to the benefits of California's postsecondary system as his or her counterpart in an exclusive private or magnet public school? If not, we should recognize that we are rewarding accidents of birth and that our current system of admissions to the University of California is, in truth, determined by ZIP code.

Editor's note: Though this piece appeared in 1989, the observations are still largely accurate. In addition, this predates the raucous debate around affirmative action in 1996. The recommendation of assessing performance on a campus-by-campus basis rather than statewide is being explored in several quarters.

Source: Sonia Maasik and Jack Soloman, eds., *California Dreams and Realities*, 2nd ed. (Boston: Bedford/ St. Martin's, 1999). Originally published in 1989 by Pacific News Service. Reprinted by permission.

SUMMARY

This chapter has explored the policy framework surrounding California's public education system. Education policy is a function of local decision making within a framework defined by the state and heavily influenced by the federal government. Further influence is ensured through funding agencies that require specific actions and policies in exchange for grant dollars. While the state maintains fairly tight control over postsecondary education (community colleges, the California State Universities, and University of California campuses), K–12 education remains fundamentally a local issue. The federal government is responsible for assuring equality of access; the state is responsible for establishing curricular priorities and financial oversight; and local K–12 districts are primarily responsible for short- and long-term policies affecting their students. The case studies illustrate how different districts pursue different challenges, emphasizing the idiosyncratic nature of education policy.

NOTES

1. See, for example, Nick Anderson, "Davis Promises Fast Start on Sweeping Education Agenda," *Los Angeles Times* (November 5, 1998): S1.
2. For more history of the Master Plan for Higher Education, see Ethan Rarick, *California Rising: The Life and Times of Pat Brown* (Berkeley: University of California Press, 2005).
3. National Education Association, *Rankings & Estimates*, 2005, www.morganquitno.com/ed5samp1.pdf.
4. Maria L. LaGanga, "Bilingual Ed Initiative Wins Easily," *Los Angeles Times* (June 3, 1998): A1.
5. B. Mantel, "No Child Left Behind." *Congressional Quarterly Researcher* 15 (May 27, 2005): 469–492.
6. Samuel Freedman, "Despite a Doctorate and Top Students, Unable to Teach," *New York Times* (October 11, 2006): B8.
7. Vista Chamber of Commerce, *Vista: Acclaimed as "A Dynamic Beauty,"* http://vistachamber.org/community_info/city_of_vista.htm.
8. Vista Chamber of Commerce, *Vista: Acclaimed as "A Dynamic Beauty,"* http://vistachamber.org/community_info/city_of_vista.htm.
9. Peter West, "California Board Defers Action on Religious Tenets in Science Classes," *Education Week on the Web* (June 2, 1993), www.edweek.org.

10. Peter West, "New Tactic Used to Push Teaching Creation Theory," *Education Week on the Web* (September 8, 1993), www.edweek.org.
11. "City of Richmond Population Profile" (February 7, 2007), www.ci.richmond.ca.us/DocumentView.aspx?DID=301&DL=1.
12. West Contra Costa Unified School District, *About WCCUSD—Quick Facts*, www.wccusd.k12.ca.us/about/quickfacts.shtml.
13. Peter Schmidt, "Judge Halts Plan to Close Schools in California District," *Education Week on the Web* (May 8, 1991), www.edweek.org.
14. Peter Schmidt, "State Auditors in California Discover 'Serious' Flaws in Troubled District's Financial-Management," *Education Week on the Web* (May 22, 1991), www.edweek.org.
15. Peter Schmidt, "Judge Halts Plan."
16. Los Angeles Unified School District, *2006–2007 Fingertip Facts*, http://notebook.lausd.net/pls/ptl/docs/PAGE/CA_LAUSD/LAUSDNET/OFFICES/COMMUNICATIONS/.
17. Ibid.
18. "The Mayor Takes Charge," *Economist* (April 29, 2006): 31–32.
19. Peter Schmidt, "L.A. Breakup Plans Gather Head of Steam," *Education Week on the Web* (October 25, 1995), www.edweek.org.
20. Patrick McGreevy and Richard Fausset, "Mayor Reasserts Bid to Take Over L.A. Schools," *Los Angeles Times* (October 7, 2005): A29.
21. Duke Helfand and Howard Blume, "Mayor, Next Supt. Pledge Cooperation," *Los Angeles Times* (October 26, 2006): B1.

CHAPTER 14

Environmental and Energy Policy

Featured Reading / Pages 182–183
Barry Commoner
The Closing Circle: Nature, Man, and Technology

Ecology has become the political substitute for the word "motherhood."

—Jesse Unruh, former Democratic leader of the California state assembly

We have met the enemy and he is us.

—Pogo

Environmental policy provides an example of policy success in California. Rich in both environmental resources and environmental problems, California has long battled environmental challenges. From its pristine coastal redwood forests in the north to the warm sandy beaches of the south, from the Sequoias in the Sierra Nevada to the desolate beauty of Joshua Tree, Mojave, and Death Valley, from the ruggedness of the Channel Islands to the windswept Monterey Peninsula, from the muddy Sacramento Delta to the fertility of the Central Valley, California overflows in natural beauty and biological diversity. Yet at the same time, California's vast industrial and agricultural infrastructure, its massive urban areas and encroaching sprawl, its densely populated coastline, its military bases, and its transportation corridors, all present significant environmental challenges that the state is only now coming to terms with. California's environmental dilemma is, at its core, a contest over scarce resources.

California has the largest population, the largest economy, and some of the most serious environmental problems of any state in the nation. These issues are, of course, interrelated. The challenge facing policymakers is how to accommodate an increasing population while maintaining healthy economic growth and simultaneously improving environmental quality. This discourse, not surprisingly, is extremely divisive, with different interests pushing in very different directions. This chapter explores California's environmental and energy challenges and the policies that have succeeded—at least in part—in stemming the tide of environmental degradation.

Specific attention is paid to air pollution policy in Southern California, water quality in the San Francisco Bay–Delta Area, and evolving transportation policy in the greater Los Angeles area.

AIR QUALITY

Air quality throughout the state differs widely. Los Angeles and its neighbors in the South Coast Basin experience the most degraded air quality in the nation after Houston. Yet a significant portion of the state remains out of compliance with Federal Air Quality Standards. As Figure 14.1 illustrates, ozone levels vary widely throughout the state. The Southern California basin is "extreme" in its nonattainment status, representing the most severe air pollution in the nation. But Northern and Central California are not smog free. The metropolitan Sacramento area, including Sacramento, Yolo, and Solano Counties, are designated "serious," and California's Central Valley is designated "serious." San Bernardino and Riverside Counties are "severe"; Santa Barbara County and Ventura County are "moderate"; and San Diego, Butte, Yuba, and Imperial are "transitional." The remaining areas are in compliance with federal ozone standards.[1]

Air pollution provides a challenging policy area because of ambient emissions travel. The San Francisco Bay Area tends to appear smog free, but this is in large measure due to its prevailing west winds. Emissions are extremely high in the Bay Area, with its 7.3 million residents. However, its ambient air quality tends to be quite good. Just as East Bay cities suffer through San Francisco's smog contribution, Yolo and Solano Counties suffer through Bay Area emissions.

California's smog problems are a result of two primary factors: its dense population with its reliance on individual automobile transit and its vast industrial and agricultural economy. Air pollution is caused by a variety of factors and carries severe health consequences. Carbon monoxide is emitted from vehicle and stationary source exhaust. It is an odorless gas that replaces oxygen in red blood cells. It can cause angina, impaired vision, poor coordination, and dizziness. While the earth releases CO naturally, the expansive release of industrial CO emissions contributes to the greenhouse effect, throwing off the equilibrium of the earth's temperature (global warming).

Volatile organic compounds (VOCs), including reactive organic gases (ROGs), are released by the incomplete combustion of gasoline and evaporation from petroleum-based fuels, solvents, and paints. Hydrocarbons react in the sunlight with oxygen and nitrogen dioxide to form ozone, peroxyacetyl nitrate (PAN), and other photochemical oxidants. Ozone, the main component of smog, irritates the mucous membranes (eyes, nasal passages, throat, lungs) causing coughing, choking, reduced lung capacity, as well as aggravating asthma, bronchitis, and emphysema. Smog, containing hundreds of chemicals including ozone and peroxyacetyl nitrate, damages trees, crops, and building materials.

FIGURE 14.1   AIR QUALITY ATTAINMENT DESIGNATIONS FOR
OZONE LEVELS IN CALIFORNIA

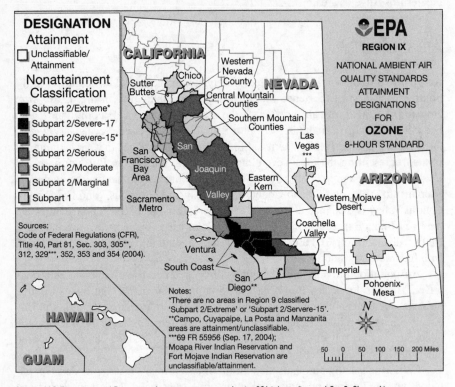

Source: U.S. Environmental Protection Agency, www.epa.gov/region09/air/maps/images/r9_o3_8hr_md.jpg.

Lead was used as an anti-knock additive in some gasolines until 1980, as a sta-bilizing agent in household and industrial paints, and as a structural component of pipes and roofing. Nonferrous smelters and battery plants also emit lead into the atmosphere. Lead, like other heavy metals, accumulates in the fat, bone, and other soft tissues of the body. The most common symptoms of lead poisoning include nau-sea and severe stomach pains. Larger accumulations cause deterioration of blood-forming organs, kidneys, and, ultimately, the nervous system. In addition, lead has been tied to learning disabilities in young children.

Oxides of nitrogen (NO_X) are a product of industrial and vehicle exhaust. It attacks the lungs, causing cellular changes resulting in lowered resistance to respira-tory infections. NO_X is a main contributor to acid rain and, when mixed with hydro-carbons, creates ozone. Particulate matter is the smoke, dust, and soot emitted from industrial processes, heating boilers, gasoline and diesel engines, coal- and diesel-burning utilities, cigarette smoke, and both organic and synthetic dusts. Larger par-ticulates clog the lung sacs, causing bronchitis and more serious pneumoconioses (diseases related to inhalation of organic and inorganic dusts), irritate mucous membranes, and clog tear ducts, damaging the surface of the eye. Microscopic particulates pass into the bloodstream, introducing carcinogens and heavy metals. Sulfur oxides (SO_X) are released in coal- and oil-burning processes. SO_X is a corrosive, poisonous gas that is associated with coughing, colds, asthma, and bronchitis, and, like nitrogen dioxide, contributes to acid rain.[2]

While few would argue that California has solved its air problems, the California Air Resources Board reports that there has been meaningful improvement in California's air over the past 25 years, as Table 14.1 illustrates. Between 1980 and 2005 the population has increased by 55 percent, and vehicle-miles traveled have increased by 146 percent. At the same time, NO_X emissions have decreased by 37 percent, and emissions of ROGs have decreased by 63 percent. Particulate matter smaller than 10 microns (PM_{10}) has increased by only 9 percent, and particulate matter smaller than 2.5 microns (PM_{25}) has decreased by a small margin. And, carbon monoxide emissions (CO) have decreased by 64 percent. Ozone exposure remains a significant problem statewide. The areas of most significant improvement for ozone exposure include the San Francisco Bay and San Diego Air Basins, while the South Coast and Sacramento Metropolitan Air Basins have experienced only mild improvement. The San Joaquin Valley Air Basin has experienced the least improvement.[3]

TABLE 14.1   STATEWIDE AMBIENT AIR QUALITY TRENDS, 1975–2010

STATEWIDE EMISSIONS TRENDS								
	1975	1980	1985	1990	1995	2000	2005	2010*
Population		23.8	26.4	29.8	31.7	34.1	37	39.2
Avg. Daily VMT		389	517.7	677.2	731.2	796.1	872.9	957.4
POPUTANT (TONS/DAY ANNUAL AVERAGE)	1975	1980	1985	1990	1995	2000	2005	2010*
NO_X	4,949	5,060	5,011	4,997	4,319	3,844	3,220	2,741
ROG	7,026	6,602	6,068	4,737	3,761	3,128	2,430	2,167
PM_{10}	1,992	2,026	2,131	2,316	2,200	2,267	2,212	2,254
PM_{25}	896	874	884	934	862	877	864	879
CO	41,866	38,189	36,145	30,221	22,832	17,515	13,766	11,408

*Data for 2010 Estimated.

Population	In millions
Avg Daily VMT	Average Daily Vehicle Miles Traveled (in millions)
NO_X	Oxides of Nitrogen
ROG	Reactive Organic Gas
PM_{10}	Particulate Matter smaller than 10 microns
PM_{25}	Particulate Matter smaller than 2.5 microns
CO	Carbon Monoxide

WATER QUALITY

Like air quality, California's water quality is a major concern as well. The same factors contributing to the poor air quality contribute to poor water quality. And as the largest farm state in the nation, California surface waters and aquifers must absorb millions of tons of pesticides and chemical fertilizers. California's manufacturing industries dump millions of gallons of contaminated waste water, and California's cities and suburbs pump out tens of millions of gallons of sewage and polluted runoff. In addition, in seeking to maximize arable land, California has lost more that 91 percent of its wetlands.[4] Wetlands are critical tidal zones that, when healthy, keep water clean by filtering out contaminants. Wetlands provide essential habitat for threatened and endangered plant and wildlife. Forty-five percent of the nation's listed endangered animals and 26 percent of its endangered plants rely on wetlands to survive.[5] California is among only seven states with this degree of loss, as Figure 14.2 illustrates.

California water quality is degraded through a variety of pollution sources. As sewer systems continue to age and deteriorate, growing populations produce increasing demands. The result is the seepage of raw sewage into aquifers. Improper discharge from septic tanks exacerbates the problem, making sewage the single largest polluter of drinking water. Waste disposal sites also pose special dangers.

Agriculture sprays millions of tons of fertilizers and pesticides on crops, which ultimately seep into water sources. Runoff from fields, feedlots, and barnyards carries potassium and nitrogen into ground and surface waters. Water diverted from rivers for irrigation is returned with excessive levels of salt and minerals, degrading drinking water sources. Colorado River water becomes increasingly sodium rich as it makes its way south, causing serious problems for communities such as Los Angeles, which rely heavily on the Colorado for drinking water. Mine runoff brings high levels of acid, iron, sulfates, copper, lead, uranium, and other hazardous materials into aquifers and streams.

The potential health effects of water pollution are serious. Nitrates from agricultural runoff can cause birth defects in infants and livestock. Chlorinated solvents from chemical degreasing agents, machinery maintenance, and chemical production are known carcinogens. Trihalomethanes, produced by chemical reactions with chlorinated water, may cause liver and kidney damage and are similarly carcinogenic. Polychlorinated biphenyls (PCBs) are produced as waste from outmoded manufacturing facilities and may cause liver damage and possibly cancer. Lead etching from old piping and solder in water systems may cause nerve damage, learning disabilities, birth defects, and possibly cancer. Coliform and pathogenic bacteria and viruses from leaking sewers and septic tanks spread gastrointestinal illnesses.

California's water quality is monitored by the State Water Resources Control Board (SWRCB). The SWRCB reports that discharges of contaminants is decreasing, the number of leaking underground storage tanks (USTs) is decreasing, and that fewer organic chemicals and pesticides are found in California's drinking water.[6] Although water quality issues vary throughout the state, as the point of estuarial destination for the state's largest watershed, the greater San Francisco Bay–Delta Area provides a useful barometer to statewide water quality.

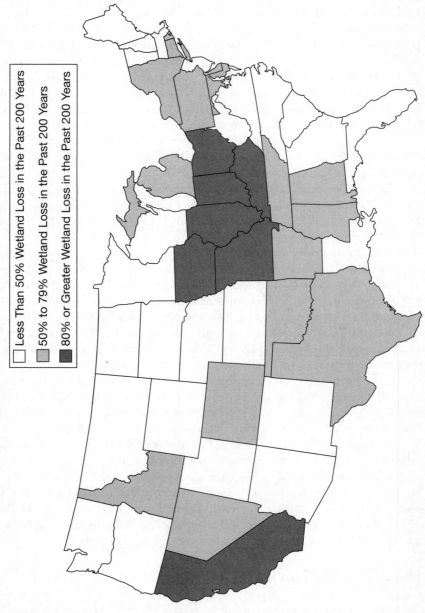

FIGURE 14.2   HISTORICAL WETLAND LOSS BY STATE

☐ Less Than 50% Wetland Loss in the Past 200 Years

▨ 50% to 79% Wetland Loss in the Past 200 Years

■ 80% or Greater Wetland Loss in the Past 200 Years

Source: US Environmental Protection Agency, Office of Water Fact Sheet Series, "Threats to Wetlands". September 2001, www.epa.gov/owow/wetlands/pdf/threats.pdf.

Bay Area Water Quality: A Statewide Barometer

The San Francisco Bay Regional Water Quality Control Board tracks the water quality for rivers, streams, estuaries, and bays in the Bay Area. They report that fish populations have suffered serious declines in all areas, with major reductions of striped bass, delta smelt, splittail, longfin smelt, and salmon. This is due to spawning habitat losses in the Delta region.[7] Bay sport fish have been impacted by chemical pollutants. White croaker, shiner surfperch, walleye surfperch, leopard sharks, brown smoothhound sharks, striped bass, sturgeon, and halibut have all tested high for PCBs, mercury, dieldrin, total DDT, total chlordane, and dioxin/furans, prompting the state to warn that Bay fish consumption should be limited. (Adults should consume no more than two Bay-caught fish meals per month; pregnant women and children no more than one.)[8]

Water and sediment is routinely tested around the Bay through the Regional Monitoring Program. During 2004 and 2005, 31 sites were tested for water toxicity, and 47 sites were tested for sediment toxicity. PCB concentrations exceeded safe levels at all sites. Pesticides DDT, dieldrin, and chlordane exceeded safe levels at several sites. Trace metals (copper, nickel, lead, mercury, and chromium) were above safe levels at many sites, particularly in the North Bay. On the positive side, the Regional Water Quality Control Board found no toxicity to fish and other aquatic organisms due to the water quality. Sediment toxicity is also widespread, even though there has been a decline in the concentrations of PCBs, pesticides, and trace metals in recent years.[9] The control board also tests groundwater around the Bay Area. Pollution is widespread, primarily due to 7,500 known leaking underground fuel tanks. There are an additional 500 sites estimated where industrial solvents have leaked into aquifers.

The most significant water quality issue in the Bay Area is aquatic habitat loss. In 1850 there were about 545,000 acres of tidal wetlands in the Bay and Delta. Today there are about 45,000 acres.[10] Historically, most of these lost wetlands were taken for agriculture. Increasingly, however, urban development is taking a serious toll, both as a consequence of habitat loss and the rise of urban creeks and non-point runoff. Urban runoff is responsible for carrying wastewater, chemical contaminants, and trash into riparian habitat, causing further water pollution and sediment problems.

Rural creeks in Marin and Sonoma Counties are polluted by dairy and agricultural runoff, bringing manure, fertilizers, and pesticides into rivers and other surface waters. Sediment "hotspots" have been created by heavy metals, solvents, pesticides, and toxic organics introduced into sediment around the Bay Area by waste water discharges and industrial runoff. The Water Control Board cautions that these hotspots may be directly toxic to any organisms in them, and the contaminants can "bioaccumulate," becoming toxic to other animals higher up the food chain.[11]

ENERGY USE AND IMPACTS

California's population increases about 1.1 percent per year, but its energy consumption increases 1.4 percent annually. Still, Californians consume less energy per capita than the nation as a whole. U.S. per capita energy consumption is just over

12,000 kWh per person, while California consumes approximately 7,300 kWh per person on an annual basis. This is up from 3,600 kWh/person in 1960, but California's per capita use has remained generally the same since 1980. California imports 84 percent of its natural gas, 58 percent of its petroleum, and 23 percent of its electricity. And, while California ranks second in total energy used, the state ranks first in residential, commercial, and transportation energy use. And the state ranks third in its industrial energy use. California's electricity is produced through several energy sources: natural gas (41 percent), coal (20 percent), hydroelectric (15 percent), nuclear (13 percent), and renewable (11 percent).[12]

California's energy use places measurable strains on environmental quality. The state's 28 million vehicles use more than 16 billion gallons of gasoline and 3 billion gallons of diesel fuel annually.[13] On-road motor vehicles produce 32 percent of the state's emissions of ROGs, 55.5 percent of CO emissions, and 47 percent of NO_x emissions.[14] The state emits an estimated 500 million tons of greenhouse gases (CO_2 equivalent). Of this, 41 percent is generated by transportation, 23 percent by industrial facilities including petroleum refineries, 10 percent by in-state electricity production, and 10 percent by out-of-state electricity generation.[15] As we discuss later in the chapter, the state's reliance on motor vehicles is not by chance—it is the result of key transportation decisions made in the 1930s through 1960s—and the lack of any transportation decisions in the 1970s and 1980s.

California's energy use and production have not been without problems. In the 1970s there were two oil crises. The first, in 1973, was a result of oil producing nations withholding supply from the United States as a result of U.S. support for Israel during the Yom Kippur War. The second, in 1979, was a result of market panic following the Iranian Revolution. In both cases, the nation's dependence in foreign oil was brought into focus, but no long-term reductions in domestic petroleum use were sustained. California's reliance on imported oil for its huge fleet of motor vehicles put it into a particularly difficult spot. In 1979 gasoline was rationed for the first time since World War II. But the greatest shock to California's energy infrastructure was the state's electricity crisis of 2000–2001. And while the oil crises of the 1970s may be attributed to the nation's growing dependence on foreign oil and geo-politics, the electricity crisis was a result of domestic corporate greed and market failure.

California's electricity crisis, also known as the Western energy crisis, exploded on June 14, 2000, as blackouts cut power to 97,000 people in the San Francisco Bay Area during a heat wave. Between January and May 2001 several blackouts cut power to between several hundred thousand to a million and a half Californians with then Governor Gray Davis declared a state of emergency in January 2001. In examining the crisis, the Federal Energy Regulatory Commission (FERC) concluded that the Western energy market was dysfunctional, allowing energy trading corporations such as Enron to manipulate supply and demand. The dysfunction in the market began as early as 1996, as California began to deregulate the energy market in an attempt to increase competition. In so doing, the FERC concluded, California created inconsistent trading rules. As Californians suffered through blackouts, Enron earned profits exceeding $500 million in 2000 and 2001.[16]

POLICY RESPONSES

Environmental policy responses in California are textbook illustrations of federalism in action. Like most other states, California only acted to improve environmental quality after the federal government required the state to do so. As a consequence, most of California's environmental policy responses are state elements of federal programs. Responses to the policy areas of air quality, water quality and water quantity, and solid and hazardous waste follow.

Air Policy

California air policy is facilitated at the state level by the California Air Resources Board (CARB) and addressed locally by 34 air pollution districts. As a consequence of the variation in air quality throughout the states, CARB and the EPA requires that regional air quality control districts create plans specifically designed for problems in their area. The local air pollution control districts set emission levels and grant emission permits for stationary sources, as well as managing transportation control measures for their respective regions. Each district develops its own air policy management plan to combat the unique air quality problems in its region. Depending on the level and type of airborne pollutants in a district, the local control board may regulate manufacturers, power plants, refineries, gasoline service stations, and auto body shops. If the Bay Area is the barometer for statewide water quality, the Los Angeles Basin is surely the barometer of air quality management in the state.

Los Angeles: A Case in Point

Like many other jurisdictions, California was slow to comply with the 1970 federal Clean Air Act Amendments. California's State Implementation Plan (SIP), accepted by the EPA under the Reagan administration, argued that Southern California simply could not meet federal standards. Ironically, it was this weak SIP that initiated California's evolution as the leader in innovative clean air policy. The acceptance of California's SIP allowed environmentalists to challenge the EPA's weak implementation of the Clean Air Act in court. Perhaps as a consequence of its growing urban density and increasingly degraded environment, California has emerged as a leader in creative environmental policymaking. This is especially true in Southern California's air quality policy.

In 1987, after discussions with the EPA broke down, the Ninth Circuit Court of Appeals in San Francisco ordered the EPA to reject California's 1984 SIP. Facing potential sanctions, including the loss of federal highway and sewer funds, and with prodding from Representative Henry Waxman (D–Los Angeles), the California Air Resources Board (CARB), the South Coast Air Quality Management District (SCAQMD), and the Southern California Association of Governments (SCAG) created the initial Air Quality Management Plan for Southern California (SCAQMP) in 1989.

SCAQMP mandates specific controls to be in place by 2010. The first part of the plan (Tier I) includes 123 immediate controls that were to be implemented by the year 2000. These controls focused on immediate changes based on technologies available at the time, such as reformulating commercial and household paints and solvents to reduce hydrocarbon emissions, regulating charcoal broilers in restaurants, requiring emission control equipment for bakeries and dry cleaners, and more effectively inspecting motor vehicles. In addition, the SCAQMP requires large employers—those employing 100 people or more—to provide employees with incentives for carpooling and public transit use.

The second section of the plan (Tier II) depended on the development of new technologies and was to be implemented over a 15-year period. This portion of the plan mandates that 40 percent of private vehicles and 70 percent of commercial trucks and buses were required to run on nonpetroleum fuels, such as methanol, by 1999. Two percent of all cars sold in 1998, and 10 percent sold in 2003, had to meet zero-emission standards. With available technology, only electric vehicles are able to meet that standard. The plan also includes the construction of housing hubs closer to job centers and improved mass transit and carpooling.

The final portion of the plan (Tier III) requires the further evolution of new technologies and therefore focuses on research and development; it includes the establishment of the Office of Technology Assessment. The specific controls in this section of the plan include the conversion of motor vehicles to "extremely low-emitting" engines, which may preclude the use of the internal combustion engine.

By 1991 the SCAQMD adopted a revised SCAQMP. The 1991 plan maintains the basic structure of the 1989 plan but establishes several new control measures that include the application of more advanced technologies, such as the Phase 2 reformulated fuels program, for reducing stationary and mobile emissions. In addition, the 1991 plan includes eight specific measures for controlling transportation-related emissions by reducing government-related vehicle miles and vehicle trips. In 1994 the plan was redesigned to fulfill the requirements of federal Clean Air Act Amendments (1990) and the California Clean Air Act (1988). Structurally, the 1994 plan is similar to the earlier versions. Tier I measures are now divided into "short-term" and "medium-term" measures (which were to be implemented between 1994 and 2005). Tier II and III measures are now consolidated as "long-term" measures. Control changes are a little more substantial. In addition to the controls mentioned, the plan imposes more stringent emissions and fuel quality standards, accommodating the California Air Resources Board—the statewide agency—low-emission-vehicle (LEV) and clean fuels regulations. Stationary sources require greater application of "technologically feasible" control equipment. The plan also requires the adoption of new technologies that "may reasonably be expected to be utilized by the year 2010."[17]

Ships, trains, aircraft, and farming and construction equipment continue to be regulated primarily by the federal EPA and CARB. The EPA released a court-ordered federal implementation plan in February 1994, requiring greater federal air quality standards. The standards were adopted by the new SCAQMP. Although the FIP was ultimately withdrawn as a concession to the new Republican Congress, the SCAQMP continues to require additional measures for non-road sources, including recreational boats and vehicles to meet these standards. In addition, several new implementation strategies were included in the 1994 plan, including increased use of market incentives, greater use of permitting, greater education programs, equipment standards, and greater communication between the local agency (the SCAQMD) and state (CARB) and federal (EPA) agencies. Several market incentives have been written into the plan. The plan expands the RECLAIM (Regional Clean Air Incentives Market) program, a "bubble" policy requiring aggregate control of a facility's emissions rather than command and control of specific emissions within the facility. RECLAIM also creates a pollution permit market where participants can sell unused pollution rights. Further, the plan establishes a wider program of tax credits for companies that reduce vehicle emissions. Perhaps most creative is the plan to develop a model of emission-based registration fees and sales taxes to encourage financial incentives for emissions reduction.

Educational outreach programs are utilized to help bring newly regulated small source categories (e.g., dry cleaners, bakeries) into compliance. Because the district is attempting to create a better working relationship with the business community in the South Coast Basin, information on alternative products, cleaner processes, and equipment modifications is being distributed so as to encourage greater emissions reductions. In addition, the plan encourages public education campaigns in order to encourage environmentally friendly behavior changes, including maximizing mass transportation use and minimizing residential emissions such as BBQs and fireplaces. The most recent version, adopted in 1997, scales back the innovative approaches that characterized the earlier versions. Placing a greater emphasis on "flexible, alternative approaches," the 1997 version backs off from some standards (e.g., ozone) and replaces remaining command and control structures with incentive-based regulations. On the positive side, the new version accommodates the new federal requirements for particulate matter (PM_{10}). In 2003 and again in 2007 the Air Quality Management Plan was updated, making small changes that align California's ozone and PM10 standards with the federal standards. Similarly, the updates incorporate state and federal planning requirements into the AQMP.

Southern California's South Coast Air Quality Management Plan (SCAQMP) leaves the federal air quality model and institutes a stringent 20-year plan to reduce smog. The commitment of the South Coast Basin to reduce emissions through a four-point plan involving conservation, alternative fuels, mass transit, and a shift in residential and economic social patterns makes the plan the strongest clean air program in the world.

Water Policy

The SWRCB was established in 1967, with the mission of ensuring the "highest reasonable quality of waters of the state, while allocating those waters to achieve the optimum balance of beneficial uses."[18] The board is made up of five full-time members, appointed to four-year terms by the governor and confirmed by the senate.

The state board shares authority with the nine regional water quality control boards. The regional boards are responsible for developing and enforcing water quality basin plans consistent with the state's water policies and objectives, and addressing the local differences in climate, topography, geology, and hydrology. The regional boards each have nine part-time members appointed by the governor and confirmed by the senate. The regional boards have specific authority to "issue waste discharge requirements, take enforcement action against violators, and monitor water quality."[19] Water quality problems throughout the state necessitate strong policy, but the state requires that these policies balance the need to improve quality with the needs of industry, agriculture, and municipal districts.

State water agencies are currently implementing several programs aimed at specific problems. The federal Clean Water Act (1987) provides the standards and framework through which the state must operate. The Clean Water Act requires the state to improve waste treatment facilities, manage and treat non-point runoff (urban runoff), and develop estuary management programs. In addition, the state has developed an aggressive watershed management program, an underground storage tank cleanup program, and through the California Coastal Act and the resulting Coastal Commission, an aggressive coastal management program.

Waste Policy

Californians generate over 37 million tons of municipal solid waste every year, about 90 percent of which is buried in the state's 670 landfills. Waste policy has traditionally been seen as a local issue, resulting in widespread landfills and incinerators. This has created serious problems over time: Toxic leachate percolates from landfills, posing serious groundwater threats; escaping gases have been shown to contain toxic contaminants and noxious odors. Most existing landfills are in violation of state and federal operating requirements. All of this is exacerbated by California's increasingly dense population, making open spaces more and more rare. As a result, the state has stepped in and taken charge of solid waste policy.

The Integrated Waste Management Act of 1989 (IWMA, also referred to as AB 939) identifies five components to an integrated waste management program for the state: source reduction; recycling; composting; waste to energy; and continued landfilling, albeit at lower volumes. The law required cities and counties to divert at least 25 percent of their waste by 1995 and 50 percent by 2000, relative to the 1990 waste stream. IWMA establishes source reduction, recycling, and composting as policy priorities over landfilling and incineration. The statute replaces the old industry-oriented waste management board with six full-time members. The governor is required to appoint one member representing the solid waste industry, one member representing the environmental community, and two "public" members; the speaker of the assembly and the Senate Rules Committee each have one discretionary appointment. The new Integrated Waste Management Board holds greater authority to enforce compliance through punitive fines of as much as $10,000 per day to non-compliant jurisdictions.

The rate of waste diversion in 1989 was 12.5 percent. Most counties were able to exceed the 25 percent reduction by 1995. By January 2000 the statewide rate of diversion was 33 percent, short of the 50 percent goal but well above the 27 percent national average.[20] By 2005, however, the statewide diversion rate was 52 percent.[21] As counties have come into compliance, municipal recycling centers have increased by 155 percent. But, this may be the easy part. Reducing incoming waste remains a major challenge. Creating markets for recovered materials continues to be a major effort for the board.

Energy Policy

As in so many other areas of policy, California has emerged as a leader in energy policy responses. The state was one of the first to leave the federal model and begin developing its own path to energy sustainability. Following the electricity crisis of 2001, it became clear that energy sustainability was an area that would require state leadership. While federal models continue to focus on fossil fuel production and importation, California's experience demonstrated that while maintaining a steady flow of traditional energy resources was necessary, increasing the efficiency of our energy use and expanding our use of renewable energy resources were critical components of the state's energy and environmental demands. In 2003 California's three energy agencies—the California Energy Commission (CEC), the California Power Authority (CPA), and the California Public Utilities Commission (CPUC)—created the California Energy Action Plan (EAP), which articulated explicit energy goals with a related six-point action plan to achieve those goals.

The primary Energy Action Plan goal is to "ensure that adequate, reliable, and reasonably-priced electrical power and natural gas supplies, including prudent reserves, are achieved and provided through policies, strategies, and actions that are cost-effective and environmentally sound for California's consumers and taxpayers."[22] The plan includes six subsidiary goals:

1. Meet California's energy growth needs while optimizing energy conservation and resource efficiency and reducing per capita electricity demand.
2. Ensure reliable, affordable, and high-quality power supply for all who need it in all regions of the state by building sufficient new generation.
3. Accelerate the state's goal for renewable resource generation to 2010.
4. Upgrade and expand the electricity transmission and distribution infrastructure and reduce the time before needed facilities are brought online.
5. Promote customer- and utility-owned distributed generation.
6. Ensure a reliable supply of reasonably priced natural gas.

The related actions the agencies committed to include:

1. Optimize energy conservation and resource efficiency.
2. Accelerate the state's goal for renewable generation.
3. Ensure reliable, affordable electricity generation.

4. Upgrade and expand the electricity transmission and distribution infrastructure.
5. Promote customer- and utility-owned distributed generation.
6. Ensure reliable supply of reasonably priced natural gas.

The Energy Action Plan is designed to be the philosophical core of the state's emerging package of energy policies. These policies are further refined in the second Energy Action Plan (EAP II), released in September 2005. EAP II calls for coordinated action from all state agencies in an effort to develop a long-term solution to the state's energy needs. EAP II defines its purpose as follows:

> Our overarching goal is for California's energy to be adequate, affordable, technologically advanced, and environmentally-sound. Energy must be reliable—provided when and where needed and with minimal environmental risks and impacts. Energy must be affordable to households, businesses and industry, and motorists—and in particular to disadvantaged customers who rely on us to ensure that they can afford this fundamental commodity. Our actions must be taken with clear recognition of cost considerations and trade-offs to ensure reasonably priced energy for all Californians. We need to develop and tap advanced technologies to achieve these goals of reliability, affordability and an environmentally-sound energy future. These goals affirm the original objectives of EAP I.[23]

In order to achieve this, EAP II establishes the following nine action areas, in order of priority:

1. Increase energy efficiency in all sectors.
2. Increase efficiency in assessing and responding to variation in electricity demand.
3. Develop renewable energy resources.
4. Improve the capacity and reliability of the electricity infrastructure.
5. Promote affordable and environmentally responsible wholesale and retail electricity markets with sound market rules.
6. Reduce demand for natural gas to ensure sustainable and affordable supply.
7. Take steps to build an efficient, multi-fuel transportation market to serve the state's future transportation needs.
8. Encourage research, development, and demonstration (RD&D) projects in technologies that will allow California to achieve its policies to make energy efficiency, demand response, and renewable resources more effective and cost-competitive.
9. Clearly establish California's leadership in and commitment to the fight against climate change.

These actions frame several of Governor Schwarzenegger's executive orders and establish a blueprint for legislative action. Whether the state can achieve all of the benchmarks of EAP and EAP II is yet to be seen. However, California's energy vision is robust and likely to establish a model for other states to follow.

The Closing Circle: Nature, Man, and Technology

Barry Commoner

The environment has just been rediscovered by the people who live in it. In the United States the event was celebrated in April 1970, during Earth Week. It was a sudden, noisy awakening. School children cleaned up rubbish; college students organized huge demonstrations; determined citizens recaptured the streets from the automobile, at least for a day. Everyone seemed to be aroused to the environmental danger and eager to do something about it.

They were offered lots of advice. Almost every writer, almost every speaker, on the college campuses, in the streets and on television and radio broadcasts, was ready to fix the blame and pronounce a cure for the environmental crisis. Some regarded the environmental issue as politically innocuous:

Ecology has become the political substitute for the word "motherhood."

—Jesse Unruh, Democratic Leader of the State of California Assembly

Some blamed pollution on the rising population:

The pollution problem is a consequence of population. It did not much matter how a lonely American frontiersman disposed of his waste. . . . But as population became denser, the natural chemical and biological recycling processes became overloaded. . . . Freedom to breed will bring ruin to all.

—Garrett Hardin, Biologist

The causal chain of the deterioration [of the environment] is easily followed to its source. Too many cars, too many factories, too much detergent, too much pesticide, multiplying contrails, inadequate sewage treatment plants, too little water, too much carbon dioxide-all can be traced easily to *too many people*.

—Paul R. Ehrlich, Biologist

Some blamed affluence:

The affluent society has become an effluent society. The 6 percent of the world's population in the United States produces 70 percent or more of the world's solid wastes.

—Walter S. Howard, Biologist

Some blamed man's innate aggressiveness:

The first problem, then, is people. . . . The second problem, a most fundamental one, lies within us—our basic aggressions. . . . As Anthony Storr has said: "The sombre fact is that we're the cruelest and most ruthless species that has ever walked the earth."

—William Roth, Director, Pacific Life Assurance Company

A minister blamed profits:

Environmental rape is a fact of our national life only because it is more profitable than responsible stewardship of earth's limited resources.

—Channing E. Phillips, Congregationalist Minister

While a historian blamed religion:

Christianity bears a huge burden of guilt. . . . We shall continue to have a worsening ecologic crisis until we reject the Christian axiom that nature has no reason for existence save to serve man.
—Lynn White, Historian

A politician blamed technology:

A runaway technology, whose only law is profit, has for years poisoned our air, ravaged our soil, stripped our forests bare, and corrupted our water resources.
—Vance Hartke, Senator from Indiana

While an environmentalist blamed politicians:

There is a peculiar paralysis in our political branches of government, which are primarily responsible for legislating and executing the policies environmentalists are urging.... Industries who profit by the rape of our environment see to it that legislators friendly to their attitudes are elected, and that bureaucrats of similar attitude are appointed.
—Roderick A. Cameron, Environmental Defense Fund

And one keen observer blamed everyone:

We have met the enemy and he is us.
—Pogo

Earth Week convinced me of the urgency of a deeper public understanding of the origins of the environmental crisis. . . . [They] can be organized into a kind of informal set of "laws of ecology. . . ."

The First Law of Ecology: *Everything Is Connected to Everything Else . . .*
The Second Law of Ecology: *Everything Must Go Somewhere . . .*
The Third Law of Ecology: *Nature Knows Best . . .*
The Fourth Law of Ecology: *There is No Such Thing as a Free Lunch . . .*

Source: Barry Commoner, *The Closing Circle*. Copyright © 1971 by Barry Commoner. Reprinted by permission of Alfred A. Knopf, a division of Random House, Inc.

SUMMARY

Perhaps as a consequence of the state's poor environmental quality, California has developed innovative approaches in a variety of areas. The regional clean air and clean water plans, as well as the statewide solid waste plan, are promising innovations. Most innovative, perhaps, is the state's response to air pollution. The South Coast Air Quality Management District's plan for bringing Southern California into compliance with federal standards is widely recognized as the most aggressive approach in the nation. Unlike the federal air quality model, it institutes a stringent 20-year plan to reduce smog through a four-point plan of conservation, alternative fuels, mass transit, and a shift in residential and economic social patterns. Urbanized states across the nation are watching California's air policy approach to see whether it provides a model worth emulating. And, the state's EAP and EAP II define an aggressive approach to achieving energy sustainability.

California's environmental and energy future will depend on the success of its current generation of environmental policy responses. The degree to which California's aggressive policy approaches can withstand political opposition will determine statewide environmental quality over the next 30 years. As a community of diverse interests, the benefits of environmental improvement—and the costs of that improvement—will be experienced differentially by different sectors. This is the basis of politics, and in a state as contentious as California it would be foolhardy to predict the future direction of any policy area. California's environmental and energy future may in large measure depend on the ability of the state's environmental constituency to persuade rank and file Californians that cleaner air and water are more to their benefit than an unrestrained, market-driven economy.

NOTES

1. U.S. Environmental Protection Agency, *PM-10 Non-attainment State/Area/County Report*, http://134.67.104.12/e-drive/CAAA/TL1/bgilbert/1996.
2. Matthew Cahn, *Environmental Deceptions* (Albany: State University of New York Press, 1995).
3. Paul Cox, Martin Johnson, and Janelle Auyeung, *The California Almanac of Emissions and Air Quality, 2006 Edition* (Sacramento: California Air Resources Board, 2006).
4. California Coastal Commission, *The 2006 Updated Assessment of the California Coastal Management Program*, www.coastal.ca.gov/fedcd/ccmp2006assessment.pdf.
5. World Resources Institute, *The 1993 Information Please Environmental Almanac* (New York: Houghton Mifflin Co., 1992).
6. Cal-EPA, *Environmental Indicators Report*, www.oehha.ca.gov/multimedia/epic/index.html.
7. San Francisco Bay Regional Water Quality Control Board, www.swrcb.ca.gov/rwqcb2/.
8. Ibid.
9. San Francisco Estuary Institute, *The Regional Monitoring Program for Water Quality in the San Francisco Estuary*, 2006, www.sfei.org/rmp/2004to05/AMR_2004-2005_FullReport_f.pdf
10. San Francisco Bay Regional Water Quality Control Board, *Habitat Loss*, www.swrcb.ca.gov/rwqcb2/.
11. San Francisco Bay Regional Water Quality Control Board, *Sediment Hotspots*, www.swrcb.ca.gov/rwqcb2/.
12. Martha Krebs, *Public Interest Energy Research Program (PIER) Report* (California Energy Commission, 2006).
13. Ibid.
14. California Air Resources Board, *On Road Emission Inventory 2006*, www.arb.ca.gov/msei/onroad/onroad.htm.

15. Martha Krebs, *Public Interest Energy Research Program (PIER) Report.*
16. FERC, *Staff Report: Price Manipulation in the Western Markets* (Federal Energy Regulatory Commission, March 26, 2003).
17. South Coast Air Quality Management District, South Coast Air Quality Management Plan. (SCAQMP), 1994.
18. California State Water Resources Control Board, "On Road Emission Inventory," July 5, 1997, www.arb.ca.gov/msei/onroad/onroad.htm.
19. Ibid.
20. California Integrated Waste Management Board (IWMB), Publication #530-99-007, January 2000.
21. Integrated Waste Management Board, *California's 2005 Statewide Diversion Rate Estimate,* 2006.
22. Consumer Power and Conservation Financing Authority, Energy Resources Conservation and Development Commission, Public Utilities Commission, *Energy Action Plan* (adopted April 2003), www.cpuc.ca.gov/word_pdf/REPORT/28715.pdf.
23. California Energy Commission, Public Utilities Commission, *Energy Action Plan II: Implementation Roadmap for Energy Policies* (adopted September 2005), www.energy.ca.gov/energy_action_plan/2005-09-21_EAP2_FINAL.PDF.

CHAPTER 15

Immigration Policy

Featured Reading / Pages 197–198
George W. Bush
A Nation of Laws and of Immigrants

The New Colossus

Not like the brazen giant of Greek fame,
With conquering limbs astride from land to land;
Here at our sea-washed, sunset gates shall stand
A mighty woman with a torch, whose flame
Is the imprisoned lightning, and her name
Mother of Exiles. From her beacon-hand
Glows world-wide welcome; her mild eyes command
The air-bridged harbor that twin cities frame.
"Keep ancient lands, your storied pomp!" cries she
With silent lips. "Give me your tired, your poor,
Your huddled masses yearning to breathe free,
The wretched refuse of your teeming shore.
Send these, the homeless, tempest-tost to me,
I lift my lamp beside the golden door!"

—Emma Lazarus, engraved on the pedestal of the Statue of Liberty

More than a decade after Proposition 187 bitterly divided Californians, immigration policy[1] has emerged as an issue on the national political agenda. Thus, before we can focus on California's unique subtext of dealing with its own "immigrant experience," we should pay homage to the fact that in the end, given our constitutional design, immigration is ultimately a federal issue.

The United States admits more immigrants across its borders than any other nation—more, in fact, than all other nations combined. Immigration has always played a significant role in U.S. population growth; it is estimated that one-third of the nation's annual population increase results from immigration.[2] Immigrants and their children account for more than 60 million people, or one-fifth of all U.S. residents.

By 2050, if today's projections are borne out, one-third of all Americans will be either Asian or Latino.[3]

Advanced globalization has exacerbated the "push–pull" phenomenon as labor markets and economic conditions both in the U.S. and surrounding nations have intensified. The rapid de-ruralization in many developing countries combined with the deep thirst for low-skilled cheap labor to fill jobs in the U.S. workforce (that American natives have avoided) has preoccupied public policymakers. During economic booms, unauthorized immigration can be tolerated or even tacitly encouraged; during recessions and heightened globalization, legal and illegal immigrants alike can be blamed for national and state problems they may have contributed to only indirectly.

The forces of globalization have provided much of the "push." For example, average U.S. wages for production workers in manufacturing are about 8 times higher than in Mexico.[4] On the "pull" side, many U.S. employers are eager to hire them. The vast majority of illegal immigrants work in the "shadow employment market." One estimate is that 75 percent of adult illegal immigrants are in the workforce.[5] Research on illegal immigrants' patterns also demonstrated a family "pull" on joining relatives already in this country—as they provide shelter, support, and contentment of unification.

The other new reality affecting the debate on immigration reform is the spill-down of living in a post-9/11 era. Border vulnerabilities and international terrorism have replaced the older concerns that overly porous borders let in narco-traffickers and the criminal element with our past waves of illegal immigrants. We are in a new world of truth or fiction, where Islamic fundamentalists sneak into the United States disguised as Mexicans. Will our border fixation (southern, not northern) bring a more sane and rational reform of our immigration policy? If the history of the past 20 years in border enforcement is any indicator, it has produced no visible or tangible effect. Will expanding the Border Patrol or sending state National Guard units to patrol our borders stop real terrorists, or have we just demonized illegal immigrants fleeing economic (and in some cases political) oppression?

THE IMMIGRATION DEBATE

In his second term, President George W. Bush made immigration reform one of his highest policy priorities. However, he was working against a backdrop of fickle public attitudes and strange alliances (e.g., the Farm Bureau and the ACLU) and xenophobic elements within both political parties that converged to either kill or advance a comprehensive immigration reform package. Along with this goes the fact that the fates of 11 or 12 million illegal immigrants are being held in abeyance.

In 2006 the Senate leadership (both majority and minority members) banded together to push Bush's reform overhaul measure through various means that were to appease the various contentious interests surrounding immigration reform. The vehicle was a bipartisan bill sponsored by Republican Arlen Spector and Democrat Edward M. Kennedy that was to advance the president's agenda by creating a guest worker program, an "earned legalization program" (which some critics call an amnesty program in disguise), and a stronger work-site enforcement program; stiffening criminal penalties for those caught smuggling immigrants; and tightening border security. In May 2006 President Bush proposed a plan to place up to 6,000 National Guard troops along the border with Mexico for at least one year.[6]

As 2006 midterm elections approached and the Senate package of reform measures was making its way to the House of Representatives, serious doubts arose, mostly in the ranks of House Republican leaders. "We are going to listen to the American people, and we are going to get a bill that is right," said Speaker J. Dennis Hastert.[7] Representative Duncan Hunter, a Republican from San Diego, declared that the county was under siege and demanded federal dollars for a 15-foot-high wall to separate Mexico and the United States. Governors of Arizona and New Mexico declared states of emergency along the border, complaining that their repeated pleas for additional Border Patrol officers and federal money to defray the costs of illegal immigration in their states had been ignored by Washington.

In April of that year, immigrants and their supporters in the labor movement, civil rights organizations, and faith groups have banned together in a massive show of street protests in cities across America to express their pro-immigrant rights position. In Los Angeles, more than 500,000 immigrants and their supporters took to the streets, and some later organized a work and school boycott. Some claim that this had "awoken the sleeping giant"—galvanizing Latinos to "get political or else." A 2006 poll by the Pew Hispanic Center found that 54 percent of Latinos think the debate over immigration reform has worsened discrimination against them. Just 15 percent said the debate had no effect.[8]

IMMIGRATION IN CALIFORNIA'S HISTORY

Only recently has California emerged as the primary gateway state for new immigrants. Ever since its founding as a state in 1850, however, California has been at the center of the immigration debate and to a large degree has led the national policy discourse. Some argue that immigration is essential to the continued prosperity of California and the nation, while proponents of stricter immigration laws have long argued that the influx of new Californians takes a heavy toll on the state's resources and dilutes its culture. As early as 1870, drawn by the Gold Rush, fully 37 percent of California residents were foreign born.[9] By the turn of the century, 25 percent of all Californians were foreign born. This declined subsequently to a low point of 9 percent by 1960.[10] California has more illegal immigrants than any other state—an estimated 2.4 million. The California Department of Finance estimates that illegal immigration adds 73,000 people to the state's population each year, thereby accounting for 12 percent of the state's population growth this decade. Even so, California is not the destination state it once was. In the 1980s, almost half the nation's illegal immigrants lived in California; today only 23 percent do. The number of illegal immigrants has been increasing dramatically in some Southeastern and Midwestern states. Still, traditional destinations such as Texas (1.4 million illegal immigrants), Florida (850,000), and New York (650,000) continue to rank after California with the largest illegal immigrant populations.[11]

California followed much of the classic patterns of ethnocultural cleavages spinning out of the U.S. East and Midwest as territorial expansion took place. White Protestant nativists aligned themselves politically against the newly arrived urban immigrant class, composed of European ethnics (e.g., Irish, Polish, Italian), Catholics, and eastern European Jews. The political reaction in most of the nation's older cities was the rise of "ethnic party machines," which not only delivered the ethnic vote during local elections but guaranteed that immigrant communities would receive a proportionate amount of the spoils of the public largess—from pork-barrel projects to government jobs.

As quickly as the window opened for ethnic political empowerment and coalition building during the machine era, so too did the door slam on the expansion of political rights with tighter immigration restrictions and the launching of the "good government" reforms during the Progressive era. The wave of immigrants from non-European nations into California and the West produced an even stronger political response. These included the large numbers of Asian and Mexican immigrants arriving to build the railroads and harvest the fields. Western state legislatures passed a series of constitutionally suspect measures—ranging from restrictions on property rights to the denial of education, health, and economic protection. The western states—California in particular—called on Congress to enact strict immigration quotas for certain groups and eventual exclusion from entry into the United States. From the Workingmen's Party, formed in 1877 and organized against Chinese immigrants in San Francisco, to the later "fringe" movements such as the Asiatic Exclusion League of California, whose sole purpose was to pressure Congress to cut off Japanese immigration in the 1920s, California has been a wellspring for nativist and exclusionary movements since statehood.

The major political parties and West Coast state legislatures maintained a rigid system of exclusion and discrimination against Asian immigrants. Early Chinese and Japanese immigrants to California were politically disenfranchised and excluded from full participation in American life because of discriminatory laws and policies. As the major port of entry for these initial groups, California led the way in racially tinged discriminatory practices that were emulated by other states and even the national government. In 1854, for example, Chinese immigrants were prohibited from testifying in court against whites. In 1855, the state legislature imposed a $50 "head tax" on Chinese immigrants. San Francisco passed an ordinance that same year referred to as the "pigtail ordinance," requiring Chinese lawbreakers to cut their hair within one inch of the scalp. In 1871, a Los Angeles mob, which included many prominent citizens, tortured and lynched Chinese men. In 1879, the new California state constitution barred corporations from hiring Chinese employees and prohibited the employment of people of Chinese descent in any public works "except for punishment of a crime." This so-called Chinese exclusion provision remained in the state constitution until it was repealed in 1952. Also repealed in 1952 was a measure put into effect in 1913 by the Progressives called the Alien Land Law, which prohibited

Asians—but not Europeans—who were not citizens from owning land in California. In 1882 pressure from California was instrumental in the passage of national legislation barring Chinese from acquiring citizenship and banning the entry of Chinese workers for decades.[12]

With the federal exclusion of Chinese from entering the United States, California's agricultural interests started to recruit imported Japanese workers to its fields. In the vast Central Valley, more than 250 crops are grown, and cheap dependable labor to harvest the crops has always been a state mandate. In the end, however, the Japanese fared no better than did their Chinese predecessors, bearing the brunt of "yellow-peril" discriminatory policies that robbed the Japanese of their due process and citizenship rights. In 1906, for example, the San Francisco school board issued a mandatory order segregating Japanese school children in the system. During the same year, the state of California barred marriages between whites and "Mongolians." Just a few years later, an open political quarrel arose on the "Japanese question" between the Republican leadership of the state and Democratic President Woodrow Wilson. Wilson ultimately dispatched his secretary of state, William Jennings Bryan, to cajole California not to pass anti-Japanese immigrant legislation. While the state backed off, California later passed legislation in 1913 to bar noncitizen Japanese from owning property or leasing farmland. Things were no better on the jurisprudential level, with the U.S. Supreme Court deciding in *Ozawa v. United States* (1922) that Asian immigrants could be barred from becoming naturalized citizens.[13]

This dual pattern of economic recruitment and social demonization played out through the development of California, the West, and indeed the rest of the United States. By 1924, immigration from Japan was effectively halted and new immigrant communities were recruited to replace them, including Filipino and Mexican laborers. When the Great Depression hit California, nativist sentiments awoke once again—resulting in the deportation of hundreds of thousands of Mexican agricultural workers. This exclusionary impulse is in constant tension with the insatiable desire for cheap labor to fuel the state's economic growth. Not long after the mass deportation of Mexicans during the depression, California's agricultural sector—the state's largest and most politically powerful industry—persuaded Congress during World War II to establish the Bracero guest worker program that brought Mexican immigrants back across the border. This flip-flopping policy toward immigrants followed the nation's economic cycles of expansion and contraction, with California and the West leading the nation's immigration policy thrust.

California's phenomenal growth over the past century was a direct consequence of a constant supply of cheap immigrant labor. During the 1980s, nearly one-fourth of all immigrants to the United States settled in California, and more than half of the 3 million undocumented immigrants granted amnesty under the 1986 Immigration Reform and Control Act (IRCA) settled in California. More immigrants arrived in California in the 1980s than in the previous three decades combined. By 2000, more than 26 percent of California residents were foreign-born; a 37 percent increase from 1990. In Los Angeles County alone, estimates are that nearly 40 percent of the population is foreign born.[14] California's historic immigration patterns have created a dysfunctional political culture that continues to be unable to successfully integrate new waves of immigrants as policy stakeholders.

BACK TO THE FUTURE: PROPOSITION 187 AND BEYOND

Every now and then, an initiative comes along that galvanizes the public to such an extent that it becomes the engine that drives an entire election. Proposition 13 (property tax relief) served that function in 1978. So did . . . Proposition 140 (term limits) in 1990. This year it was Proposition 187—the initiative that denies educational, social, and medical services to those who cannot prove American citizenship.[15]

Nativist sentiments continue to rise up again and again in California to carry the immigration issue onto the national agenda. This is more than just a debate over legal status. Nation-states throughout the world are puzzling over the impacts of migration. Many nations that once welcomed immigrants freely are now ambivalent. This includes Australia, Canada, New Zealand, Germany, and the United States—to mention a few. In the case of the United States, individual states are sometimes at odds with the federal government's immigration policies. *The Field Poll* recently found that 70 percent of California voters support comprehensive reform that includes secure borders, guest workers, and legalization of undocumented immigrants. In California, Nancy H. Martis captures this tension:

As certain as the seasons, issues surrounding illegal migrants and their rights in society come around again and again. . . . In 1913, the Legislature made no apologies when it ultimately passed a law designed to prevent Asian immigrants from owning and leasing land despite its clear intention to suppress undocumented residents. The law was signed by Progressive Governor Hiram Johnson over the objection of President Woodrow Wilson.[16]

Proposition 187: A Defining Moment in Time

In 1994, Governor Pete Wilson made Proposition 187 a cornerstone of his successful reelection campaign. Proposition 187—entitled "SOS" (Save Our State) by proponents—was designed to stop "illegal aliens" from entering the state. But, like past immigration reforms, the policy goes well beyond attacking the problem of undocumented immigration. There were three major provisions to the measure. First, it would have made undocumented immigrants ineligible for public social services, public health care services (except for emergency services mandated by federal law), and public school education at the elementary, secondary, and postsecondary levels. Second, it would have required that "all persons employed in the providing of (public) services shall diligently protect public funds from misuse" by excluding anyone who has not been "verified" to be in the country legally. State and local agencies would have been required, under the measure, to report persons who are *suspected* undocumented immigrants to the California attorney general and the

Immigration and Naturalization Service and maintain records of such reports. The law stated:

> If any public entity in this state to whom a person has applied for public social services determines *or reasonably suspects*, based upon the information provided to it, that the person is an alien in the United States in violation of federal law, the following procedures shall be followed by the public entity: (1) The entity shall not provide the person with benefits or services. (2) The entity shall, in writing, notify the person of his or her apparent illegal immigration status, and that the person must either obtain legal status or leave the United States. (3) The entity shall also notify the State Director of Social Services, the Attorney General of California, and the United States Immigration and Naturalization Service of the *apparent* illegal status, and shall provide any additional information that may be requested by any other public entity. (emphasis added)[17]

Finally, Proposition 187 would have made it a felony to manufacture, distribute, sell, or use false citizenship or residency documents.

Proponents of Proposition 187 argued that the proposal would end "the illegal alien invasion" and ultimately "save our state."[18] For them, this "invasion" has cost taxpayers in excess of $5 billion a year for welfare and medical and educational benefits, which acts as "magnets" to draw undocumented immigrants to the state in the first place. Further, the federal government has been derelict in its duties to control the nation's borders, so the people of California must "send a message" to Washington. Opponents of Proposition 187 argued that while undocumented immigration may be a problem for the state, Proposition 187 is not the solution. Further, they point out that under *Plyler v. Doe* (1982), denying children of undocumented immigrants educational services is unconstitutional. Further, opponents were concerned about the ethical and practical implications of cutting medical services to this population, pointing out that untreated health problems would exacerbate existing public health concerns. But most importantly, the proposition's vague language of "reasonable suspicion" underscored the concern of many that Latinos and other ethnic minorities—immigrant or not—would become a vulnerable class of citizens.

The 1994 Vote and the Issue of Illegal Immigration

Voters in the general election of 1994 produced an electoral earthquake in the body politic, shifting control of Congress to the Republicans and throwing many incumbent Democrats from the state legislature. Clearly, voters were angry with "politics as usual" and eager to upset the status quo, much as they did two years prior, with the election of President Clinton. California's divided government between a sitting Republican governor and a Democratic controlled legislature produced little substantive policy momentum.

As late as November 1993, the California Opinion Index barely measured immigration as a voter's concern. In fact, of the 28 major issues California voters identified as a concern, immigration came in at 19. Crime, the state's economy, the spread of AIDS, and public schools all ranked above it. At the same time, Pete Wilson trailed his Democratic challenger, Kathleen Brown, by 23 percentage points. In an amazing comeback, Wilson went on to defeat Brown by close to 1.4 million votes (Wilson's 55 percent to Brown's 41 percent). Wilson's win was credited to his ability to associate his campaign with crime and anti-immigration themes—specifically through two ballot initiatives: Propositions 184 and 187. Wilson effectively controlled the campaign agenda, deflecting attention away from the state's early 1990s recessionary economy, an issue on which he ordinarily would have been extremely vulnerable.

Wilson's campaign message clearly resonated with the electorate. Stressing the themes of less government spending, law and order, lower taxes, and controlling illegal immigration appealed to groups that were overrepresented at the polls—older white voters. Teaming up with conservative Assemblyman Richard Mountjoy and Congressman Dana Rohrabacher, Wilson made Proposition 187 the foundation of his campaign. The campaign whipped up a dormant xenophobia that is never far from California's political culture. Campaign literature screamed: "Proposition 187 will ultimately end the ILLEGAL ALIEN invasion" (emphasis in the original).[19] By the end of the campaign, voters believed that the issue of illegal immigration was important. Sixty-four percent of white voters favored 187, while 73 percent of Latino voters voted against it. African-American and Asian voters were almost evenly split. Clearly, voters sought to "send a message," as Table 15.1 illustrates.

The Death of Proposition 187

In November 1995 U.S. District Judge Mariana R. Pfaelzer threw out significant portions of Proposition 187, ruling them unconstitutional and setting in motion a protracted legal battle. Judge Pfaelzer ruled that Sections 4, 5, 6, 7, and 9 of the initiative were invalid because they were preempted by federal laws. In these sections,

TABLE 15.1   REASONS GIVEN FOR SUPPORTING PROPOSITION 187

	LIKELY YES VOTERS
It will send a message to federal government to do more to protect our national borders.	90%
It will free up money for the education of the children of legal residents.	78
It will reduce the number of illegal immigrants who move here to have their children born as U.S. citizens.	76
It will send a message to federal government to pay for the costs associated with illegal immigrants.	74
It will deter illegal immigrants from coming to California in the first place.	71
It will create more job opportunities for legal residents.	69
It will help reinforce English as our common language.	62
State government will save millions of dollars that are now being spent on illegal immigrants.	61
It will make it easier to preserve the American way of life.	56

Source: *The Field Poll*, no. 1734 (October 17, 1994): 5.

Judge Pfaelzer found that the state could not bar illegal immigrants from health care and social welfare services (since most of these services were federally funded), to which they were otherwise entitled under existing federal laws. The judge also ruled that the prior precedent, *Plyler v. Doe* (1982), should be followed in application to this initiative and therefore the exclusion of children of illegal immigrants from public elementary and secondary schools under Section 7 was invalid.

At the same time Judge Pfaelzer only partially struck down Section 8 of the initiative, which would have excluded illegal immigrants from public postsecondary educational institutions. She ruled that the state does not have to provide postsecondary education to persons who are not authorized under federal law to be in the United States. However, a subsection that required admissions officials to report any illegal immigrant to authorities was ruled to be preempted by federal law. Beyond this, the judge let stand three other sections pertaining to severability and the criminal sanctions applying to the manufacture, sale, and use of false citizenship documents. On the sections ruled invalid, Pfaelzer stated that the measure's provisions "directly regulate immigration by creating a comprehensive scheme to detect and report the presence and affect the removal of illegal aliens . . ." and that "the state is powerless to enact its own scheme to regulate immigration."[20]

In short, Proposition 187 was effectively ruled unconstitutional. All that remained were two relatively minor laws that establish state criminal penalties for the manufacture and use of false documents. In July 1999, Governor Gray Davis reached an agreement with civil rights organizations and agreed to drop litigation and further appeal, effectively killing Proposition 187 for good.[21]

As California's economy has rebounded from recession, people seem less concerned about immigration—legal or otherwise. Republican presidential candidate Bob Dole counted on a tough immigration reform proposal to win the state in the 1996 election (as Pete Wilson had done so successfully two years earlier), but the issue won him little support outside the ranks of the most dedicated Republican faithful. Dole lost the California vote to Bill Clinton in an election in which just 7 percent of Californians identified illegal immigration as a major issue influencing their vote.[22] Two years later, Attorney General Dan Lungren tried the same Wilson-style campaign in his bid for governor, losing by a landslide to Democrat Gray Davis. In 2003 during the recall election of Gray Davis, the prominent Democrat seeking to succeed him, Lieutenant Governor Cruz Bustamante attacked Schwarzenegger as "anti-immigrant." Immigrant issues had become a central part of the recall campaign and played out profoundly among the state's Latino population, who amount to approximately 16 percent of the California electorate. The irony, of course, was that Bustamante, a grandson of Mexican immigrants, and Schwarzenegger, who came to the United States as a legal immigrant from Austria during the 1960s, both claimed the mantle of compassion for the immigrant population in California. The differences played out in their policy positions. Schwarzenegger admitted voting for Proposition 187 (which he later said was a mistake), and Pete Wilson (the champion of Proposition 187) served as co-chair of Schwarzenegger's election campaign. Schwarzenegger was also criticized about his membership on the advisory board of

U.S. English, a group that supports making English the country's official language. Despite the attacks by his Republican and Democrat rivals, Schwarzenegger went on to win the special recall election, with over 30 percent of the Latino vote.

In the early part of his first term, there was a good bet going that the moderate GOP governor who saw his state as a "purple" one (not conservative "red" or liberal "blue") would be able to deliver more federal dollars to help California address the additional costs and burdens that illegal immigration was associated with. Schwarzenegger did spend a lot of personal face time lobbying his Washington GOP colleagues, delivering a few extra concessions from the feds (mostly to address the costs of capturing and housing the criminal immigrant element and a good chunk of anti-terrorism dollars, which aided in stronger border control).

Besides the mantra of "blame Washington" when it comes to responding to illegal immigration, Schwarzenegger's early administration also used the tactic of "wait for Washington" to deflect many hot-button policy issues. For example, Senator Gil Cedillo, a Los Angeles Democrat, has pushed numerous times to have the state issue driver's licenses to the estimated 2 million illegal immigrants who commute to work, take their kids to school, and go to the doctor. Opponents claim that issuing licenses would help terrorists open bank accounts and board planes. They also say that those here illegally should not be rewarded with driving privileges. Governor Schwarzenegger has vetoed this legislation passed by both Democratic-controlled state houses. The governor sidestepped one of the most contentious immigration issues, saying he wanted to defer future talks on driver's licenses for illegal immigrants until federal officials develop national standards to overhaul the entire intelligence network. The governor cited language in the intelligence bill that directs the federal Departments of Transportation and Homeland Security to develop national standards for driver's licenses. Interestingly, as California now waits for Washington to act, other states such as Tennessee have moved ahead in issuing licenses that are not valid other than for driving-related purposes.

Schwarzenegger took some heat from his conservative GOP base for his bold pronouncements that he wanted to put immigrants on a path toward citizenship. He sought middle ground in the immigration debate and focused on national policy. The answer, Schwarzenegger said, is to secure the borders and create a guest worker program, but insisted that "amnesty is not the answer . . . but it is not realistic either to round up 12 million people and send them home."[23]

The price Republicans paid for Wilson's initiatives is now political legend. Proposition 187 spurred such a backlash against the GOP that, in California, it has been reduced to minority party status—Arnold Schwarzenegger's first term election notwithstanding. Schwarzenegger has avoided the mistakes of the past and will not be another Pete Wilson—even as he takes the slings-and-arrows of his fellow party loyalists. The governor wants to elevate what has become a nasty public debate and see it conducted "in a civil way without prejudice and without hatred." Schwarzenegger said to the editorial board of the *San Diego Union-Tribune* that Californians are "making a big mistake" if they focus their anger on "Mexico or Mexicans or Latinos or whoever is coming through the south."[24]

Schwarzenegger joined President George W. Bush's call for comprehensive immigration reform. Yet the governor diverged from Bush's plan in what was to be a collective national response to deploy National Guard troops to guard the 2,000-mile southern border. As commander-in-chief over the California National Guard, Schwarzenegger will not send state National Guard troops to other states, especially since they are often used for fighting national disasters such as fires and therefore would be stretched pretty thin. The governor has asked the federal government to pay all costs of the mission and made it clear that troops are deployed on a strictly temporary basis. Troops returning from Iraq and Afghanistan are excluded from border duty.

Nationally, in the November 2006 election, power shifted when the Democrats took control of both the House and the Senate. What was left as unfinished business was a comprehensive immigration reform initiative. Under the Republican control Congress, the House passed a bill that would tighten border security and crack down on illegal workers. The Senate supported legislation that would establish a guest worker program and allow illegal immigrants already in the country to work towards citizenship. Unable to compromise on a comprehensive measure, the House put forth a bill to require photo identification to vote and to deport illegal workers. The Senate left hanging a bill approved by the House that proposed a 700-mile fence along the Mexican border.

The entire issue of a comprehensive national immigration measure is now up for grabs yet again. In the transition period between congressional sessions, there were attempts to fashion a bipartisan consensus towards a measure that would include tighter border security and a guest worker program. Senator Edward Kennedy (the new Democratic chair from Massachusetts of the Senate Immigration, Border Security and Citizenship subcommittee), Senator John McCain (R–Arizona), and Representatives Jeff Flake (R–Arizona) and Luis V. Gutierrez (D–Illinois) were pushing for a bipartisan compromise during the final months of the Bush administration. At the same time, many House Democrats were newly elected moderates who campaigned against legalizing illegal immigration. In the 2008 election, Republicans tried in vain to woo back Latino voters who supported them at a rate of just 29 percent in 2006 (compared to 44 percent in the 2004 elections).

It was a Pyrrhic victory under the new Democratically controlled 110th Congress. A comprehensive immigration reform measure was brought back from the dead. The measure included border security provisions that would have added thousands of new border agents, along with high-tech security devices such as cameras and radar. It would have created a work-site system to verify that all workers have legal status. Republicans pushed to add $4.4 billion in funding to accomplish these goals. The measured was two-tiered stepped, in that once the borders were more secure, a temporary worker program would have brought in 200,000 workers a year, under a new "Z visa" that would have given preference for eligible illegal immigrants whose skills and education would benefit America's development. The fate of 12 million undocumented immigrants was also addressed; however, neither party would call this a "blanket amnesty program."

In the end, the bill could not overcome the fatal objections of the left or the right. The bill failed on a procedural vote to close debate and move the measure forward: 46–53, 14 votes short of the 60 needed. Many of the 15 Democrats who voted to block the bill saw it as needlessly punitive, while many of the 37 Republicans who opposed the bill complained that it was not strict enough.

With no national immigration reform and the general consensus that the status quo is unacceptable, cities and states will feel the pressure to take some "patchwork" measures to address the immigration debate. Given this new reality, the Schwarzenegger stalling tactic of "wait for Washington" will no longer carry the day. Parts of the comprehensive packages failed that have particular relevance to California—such as the agricultural jobs initiative, a special program for farm workers, and the Dream Act, which would give illegal migrant children a way to earn citizenship if they are in school or the military—may have a chance to be reintroduced as stand-alone legislation. Still, the main action has devolved unfortunately (or fortunately) to the other jurisdictional "laboratories of democracy" to try their skills at solving some part of this constitutional hot potato.

If politicians were to step outside the closed framework of addressing anxieties and look deeper into more cogent policy solutions, perhaps Californians could set the national model for others to emulate. One path has already been advanced by the state of California's bipartisan Little Hoover Commission, which has advanced a residency program that would reward *behavior* of immigrants and encourage them to become responsible members of the political community. The program would offer access to driver's licenses, in-state tuition, health care, job training, and housing to immigrants who stay out of the criminal justice system, pay taxes, learn English, make sure their children attend school regularly, participate in local civic efforts, and demonstrate willingness to become citizens.[25]

A Nation of Laws and of Immigrants   *George W. Bush*

I've asked for a few minutes of your time to discuss a matter of national importance: the reform of America's immigration system.

The issue of immigration stirs intense emotions and in recent weeks, Americans have seen those emotions on display. On the streets of major cities, crowds have rallied in support of those in our country illegally. At our southern border, others have organized to stop illegal immigrants from coming in. Across the country, Americans are trying to reconcile these contrasting images. And in Washington, the debate over immigration reform has reached a time of decision. Tonight, I will make it clear where I stand and where I want to lead our country on this vital issue.

We must begin by recognizing the problems with our immigration system. For decades, the United States has not been in complete control of its borders. As a result, many who want to work in our economy have been able to sneak across our border, and millions have stayed.

Once here, illegal immigrants live in the shadows of our society. Many use forged documents to get jobs, and that makes it difficult for employers to verify that the workers they hire are legal. Illegal immigration puts pressure on public schools and hospitals, it strains state and local budgets and brings crime to our communities. These are real problems, yet we must remember that the vast majority of illegal immigrants are decent people who work hard, support their families, practice their faith and lead respectable lives. They are part of American life, but they are beyond the reach and protection of American law.

We're a nation of laws, and we must enforce our laws. We're also a nation of immigrants, and we must uphold that tradition, which has strengthened our country in so many ways. These are not contradictory goals. America can be a lawful society and a welcoming society at the same time. We will fix the problems created by illegal immigration, and we will deliver a system that is secure, orderly and fair.

Editor's note: This is an excerpt from a transcript of President Bush's speech on immigration, as recorded by the *New York Times*.

Source: *New York Times* (May 16, 2006): A22.

SUMMARY

Because of the disproportionate impact of immigration on the Golden State, the nation's immigration policies have been especially important in California. California has been a destination of choice for immigrants from around the globe as well as for migrants from other states. The state's opportunities, resources, and promise of a better life have guaranteed that people will continue arriving here, even during times when shifting political attitudes create a chilly climate for immigrants. Since its statehood, California's immigration policy has swung between extremes, reflecting dual realities: Immigrants are essential components of the state's economic growth, and California's political culture has long demonized newcomers. "Welcome to California— Now Go Home!"[26] California remains an ideal, to be pursued by people seeking a better life—whether native born or foreign born. This is unlikely to change anytime soon.

NOTES

1. Portions of this chapter on immigration policy have been printed in Michael Preston, Bruce Cain, and Sandra Bass, eds., *Racial and Ethnic Politics in California* (Berkeley: Institute for Intergovernmental Studies, 1997).
2. William O'Hare, "America's Minorities: The Demographics of Diversity," *Population Bulletin* 47, no. 4 (Washington, DC: Population Reference Bureau, 1992).
3. Tamar Jacoby, ed., *Reinventing the Melting Pot* (New York: Basic Books, 2004), p. 6.
4. Based on Bureau of Labor Statistics, *International Comparisons of Hourly Compensation Costs for Production Workers in Manufacturing, Supplementary Tables* (Washington DC: Bureau of Labor Statistics, 2007), www.bls.gov/news.release/ichcc.t02.htm.

5. Lindsay B. Lowell and Richard Fry, *Estimating the Distribution of Undocumented Workers in the Urban Labor Force: Technical Memorandum* (Washington, DC: The Pew Hispanic Center, 2004).

6. Jim Rutenberg, "President Calls for Compromise on Immigration," *New York Times* (May 16, 2006): A1.

7. Carl Hulse, "House Plans National Hearings Before Charges to Immigration," *New York Times* (June 21, 2006): A1.

8. Roberto Suro and Gabriel Escobar, "2006 National Survey of Latinos: The Immigration Debate." Washington, DC: Pew Hispanic Center, www.pewhispanic.org/files/reports/68.pdf

9. Doris Marion Wright, "The Making of Cosmopolitan California: An Analysis of Immigration, 1848–1870," *California Historical Society Quarterly* XIX (December 1940): 332.

10. Dowell Myers, *The Changing Immigrants of Southern California*, Research Report LCRI-95-94R (Los Angeles: University of Southern California, School of Urban and Regional Planning, October 25, 1995), p. 1.

11. Hans P. Johnson, "Illegal Migration," in *At Issue* (San Francisco: Public Policy Institute of California, April 2006), p. 2.

12. Morton Grodzins, *Americans Betrayed* (Chicago: University of Chicago Press, 1949), and Roger Daniels, *The Politics of Prejudice* (New York: Atheneum, 1968).

13. Yuji Ichioka, "Early Japanese Quest for Citizenship: The Background of the 1922 Ozawa Case," *Amerasia Journal* 4 (1977): 1–22.

14. Nolan Marone, Kaari Baluja, Joseph Costanzo and Cynthia Davis, "Foreign-Born Population: 2000," (Washington, DC: US Census Bureau, 2003), www.census.gov/prod/2003pubs/c2kbr-34.pdf.

15. Nancy Martis and A. G. Black, "Proposition 187," *California Journal* (December 1994): 20.

16. Ibid., p. 9.

17. Ballot text of California's Proposition 187 (1994).

18. "Argument in Favor of Proposition 187," *California 1994 Voter's Guide.*

19. Ibid.

20. Paul Feldman, "Major Portions of Proposition 187 Thrown Out by Federal Judge," *Los Angeles Times* (November 21, 1995): A1.

21. Patrick J. McDonnell, "Davis Won't Appeal Prop. 187 Ruling, Ending Court Battles; Litigation," *Los Angeles Times* (July 29, 1999): A1.

22. Maria La Ganga and Dave Lesher, "Dole to Push Tough Stand in California Swing," *Los Angeles Times* (October 26, 1996): A1.

23. Governor Arnold Schwarzenegger, "Keep the Immigration Debate Civil," *Los Angeles Times* (September 12, 2006): A15.

24. Ruben Navarrette, Jr., "Prejudice in the Immigration Debate," *San Diego Union-Tribune* (August 2, 2006): B7.

25. This case is strongly made by Peter Skerry. See his opinion editorial "How to Grab Back Control on Illegal Immigration," *Los Angeles Times* (August 20, 2006): M1.

26. Bumper sticker popular during the summer of 1984, when Los Angeles hosted the Summer Olympics.

There were small acts of cruelty to go with the larger violations of constitutional rights. Norman Mineta, later a congressman from California, was just ten years old when his family was loaded onto a train in the San Jose freight yards. He was wearing his Cub Scout uniform and carrying his baseball bat and glove, the American-born son of a prominent Japanese businessman who had lived in the area for forty years. Several of young Norman's schoolmates came to the tracks to say good-bye, just in time to see the armed guards confiscate his baseball bat because, they said, it could be used as a weapon. It was a world turned upside down for these law-abiding, productive, and respectable families.

Tom Brokaw, from *Shame*

The history of United States is a history of the American people's constant battle for the sacred rights of life and liberty. "All men are created equal" signified the ideal status of all humans. Yet, for almost 90 years after the Declaration of Independence was signed, slavery remained legal; it ended with the passage of the Thirteenth Amendment in 1865. Over the next 100 years, U.S. society expanded, with sustained economic growth, along with deepening discrimination toward blacks, especially in the South. The Civil Rights Act of 1964 guaranteed the individual right of every U.S. citizen to vote, and it banned discrimination in public facilities, in government, in education, and in employment based on race, color, religion, gender, or national origin. The passage of this federal law was a result of the 1960s nonviolent protests led by Martin Luther King, Jr., which were originally conceived to protect the rights of black men; the Civil Rights Act was broader, protecting the civil rights of everyone, including women (for the first time). Later, the protection was extended to disabled persons (via the Americans with Disabilities Act, 1990) and to a more limited degree to people with a different sexual orientation.[1]

Because California was not admitted to the Union until 1850, California avoided many of the controversies over slavery and civil rights that had troubled the rest of the nation. Its acceptance into the Union as a free state meant that it would never experience the institutional dehumanization of a slave society. California's role in the Civil War was as banker for the Union, providing rich gold reserves but avoiding the bloody human cost. By 1876, just a few years before California drafted its second constitution, the U.S. Constitution had been permanently altered by the addition of the Thirteenth, Fourteenth, and Fifteenth Amendments. Equal protections were thus handed to California as a fundamental legal principle.[2]

Still, life was not easy for people of color in the latter part of the 1800s. In the areas of suffrage, education, and the right to provide testimony in court, equality was delayed for many of the state's minority communities.[3] From the passage of its first public school laws in 1851, California exhibited an unwillingness to provide schools that would "mix the races." By 1870 California segregated white students from black, Indian, Chinese, and Latino students. While minorities had the right to vote after 1870, the state legislature did not formally ratify the Fifteenth Amendment until 1962, almost a century after it became part of the U.S. Constitution. Legislative roadblocks were established to prohibit blacks, Native Americans, and Chinese residents from testifying in court. Public law required the following:

> No black or mulatto person or Indian shall be permitted to give evidence in favor or against any white person. Every person who shall have one-eighth part or more Negro blood shall be deemed a mulatto, and every person who shall have one-half Indian blood shall be deemed an Indian.[4]

These impediments demonstrate how the drama of differentness played out early in California's development and how concomitant political power was distributed or denied.

CIVIL RIGHTS POLICY IN CALIFORNIA

The fight for civil rights in California is not merely pro forma. Though avoiding the Jim Crow past of many states, California's racial demons are just as real.[5] An early example of legal discrimination toward certain nationalities is the 1882 Chinese Exclusion Act,[6] which was in effect for more than 60 years, barring Chinese people from coming to or returning to California. This discrimination was repealed by the passage in 1943 of the Chinese Exclusion Repeal Act.[7] However, the most dramatic, perhaps, was the internment of Japanese Americans during World War II. Roosevelt's Executive Order #9066 (1942) authorized the secretary of war to exclude "all persons of Japanese ancestry, both alien and non-alien" from the Pacific Coast area on a plea of military necessity. Though not a state law, the exclusion order resulted in curfews, detention, and ultimately relocation of Japanese Americans and Japanese residents throughout California and Hawaii. It is widely recognized that the military justification was suspect and that local interest groups fought hard to remove the Japanese for nonmilitary reasons. Supreme Court Justice Murphy argued as follows:

> This exclusion of "all persons of Japanese ancestry, both alien and non-alien," from the Pacific Coast area on a plea of military necessity in the absence of martial law ought not to be approved. Such exclusion goes over "the very brink of constitutional power" and falls into the ugly abyss of racism.[8]

Mr. Austin E. Anson, managing secretary of the Salinas Vegetable Grower-Shipper Association, stated the following in the *Saturday Evening Post*:

> We're charged with wanting to get rid of the Japs for selfish reasons. . . . We do. It's a question of whether the white man lives on the Pacific Coast or the brown men. They came into this valley to work, and they stayed to take over. . . . They undersell the white man in the markets. . . . They work their women and children while the white farmer has to pay wages for his help. If all the Japs were removed tomorrow, we'd never miss them in two weeks, because the white farmers can take over and produce everything the Jap grows. And we don't want them back when the war ends, either.[9]

It was not until the 1960s that California embarked on an explicit path to remedy discrimination. With the passage of the federal Civil Rights Act in 1964 and the Voting Rights Act of 1965, the state responded with its own anti-discriminatory legislation. Under the Unruh Civil Rights Act, the state reaffirmed federal civil rights mandates. The act prohibited discrimination in public accommodations on the grounds of race, color, religion, gender, or national origin; sexual orientation was added in the 1990s. It further prohibited discrimination in employment hiring and firing, and it prohibited discrimination in the sale or rental of housing. *De jure* ("under the law") legal guarantees tell only part of the story, however. *De facto* ("in fact") bigotry and discrimination on the community level is just as important. Despite the significance of *Brown v. Board of Education of Topeka* (1954), *Green v. School Board of New Kent County* (1968), and *Swann v. Charlotte-Mechlenburg Board of Education* (1971), California's public schools remained largely segregated well into the 1970s. Eventually they saw court-ordered integration through a program of mandatory busing.

Busing created a backlash that continues today. Anti-busing leaders in California argued that busing conflicted with neighborhood rights and that integrating less-prepared "inner city" students into high-performing suburban campuses would "dumb down" educational standards. Bobbi Fiedler, an anti-busing activist from L.A.'s San Fernando Valley, used the issue as a launching pad to win a congressional seat. Anti-busing sentiment had a profound impact on California communities across city–suburban–rural lines. White families started leaving the integrated school districts in droves to avoid forced busing—establishing "white flight" as the *de facto* response to *de jure* protections.

The battles over urban secession, school standards, and district control that are common today are a direct outgrowth of the busing controversy. What we are left with is a profound reflection about government's inability to sustain civil and human rights legislation in the face of a hostile and vocal minority. Subsequent federal supreme courts have retreated from pressing full integration and equality of education in the face of hostile and vocal minorities. School desegregation remained a back-burner issue in the 1980s and 1990s, not only within the courts but also in Congress and in the state legislatures. By the time the twenty-first century rolled in, the issue of "inferior" versus "superior" school districts (based largely on racial and economic status) had replaced the busing controversy of past decades. This was clearly amplified in 2006, when Los Angeles Mayor Antonio Villaraigosa decided to go to the state legislature to seize control of the Los Angeles Unified School District, due to these schools' historic underperformance.

Ending Discrimination Through Affirmative Action

The phrase *affirmative action* was first used by President Lyndon Johnson. Johnson argued that discrimination was sufficiently ingrained in U.S. culture that taking affirmative (rather than passive) action was necessary. His 1965 Executive Order 11246 required federal contractors to take affirmative action to ensure that applicants are employed and employees are treated during employment without regard to their race, creed, color, or national origin.

In 1967, Johnson expanded the executive order to include women. Affirmative action has come to refer to specific programs designed to expand access to education and the workplace to members of historically underrepresented groups. The National Organization for Women says that "affirmative action levels the playing field so people of color and all women have the chance to compete in education and in business."[10] Affirmative action programs have sought to expand the number of applicants from underrepresented groups and have given preference to members of specified communities in an effort to increase the numbers of women, African Americans, Latinos, and Asians in competitive educational and professional environments. Thus, if equality under the law sags under the weight of *de facto* discrimination, proponents argue "affirmative action is the bridge between changing the laws and changing the culture."[11] Since the late 1960s, affirmative action has taken many forms and has proven quite controversial.

The Bakke Case

Affirmative action was first challenged in the *Bakke* (1978) case. Allan Bakke, a white man, was rejected from UC Davis Medical School, although his grades and test scores were higher than those of students accepted to the 16 slots reserved for underrepresented applicants. (UC Davis had a special-admissions program that held aside 16 of the 100 medical school slots for members of underrepresented communities.) Bakke filed suit in state court, claiming he was a victim of racial discrimination. The California supreme court upheld Bakke's legal challenge, and the state—on behalf of the University of California—appealed the case to the U.S. Supreme Court. In *Regents of the University of California v. Bakke* (1978),[12] the Court ruled 5–4 that while racial preference can be used as a factor, a specific quota like the 16 percent quota used at UC Davis was unconstitutional and that Bakke should be admitted. Four justices supported the constitutionality of racial quotas (or *set-asides*) as a remedy for historical discrimination under the Civil Rights Act of 1964. Four justices opposed the quota system under their reading of the Fourteenth Amendment. Justice Lewis F. Powell, Jr., cast the swing vote. The final legal result was that while Bakke was admitted as an individual, the system of admissions used at UC Davis Medical School was declared constitutionally flawed. The *Bakke* decision was extremely important in determining that race and other factors could be used to allow a "preferential admission" program to ensure a diverse student body. A more refined affirmative action program would therefore be constitutionally maintained, not only in California's higher educational system but throughout the rest of the nation.

By the late 1980s several court cases undercut *Bakke*, giving greater standing to claims of reverse discrimination, invalidating minority set-asides in cases where past discrimination against minorities was unproven, and limiting the use of statistics to demonstrate past discrimination, since statistics are aggregate and cannot legally prove intent.[13] While the Civil Rights Act of 1991 confirmed many of the principles of affirmative action as an important remedy to discrimination, the future of affirmative action is in jeopardy.

Twenty-five years after *Bakke*, in June 2003, affirmative action was tested again in the Supreme Court. A white Michigan resident, Barbara Grutter, applied to the University of Michigan Law School and was ultimately denied admission. In December 1997, she filed suit, alleging that the university had discriminated against her on the base of race, in violation of the Equal Protection Clause of the Fourteenth Amendment to the U.S. Constitution and Title VI of the 1964 Civil Rights Act. In March 2001, Grutter prevailed in U.S. District Court in Detroit. Judge Bernard Friedman concluded that use of race in admission decisions is unconstitutional.[14] In 2002, the Sixth Circuit Court of Appeals reversed the District Court's decision.[15] In June 2003, the case was appealed to the Supreme Court. Justice O'Connor delivered the 5–4 opinion that the U.S. Constitution doesn't prohibit a university's "narrowly tailored use" of race in admission decisions and cited Grutter's claim, based on Title VI of 1964 Civil Rights Act, as invalid. The Supreme Court affirmed the judgment of the Court of Appeals.[16]

The *Grutter* decision further split the nation over affirmative action. For Republicans, the key point was that the Supreme Court's decision struck down a rigid quota system in university admissions, but for the Democrats, the victory was that race could be used as a factor in making admission decisions.[17] At best, this was a Solomonic decision.

Proposition 209: The California Civil Rights Initiative (CCRI)

In the midst of the rancor over California's role in the 1996 presidential elections, opponents of affirmative action turned in some 1.1 million signatures on a ballot proposition to prevent race, ethnicity, or sex from being used as the basis for "discriminating against, or granting preferential treatment to, any individual or group."[18]

Proposition 209 sought to dismantle the state's longstanding commitment to affirmative action. The proposition stated:

> The state shall not discriminate against, or grant preferential treatment to, any individual or group on the basis of race, sex, color, ethnicity, or national origin in the operation of public employment, public education, or public contracting.[19]

Critics argued that Proposition 209 was disingenuous, saying that discrimination was already banned by federal civil rights laws and pointing out that the third clause of the initiative presented an explicit attack on the protections against sexual discrimination ensured by Title X of the Civil Rights Act. The third clause of Proposition 209 declared:

> Nothing in this section shall be interpreted as prohibiting bona fide qualifications based on sex which are reasonably necessary to the normal operation of public employment, public education, or public contracting.[20]

What "bona fide qualifications" are "reasonably necessary" was not defined. Because public safety agencies (e.g., police, fire departments) have traditionally used this line of argument to exclude women, this language elicited protest.

This initiative and later public policies continued to stir controversy even at the dawn of the twenty-first century because they target equity programs that are largely responsible for giving traditionally underrepresented communities (e.g., women, blacks, Latinos, Asians) greater access to education, business, and professions. Advocates of Proposition 209 argued that affirmative action programs had served their purpose but that they are no longer appropriate. Opponents—mainly Democrats—saw the initiative as a "wedge issue," just as Proposition 187 (the anti-immigration initiative) had been. California had been critical in Clinton's election victory in 1992, and this issue threatened to divide the state electorate, which was leaning toward Clinton once again in 1996.

FROM PROPOSITION 209 TO THE PRESENT

As California goes, so goes the nation. Two years after Proposition 209 was ratified in California, Washington became the second state to abolish affirmative action when voters approved Initiative 200. After the vote, UC Regent Ward Connerly—who help finance and campaign for the Washington initiative—announced that the initiative process provided the best vehicle to further the anti-affirmative action movement. Later, Connerly would back similar initiatives in other states.[21] However, a nationwide grassroots movement to roll back affirmative action is still far from certain. Voters in Houston, Texas, rejected a citywide initiative to ban affirmative action, and activists in Florida failed to gather enough signatures to place a version of Proposition 209 on that state's ballot (although in 2000, Florida changed its college admissions programs such that it essentially eliminated affirmative action). In January 2006 language banning racial preferences in public education and hiring for the so-called Michigan Civil Rights Initiative (MCRI) was approved for the vote that year. Michigan voters approved Proposition 2 by a margin of 58 percent to 42 percent.

Although Proposition 209 became California state law, the battle over affirmative action programs in the state is far from over. In 1998 San Francisco's Board of Supervisors balked at CCRI, voting to extend—and even expand—the city's affirmative action program. In a plan backed by Mayor Willie Brown, San Francisco upheld its Business Enterprise program, giving preferences to minority- and women-owned businesses—as well as local businesses—in the awarding of city contracts. Even under this 10-year-old program, 89 percent of construction dollars went to firms owned by white men. Supervisor Amos Brown, who sponsored the plan, remarked, "It's not about giving anyone anything they don't deserve in a just society. This legislation is about inclusion."[22] Charging that the San Francisco program contradicts the will of the majority of the state's voters, Ward Connerly vowed a legal challenge.

At the University of California, where the rollback of affirmative action began, policy was in constant flux. The Board of Regents would eventually move to modify UC admission requirements to circumvent Proposition 209, even though they could not overturn its restrictions.[23] The declining minority enrollments at UC Berkeley tell the story. Just two years after Proposition 209 was passed, only 3.5 percent of incoming freshmen were African American and 7.5 percent were Latino. These figures were approximately half of what they were the previous year.[24]

Our discussion and analysis of the fate of affirmative action in California and beyond leaves us with two major questions: Should any subset of Americans receive preference in education, jobs, or government contracts because of skin color or gender? Alternatively, have affirmative action programs, which began in the 1960s to help blacks, Latinos, and Native Americans overcome generations of discrimination, succeeded in eliminating their disadvantages in gaining access to education and the upper ranks of the workforce? Some say that affirmative action is a compromise—giving up on colorblindness in order to obtain integration. Are colorblindness and integration two values in conflict with each other? According to Jeffrey Lehman, former dean of the University of Michigan Law School:

> Unfortunately, those values are in conflict. The admissions pool at the most selective universities reflect the cumulative effect of history, sociology and economics, public investments and private choices. Because those variables are not race-independent, a colorblind admissions process is unlikely to produce meaningful racial integration.[25]

Today, in reflecting on the passage of Proposition 209, the diversity question within higher education and other public sector programs continues to play out. California has always been (rightly or wrongly) viewed as the harbinger of a multicultural/multiethnic/multilingual future in America. Can the state achieve real racial integration in its elite-training career institutions *and* maintain a colorblind admissions policy that is not race dependent?

A decade after the passage of Proposition 209, the numbers speak for themselves: census data from 2000 confirm that the United States is 14 percent Latino and

13 percent African American. California is 35 percent Latino and 7 percent African American. Since the passage of the proposition, entering classes at the two flagship UC campuses, Berkeley and UCLA, have put admissions of Latinos between 11 percent to 14 percent and of African Americans between 2 percent and 4 percent. Out of the 4,422 students in UCLA's freshman class of 2006, 100 were black.[26] In September 2006 UCLA announced that it would shift immediately to a "holistic" admissions process in which student's academic records will be viewed in light of their personal experiences and challenges (and presumably within the spirit and law imposed by Proposition 209).[27] UC Berkeley adopted holistic review several years ago and has since seen its number of underrepresented minority students rise. Ironically, more than half of UCLA's student population are minority students—with Asian American students representing a larger percentage of the UCLA population than they do overall in the state's demographics.

Is it time for a new ballot initiative that would amend Proposition 209 to authorize the kind of conservative affirmative action that has become the national norm? Affirmative action may not be the perfect fix to California's long history of unequal access, but without an alternative, California's underrepresented minority populations are likely to lose even more ground.

BEYOND RACE: THE QUEST FOR GENDER AND SEXUAL ORIENTATION PARITY IN CALIFORNIA

"Identity politics" became a politically correct buzz phrase in the 1990s, a decade epitomized by escalating tensions in California between majority and minority groups. Identity politics has generally been described as the tendency for each minority group to define issues solely or primarily in terms of their own group interests, values and priorities.[28] The terminology of identity politics was long used to analyze the politicization of racial and ethnic groups. By the late 1970s however, especially in California (as a major national trendsetter), women and the gay, lesbian, bisexual, and transgender (GLBT) communities adopted their own version of identity politics in the quest for fuller civil right inclusion.

Women and Equal Rights in California

California women (under Hiram Johnson's administration in 1911) were given the right to vote—nine years before the United States adopted the Nineteenth Amendment. Yet they have long been denied equal rights and political power. Male-dominated institutions have long placed a gender-based "glass ceiling" on the recruitment and advancement of women. In the past, women were confined to household chores and child care and, later, as they entered the labor market post-World War II, they were relegated to "women's work" (e.g., as flight attendants, nurses, teachers).

Ironically, women have been the majority of the population of the state even since the mid-1950s. What they have lacked is political strength and a feminist consciousness. There have been women serving in elected positions in the California state assembly since 1918. It was not until 1976, however, that the state senate had its first woman senator. Rose Ann Vuich was a second-generation Serbian American from the farm town of Dinuba, located on the outskirts of Fresno, California. According to Terry McHale:

> Her political career was launched in 1976 when she was chosen to replace the presumed Democratic candidate, who had withdrawn from the race.
>   It was assumed that her Republican opponent, an Assemblyman, was unbeatable. The Democratic Caucus viewed Vuich as sincere, but naïve. They thought her inde-fatigability and grassroots understanding of the district was more old-fashioned than practical and remained unconvinced that she could compete with her opponent's con-nections and political wiles. As a result, Vuich had little money for her campaign. However, she had enough for a thirty-second television piece mocking her opponent for voting to fund Southern California freeways while failing to appropriate money for Highway 41 in their own district. She blamed him publicly for the "freeway to nowhere." The criticism caught fire and the "Freeway Lady" won the race.
>   As the state's first female Senator, Rose Ann Vuich made a habit ringing a bell several times a day when colleagues addressed the collective members of the Senate as "Gentlemen," failing to note that the chamber was no longer an exclu-sively male domain. And it was Vuich's election, not the Capitol's extensive retro-fit in the 1970s, that made necessary the conversion of a closet into a women's bathroom. The bathroom, located behind the Senate floor, is still referred to as "The Rose Room." Vuich was not a commanding speaker, yet she had a piercing intelligence and could handle the spotlight when necessary. On the issues, she was key vote against a costly Los Angeles prison and said no to the confirmation of Dan Lungren (future attorney general and Republican nominee for governor) for state treasurer. The latter drew the wrath of statewide politicians who vainly sought a strong candidate to oppose her.
>   Vuich, who reflected the conservative make up of her district, was re-elected three times. A strong advocate for agriculture, she made a habit of bringing fresh produce to the Senate and withholding it from hungry colleagues until she explained how beneficial the agricultural industry was to the overall health of our state.
>   After sixteen years in Senate, a time when she proved that graciousness was not a sign of weakness and that being a woman was not a barrier to providing daring lead-ership, she retired in 1992. The election of Rose Ann Vuich, the farm kid from the Central Valley, marked the beginning of positive change when subsequent women legislators joined her in shaping the past quarter century. She will forever remain a symbol of great leadership to all women.[29]

The first woman in California to hold statewide office was Ivy Baker Priest, who was elected state treasurer in 1966 and held the office for two terms. In 1974 the City of San Jose elected the state's first woman mayor.

As they have elsewhere, women have had a difficult time gaining access to polit-ical power in California. They were long underrepresented in those main funneling careers that legislators usually pursue. They lacked financial resources and the elec-toral tools that normally propel qualified, ambitious candidates into office. With the passage of term limits set forth by Proposition 140, there was supposed to be a more equal playing field for "new blood" to compete in competitive districts. The record has been a mixed bag: There are certainly more women and underrepresented minorities now in the legislature. The evidence, however, is still murky as to whether the quicker cycling of new members via term limits has produced better representation or—equally critical—better public policies.

The California Legislative Women's Caucus was formed in 1985 by nine Democrats and six Republicans. Its purpose is to "encourage collegiality, participation in cooperation among elected women in California government and to promote the interests of women, children and families through legislation."[30]

Advances in gender equality have been made in California over the past three decades. One can even attribute the feminization of human services as a by-product of the women's movement benefiting *all* Californians—including families and children.

What does a "women's legislative agenda" look like today? Essentially, we can divide this into four major categories:

1. **Family**—Issues pertaining to children, foster care, adoption, child care, and custody.
2. **Work**—Issues related to pay equity, fair treatment in the workplace, sexual harassment, and family leave from work (see example below).
3. **Health**—Issues related to female-specific cancer, sexual education, contraception (e.g., morning after pill), stem cell research, and reproductive rights (see example below).
4. **Safety**—Issues pertaining to domestic violence, rape/sexual assault, prison treatment, and prostitution.

Two examples show the influence the women's movement has had on the contemporary California political landscape.

FAMILY LEAVE. On July 1, 2005, a groundbreaking new paid-leave law went into effect in California, making it easier for employees to spend time with new infants or to care for ailing relatives. The family leave law provides employees with up to 55 percent of their regular pay for up to six weeks of leave time. This law, a first in this country in terms of national social policy, covers 13 million Californians, or nearly one-tenth of the American workforce. A study of 169 countries by the Harvard School of Public Heath found that the United States is one of only five countries that do not offer paid leave for new mothers. In California, paid leave is funded through a 0.08 percent payroll tax that is expected to generate close to $130 million a year for the program.

PARENTAL NOTIFICATION. Not only can we see proactive public policy fashioned by and primarily for women, but sometimes a "reactive" mobilization is orchestrated by the same people in order to keep bad policy from becoming law. For example, Proposition 85—the Parents' Right to Know and Child Protection Initiative— qualified as an initiative for the November 2006 ballot. The initiative would have required that a parent or legal guardian of a young woman under age 18 be notified

48 hours before the woman may legally have an abortion. If it was deemed not in the best interest of the young woman to inform her parent or legal guardian of her intentions to have an abortion, she would have been able to ask a judge for a waiver of the notification requirement. Women's health advocates argued that requiring parental permission for underage girls adds extra trauma to those in abusive or incestuous relationships and favors young women with the education and resources to go through the process. Obtaining a waiver from a judge is a difficult process for a young woman to undertake, and the results can be contingent on the personal beliefs of the judge issuing the waiver. With strong opposition from most mainstream women's and health groups in the state, the measure was defeated by 54 percent to 46 percent.

Other examples of the strength of the state's women's community abound: California is the first state to ban gender discrimination in community youth athletic programs. California has also been a trendsetter in the area of laws concerning abusive partners. A new law now allows an imprisoned woman a chance for a new trial or reduced sentence if she can prove that her crime was committed under coercion of an abusive partner. The law could mean release from prison for women who felt they would be severely beaten by their abusers if they chose not to carry out criminal acts.

The Long March Toward GLBT Equal and Civil Rights

One of the earliest gay-related references from the pre-state of California is found in Captain Alarcón's brief observation, dating to 1540, of the Native Americans in the area:

> There were among these Indians three or four men in women's apparel.[31]

In the 1777 publication of Spanish missionary Francisco Palóu's *Founding of the Santa Clara Mission*, we get another early version of the gay-themed life among the aboriginal Californians, as he chronicled the life of Junipero Serra and the nine Franciscan missions founded in California:

> Two laymen arrived at the house of a convent, one of them is unusual clothing, but the other dressed like a woman and called by them a *Joya* [Jewel] . . . The head of the Mission went to the house with a sentry and a soldier. The couple was caught in the act of committing the nefarious sin. They were duly punished for this crime, but not with the severity it properly deserved. When they were rebuked for such an enormous crime, the layman answered that the *Joya* was his wife! They were not seen again in the Mission or its surrounding after this reprimand. Nor did these disreputable people appear in the other missions, although many *Joyas* can be seen in the area of Canal de Santa Barbara; around three, almost every village has two or three [of them].[32]

While many date the struggle for GLBT civil rights to the Stonewall riots of June 1969 in New York City, California was one of the main incubators of the GLBT liberation movement. In 1951 the Mattachine Society was founded in Los Angeles to stop the police harassment against the male homosexual minority community. It later evolved, under its founder Henry Hay, into a multipurpose early civil rights organization dedicated in part to "political action" against "discrimination and oppressive legislation."[33] The first organized lesbian civil rights organization in the United

States, the Daughters of Bilitis, was found by Del Martin and Phyllis Lyon of San Francisco in 1955. One of their founding principles of purpose was "changes through the due process of law in the state legislatures."[34]

As in other law reform and civil rights movements, the fashioning of GLBT "identity politics" was a melding of the personal with the political. Being a second class citizen with diminished rights violated the social contract of fundamental human rights. Civil rights can be understood as the right of equal treatment under the laws—the right of full citizenship. These groups argued that if we are to live in a truly civil society, we must agree to respect the rights of others and subject our activities to reasonable government restrictions enacted for the good of the entire society.

Contemporary GLBT Developments in California

The debate over same-sex marriage reached the courts after the city of San Francisco unilaterally granted nearly 4,000 marriage licenses to same-sex couples in 2004. This would have made them eligible for more than 1,000 federal protection clauses, including family and medical leave, Social Security benefits, tax breaks in joint filing, long term care insurance, and the ability to sponsor a partner for immigration benefits. However, the California supreme court ordered the city to stop issuing the certificates after four weeks. Subsequently, the court decided that same-sex marriage was a constitutional right guaranteed under the state constitution. In its milestone ruling in May 2008, the California supreme court ruled in a 121-page opinion that gay and lesbian couples can legally marry. In the Republican-dominated court, the majority in a 4–3 ruling struck down the state's ban on same-sex marriage and virtually any law that discriminates on the basis of sexual orientation.

The ruling cited a 60-year-old precedent that struck down a ban on interracial marriage in California. The three dissenting justices argued that it was up to the electorate or legislature to decide whether gays and lesbians should be permitted to marry. In 2000, over 61 percent of the California electorate approved an initiative, Proposition 22, that defined only marriage between a man and woman as valid and recognized in California. Opponents of the court's majority opinion attacked it as "judicial tyranny" and argued that the court had overstepped its boundaries and created a new right out of thin air—making gay marriage a natural right.

In 2004, Massachusetts became the first state to legalize gay marriage, and the California decision had ripple effects on other state judiciaries. For example, the Iowa supreme court ruled in 2009 that denying marriage to same-sex couples violates the Equal Protection and Due Process guarantees in the Iowa state constitution. No state has ever passed a constitutional amendment to ban same-sex marriage after the court has granted marriage equality.

According to 2000 census data, California has an estimated 100,000 same-sex households, about one-quarter of them with children. Protect Marriage, a coalition of social and religious conservative groups, submitted over 690,000 valid signatures to qualify a ballot initiative, Proposition 8, on the November 2008 ballot to overturn the court's decision.

Proposition 8 passed by a narrow margin of 52 percent. It was probably the most expensive campaign for a proposition in California's history, with both sides spending in excess of $40 million. Lawsuits were immediately filed, alleging that on its face, Proposition 8 is an improper revision rather than an amendment of the California constitution because it eliminated an existing right only for a targeted minority. Under this legal argument, the California constitution cannot be changed through a simple majority vote but must first be approved by two-thirds of the legislature. The California Supreme Court upheld Proposition 8 in May 2009, but let stand the thousands of same-sex marriages performed legally before the measure's ratification.

Shame   *Tom Brokaw*

There were small acts of cruelty to go with the larger violations of constitutional rights. Norman Mineta, later a congressman from California, was just ten years old when his family was loaded onto a train in the San Jose freight yards. He was wearing his Cub Scout uniform and carrying his baseball bat and glove, the American-born son of a prominent Japanese businessman who had lived in the area for forty years. Several of young Norman's schoolmates came to the tracks to say good-bye, just in time to see the armed guards confiscate his baseball bat because, they said, it could be used as a weapon. It was a world turned upside down for these law-abiding, productive, and respectable families.

When Bob Dole of Russell, Kansas, got to know Danny Inouye of Honolulu in the same rehabilitation hospital in Michigan after the war, they had a good deal in common for two young men from such distinctly different backgrounds. Both were trying to learn to live without the use of an arm as a result of combat wounds suffered as Army lieutenants in the mountains of Italy . . . [but] Inouye's route to that hospital took a few turns not imposed on the young man from Kansas. Inouye was a Japanese American, raised in Hawaii. On December 7, 1941, Inouye, who was just seventeen, was preparing to attend church when he heard a hysterical local radio announcer explain that Pearl Harbor had been attacked.

Young Inouye was enrolled in a Red Cross first-aid training program at the time, so he went directly to the harbor and began helping with the hundreds of casualties. In effect, he was in the war from the opening moments. He stayed on duty at the Red Cross medical aid facility for the next seven days. In March 1942, the U.S. military repaid Inouye by declaring that all young men of Japanese ancestry would be designated 4-C, which meant "enemy alien," unfit for service. Inouye says, "That really hit me. I considered myself patriotic, and to be told you could not put on a uniform, that was an insult. Thousands of us signed petitions, asking to be able to enlist." The Army decided to form an all-Japanese American unit, the 442nd Regimental Combat Team. Its shoulder patch was a coffin with a torch of liberty inside. The motto was "Go For Broke." Before the war was over, the 442nd and its units would become the most heavily decorated single combat unit of its size in U.S. Army history. Daniel Inouye went on to become Hawaii's first congressman, and the first Japanese American in Congress.

...

. . . Nao Takasugi was a junior studying business at UCLA when the Japanese bombed Pearl Harbor. Suddenly, because of his ancestry, he was subject to a strict curfew: He couldn't be out before 6 A.M. and after 6 P.M. He couldn't go five miles beyond his family home in Oxnard, which ruled out UCLA, more than fifty miles away. Then, in his neighborhood, came the posting of Executive Order 9066. "Here I was," he says, "a nineteen-year-old college student full of ambition and ideals. All of that just came crashing down." The Takasugi family—the parents, four daughters, and Nao—were told to prepare whatever personal possessions they could carry in their hands and report to the railroad station in Ventura. The railroad station was bristling with armed guards. The Takasugi family, just days before a respected and productive family of American citizens, boarded for an unknown destination, their most fundamental rights stripped in the name of fear.

Nao Takasugi later earned an MBA at Wharton, became mayor and a member of the city council of Oxnard, and became a California State Assemblyman in 1992.

Senator Inouye and Assemblyman Takasugi are currently on the board of the Japanese American National Museum.

Source: Tom Brokaw, *The Greatest Generation*. Copyright © 1998 by Tom Brokaw. Reprinted by permission of Random House, Inc.

SUMMARY

The struggle for equality in California has not been easy. Ever since California became a state, communities of color, gender, and different sexual orientations have been subjected to institutional and *de facto* discrimination. The internment of Japanese Americans is but one ugly footnote in California's—and the nation's—past. The landmark civil rights legislation of the 1960s forced leaders to find new ways to break down the barriers to social and economic advancement. From *Bakke* to Proposition 209, affirmative action policies designed to advance equality first came under fire in California. Like many other policy innovations in California, the movement to end affirmative action through direct democracy is taking hold in other states.

Whether California will assertively and affirmatively develop new approaches to ensure equal access in the post-affirmative action era is not yet clear. Without doubt, there is a long way to go. The state's changing demographics may actually solve the problem more quickly than the conflicted policy approaches of the past. California Republicans (Arnold Schwarzenegger notwithstanding) have already experienced a backlash: Since 1998, Latinos and Asians have turned out to vote in record numbers against a party that had taken tough anti-immigration and anti-affirmative action positions, prompting fears among Republican leaders that these issues may be damaging in the long run—having alienated too many potential supporters. California's majority white population is expected to slip under 50 percent within the next decade. With no ethnic majority, the state's minority communities may fare better.

Still, equal protection over race, gender, sexual orientation, and class continues to create serious impediments to equality throughout the state. It is always easier to talk about recognizing people's civil rights and liberties than it is to practice these policies. In the end, the issue revolves about the distribution of power and resources. The political system never remains static—it is in constant flux, with new demands of under-represented populations who want some of the American dream. Furthermore, equal rights is not a zero-sum formula (i.e., "I got mine, so you can't have yours"). What we have witnessed in California over the past 30 or 40 years is the rise of "coalition politics," where groups ban together for a louder voice in public policy results. In reality, it is just the reversal of zero-sum: It's more of a philosophy that if one group is discriminated against, we are all affected. So, for example, hybrid coalitions have formed in California as supporters and legislative backers of the gay marriage bill— from the California Council of Churches, to the Mexican American Legal Defense and Education Fund, to Asian Americans for Civil Rights and Equality. In the end, civil rights cannot be built in a vacuum: The true mosaic of civil liberties in California must be painted in one broad landscape. Equal justice concerns are basic fibers in the state as we have evolved from our soiled past. Equal protection and equal access under the law will no doubt remain a contested terrain in California in the twenty-first century. The course is in our hands to determine whether we become a "melting pot" or more a "salad bowl" of shared American values of justice.

APPENDIX:
KOREMATSU V. UNITED STATES (1944)

Editor's note: The internment of Japanese Americans was tested in *Korematsu v. United States*. The following excerpts include the U.S. Supreme Court's majority opinion sustaining the internment, as well as a particularly harsh dissent from Justice Murphy.

MR. JUSTICE BLACK delivered the majority opinion of the Court.

The petitioner, an American citizen of Japanese descent, was convicted in a federal district court for remaining in San Leandro, California, a "Military Area," contrary to Civilian Exclusion Order No. 34 of the Commanding General of the Western Command, U.S. Army, which directed that after May 9, 1942, all persons of Japanese ancestry should be excluded from that area. No question was raised as to petitioner's loyalty to the United States. The Circuit Court of Appeals affirmed,[35] and the importance of the constitutional question involved caused us to grant certiorari.

It should be noted, to begin with, that all legal restrictions which curtail the civil rights of a single racial group are immediately suspect. That is not to say that all such restrictions are unconstitutional. It is to say that courts must subject them to the most rigid scrutiny. Pressing public necessity may sometimes justify the existence of such restrictions; racial antagonism never can.

In the instant case prosecution of the petitioner was begun by information charging violation of an Act of Congress, of March 21, 1942, 56 Stat. 173, which provides that ". . . whoever shall enter, remain in, leave, or commit any act in any military area or military zone prescribed, under the authority of an Executive order of the President, by the Secretary of War, or by any military commander designated by the Secretary of War, contrary to the restrictions applicable to any such area or zone or contrary to the order of the Secretary of War or any such military commander, shall, if it appears that he knew or should have known of the existence and extent of the restrictions or order and that his act was in violation thereof, be guilty of a misdemeanor and upon conviction shall be liable to a fine not to exceed $5,000 or to imprisonment for not more than one year, or both, for each offense."

Exclusion Order No. 34, which the petitioner knowingly and admittedly violated, was one of a number of military orders and proclamations, all of which were substantially based upon Executive Order No. 9066, 7 Fed. Reg. 1407. That order, issued after we were at war with Japan, declared that "the successful prosecution of the war requires every possible protection against espionage and against sabotage to national-defense material, national-defense premises, and national-defense utilities. . . ."

One of the series of orders and proclamations, a curfew order, which like the exclusion order here was promulgated pursuant to Executive Order 9066, subjected all persons of Japanese ancestry in prescribed West Coast military areas to remain in their residences from 8 P.M. to 6 A.M. As is the case with the exclusion order here, that prior curfew order was designed as a "protection against espionage and against sabotage." In *Hirabayashi v. United States*, 320 U.S. 81, we sustained a conviction obtained for violation of the curfew order. The *Hirabayashi* conviction and this one thus rest on the same 1942 Congressional Act and the same basic executive and military orders, all of which orders were aimed at the twin dangers of espionage and sabotage.

The 1942 Act was attacked in the *Hirabayashi* case as an unconstitutional delegation of power; it was contended that the curfew order and other orders on which it rested were beyond the war powers of the Congress, the military authorities and of the President, as Commander in Chief of the Army; and finally that to apply the curfew order against none but citizens of Japanese ancestry amounted to a constitutionally prohibited discrimination solely on account of race. To these questions, we gave the serious consideration which their importance justified. We upheld the curfew order as an exercise of the power of the government to take steps necessary to prevent espionage and sabotage in an area threatened by Japanese attack.

In the light of the principles we announced in the *Hirabayashi* case, we are unable to conclude that it was beyond the war power of Congress and the Executive to exclude those of Japanese ancestry from the West Coast war area at the time they did. True, exclusion from the area in which one's home is located is a far greater deprivation than constant confinement to the home from 8 P.M. to 6 A.M. Nothing short of apprehension by the proper military authorities of the gravest imminent danger to the public safety can constitutionally justify either. But exclusion from a threatened area, no less than curfew, has a definite and close relationship to the prevention of espionage and sabotage. The military authorities, charged with the primary responsibility of defending our shores, concluded that curfew provided inadequate protection and ordered exclusion. They did so, as pointed out in our *Hirabayashi* opinion, in accordance with Congressional authority to the military to say who should, and who should not, remain in the threatened areas.

In this case the petitioner challenges the assumptions upon which we rested our conclusions in the *Hirabayashi* case. He also urges that by May 1942, when Order No. 34 was promulgated, all danger of Japanese invasion of the West Coast had disappeared. After careful consideration of these contentions we are compelled to reject them.

. . . The judgment that exclusion of the whole group was for the same reason a military imperative answers the contention that the exclusion was in the nature of group punishment based on antagonism to those of Japanese origin. That there were members of the group who retained loyalties to Japan has been confirmed by investigations made subsequent to the exclusion. Approximately five thousand American citizens of Japanese ancestry refused to swear unqualified allegiance to the United States and to renounce allegiance to the Japanese Emperor, and several thousand evacuees requested repatriation to Japan.[36]

We uphold the exclusion order as of the time it was made and when the petitioner violated it. *Cf. Chastleton Corporation v. Sinclair*, 264 U.S. 543, 547; *Block v. Hirsh*, 256 U.S. 135, 154–155. In doing so, we are not unmindful of the hardships imposed by it upon a large group of American citizens. *Cf. Ex parte Kawato*, 317 U.S. 69, 73. But hardships are part of war, and war is an aggregation of hardships. All citizens alike, both in and out of uniform, feel the impact of war in greater or lesser measure. Citizenship has its responsibilities as well as its privileges, and in time of war the burden is always heavier. Compulsory exclusion of large groups of citizens from their homes, except under circumstances of direst emergency and peril, is inconsistent with our basic governmental institutions. But when under conditions of modern warfare our shores are threatened by hostile forces, the power to protect must be commensurate with the threatened danger.

. . . It is said that we are dealing here with the case of imprisonment of a citizen in a concentration camp solely because of his ancestry, without evidence or inquiry concerning his loyalty and good disposition towards the United States. Our task would be simple, our duty clear, were this a case involving the imprisonment of a loyal citizen in a concentration camp because of racial prejudice. Regardless of the true nature of the assembly and relocation centers—and we deem it unjustifiable to call them concentration camps with all the ugly connotations that term implies—we are dealing specifically with nothing but an exclusion order. To cast this case into outlines of racial prejudice, without reference to the real military dangers which were presented, merely confuses the issue. Korematsu was not excluded from the Military Area because of hostility to him or his race. He was excluded because we are at war with the Japanese Empire, because the properly constituted military authorities feared an invasion of our West Coast and felt constrained to take proper security measures, because they decided that the military urgency of the situation demanded that all citizens of Japanese ancestry be segregated from the West Coast temporarily, and finally, because Congress, reposing its confidence in this time of war in our military leaders—as inevitably it must—determined that they should have the power to do just this. There was evidence of disloyalty on the part of some, the military authorities considered that the need for action was great, and time was short. We cannot—by availing ourselves of the calm perspective of hindsight—now say that at that time these actions were unjustified.

MR. JUSTICE MURPHY, dissenting.

This exclusion of "all persons of Japanese ancestry, both alien and non-alien," from the Pacific Coast area on a plea of military necessity in the absence of martial law ought not to be approved. Such exclusion goes over "the very brink of constitutional power" and falls into the ugly abyss of racism.

In dealing with matters relating to the prosecution and progress of a war, we must accord great respect and consideration to the judgments of the military authorities who are on the scene and who have full knowledge of the military facts. The scope of their discretion must, as a matter of necessity and common sense, be wide. And their judgments ought not to be overruled lightly by those whose training and duties ill-equip them to deal intelligently with matters so vital to the physical security of the nation.

At the same time, however, it is essential that there be definite limits to military discretion, especially where martial law has not been declared. Individuals must not be left impoverished of their constitutional rights on a plea of military necessity that has neither substance nor support. Thus, like other claims conflicting with the asserted constitutional rights of the individual, the military claim must subject itself to the judicial process of having its reasonableness determined and its conflicts with other interests reconciled. "What are the allowable limits of military discretion, and whether or not they have been overstepped in a particular case, are judicial questions." *Sterling v. Constantin*, 287 U.S. 378, 401.

The judicial test of whether the Government, on a plea of military necessity, can validly deprive an individual of any of his constitutional rights is whether the deprivation is reasonably related to a public danger that is so "immediate, imminent, and impending" as not to admit of delay and not to permit the intervention of ordinary constitutional processes to alleviate the danger. *United States v. Russell*, 13 Wall. 623, 627–628; *Mitchell v. Harmony*, 13 How. 115, 134–135; *Raymond v. Thomas*, 91 U.S. 712, 716. Civilian Exclusion Order No. 34, banishing from a prescribed area of the Pacific Coast "all persons of Japanese ancestry, both alien and non-alien," clearly does not meet that test. Being an obvious racial discrimination, the order deprives all those within its scope of the equal protection of the laws as guaranteed by the Fifth Amendment. It further deprives these individuals of their constitutional rights to live and work where they will, to establish a home where they choose and to move about freely. In excommunicating them without benefit of hearings, this order also deprives them of all their constitutional rights to procedural due process. Yet no reasonable relation to an "immediate, imminent, and impending" public danger is evident to support this racial restriction which is one of the most sweeping and complete deprivations of constitutional rights in the history of this nation in the absence of martial law.

It must be conceded that the military and naval situation in the spring of 1942 was such as to generate a very real fear of invasion of the Pacific Coast, accompanied by fears of sabotage and espionage in that area. The military command was therefore justified in adopting all reasonable means necessary to combat these dangers. In adjudging the military action taken in light of the then apparent dangers, we must not erect too high or too meticulous standards; it is necessary only that the action have some reasonable relation to the removal of the dangers of invasion, sabotage and espionage. But the exclusion, either temporarily or permanently, of all persons with Japanese blood in their veins has no such reasonable relation. And that relation is lacking because the exclusion order necessarily must rely for its reasonableness upon the assumption that all persons of Japanese ancestry may have a dangerous tendency to commit sabotage and espionage and to aid our Japanese enemy in other ways. It is difficult to believe that reason, logic or experience could be marshalled in support of such an assumption.

That this forced exclusion was the result in good measure of this erroneous assumption of racial guilt rather than bona fide military necessity is evidenced by the Commanding General's Final Report on the evacuation from the Pacific Coast area.[37] In it he refers to all individuals of Japanese descent as "subversive," as belonging to "an enemy race" whose "racial strains are undiluted," and as constituting "over 112,000 potential enemies . . . at large today" along the Pacific Coast.[38] In support of this blanket condemnation of all persons of Japanese descent, however, no reliable evidence is cited to show that such individuals were generally disloyal,[39] or had generally so conducted themselves in this area as to constitute a special menace to defense installations or war industries, or had otherwise by their behavior furnished reasonable ground for their exclusion as a group.

Justification for the exclusion is sought, instead, mainly upon questionable racial and sociological grounds not ordinarily within the realm of expert military judgment, supplemented by certain semi-military conclusions drawn from an unwarranted use of circumstantial evidence. Individuals of Japanese ancestry are condemned because they are said to be "a large, unassimilated, tightly knit racial group, bound to an enemy nation by strong ties of race, culture, custom and religion."[40] They are claimed to be given to "emperor worshipping ceremonies"[41] and to "dual citizenship."[42] Japanese language schools and allegedly pro-Japanese organizations are cited as evidence of possible group disloyalty,[43] together with facts as to certain persons being educated and residing at length in Japan.[44] It is intimated that many of these individuals deliberately resided "adjacent to strategic points," thus enabling them "to carry into execution a tremendous program of sabotage on a mass scale should any considerable number of them have been inclined to do so."[45] The need for protective custody is also asserted. The report refers without identity to "numerous incidents of violence" as well as to other admittedly unverified or cumulative incidents. From this, plus certain other events not shown to have been connected with the Japanese Americans, it is concluded that the "situation was fraught with danger to the Japanese population itself" and that the general public "was ready to take matters into its own hands."[46] Finally, it is intimated, though not directly charged or proved, that persons of Japanese ancestry were responsible for three minor isolated shellings and bombings of the Pacific Coast area,[47] as well as for unidentified radio transmissions and night signaling.

The main reasons relied upon by those responsible for the forced evacuation, therefore, do not prove a reasonable relation between the group characteristics of Japanese Americans and the dangers of invasion, sabotage, and espionage. The reasons appear, instead, to be largely an accumulation of much of the misinformation, half-truths and insinuations that for years have been directed against Japanese Americans by people with racial and economic prejudices—the same people who have been among the foremost advocates of the evacuation.[48] A military judgment based upon such racial and sociological considerations is not entitled to the great weight ordinarily given the judgments based upon strictly military considerations. Especially is this so when every charge relative to race, religion, culture, geographical location, and legal and economic status has been substantially discredited by independent studies made by experts in these matters.[49]

The military necessity which is essential to the validity of the evacuation order thus resolves itself into a few intimations that certain individuals actively aided the enemy, from which it is inferred that the entire group of Japanese Americans could not be trusted to be or remain loyal to the United States. No one denies, of course, that there were some disloyal persons of Japanese descent on the Pacific Coast who did all in their power to aid their ancestral land. Similar disloyal activities have been engaged in by many persons of German, Italian and even more pioneer stock in our country. But to infer that examples of individual disloyalty prove group disloyalty and justify discriminatory action against the entire group is to deny that under our system of law individual guilt is the sole basis for deprivation of rights. Moreover, this inference, which is at the very heart of the evacuation orders, has been used in support of the abhorrent and despicable treatment of minority groups by the dictatorial tyrannies which this nation is now pledged to destroy. To give constitutional sanction to that inference in this case, however well-intentioned may have been the military command on the Pacific Coast, is to adopt one of the cruelest of the rationales used by our enemies to destroy the dignity of the individual and to encourage and open the door to discriminatory actions against other minority groups in the passions of tomorrow.

No adequate reason is given for the failure to treat these Japanese Americans on an individual basis by holding investigations and hearings to separate the loyal from the disloyal, as was done in the case of persons of German and Italian ancestry. See House Report No. 2124 (77th Cong., 2d Sess.) 247–252. It is asserted merely that the loyalties of this group "were unknown and time was of the essence."[50] Yet nearly four months elapsed after Pearl Harbor before the first exclusion order was issued; nearly eight months went by until the last order was issued; and the last of these "subversive" persons was not actually removed until almost eleven months had elapsed. Leisure and deliberation seem to have been more of the essence than speed. And the fact that conditions were not such as to warrant a declaration of martial law adds strength to the belief that the factors of time and military necessity were not as urgent as they have been represented to be.

Moreover, there was no adequate proof that the Federal Bureau of Investigation and the military and naval intelligence services did not have the espionage and sabotage situation well in hand during this long period. Nor is there any denial of the fact that not one person of Japanese ancestry was accused or convicted of espionage or sabotage after Pearl Harbor while they were still free,[51] a fact which is some evidence of the loyalty of the vast majority of these individuals and of the effectiveness of the established methods of combating these evils. It seems incredible that under these circumstances it would have been impossible to hold loyalty hearings for the mere 112,000 persons involved—or at least for the 70,000 American citizens—especially when a large part of this number represented children and elderly men and women.

Any inconvenience that may have accompanied an attempt to conform to procedural due process cannot be said to justify violations of constitutional rights of individuals.

I dissent, therefore, from this legalization of racism. Racial discrimination in any form and in any degree has no justifiable part whatever in our democratic way of life. It is unattractive in any setting but it is utterly revolting among a free people who have embraced the principles set forth in the Constitution of the United States. All residents of this nation are kin in some way by blood or culture to a foreign land. Yet they are primarily and necessarily a part of the new and distinct civilization of the United States. They must accordingly be treated at all times as the heirs of the American experiment and as entitled to all the rights and freedoms guaranteed by the constitution.

NOTES

1. Employment Nondiscrimination Act, H.R. 3285, 2003.
2. In fact, as early as 1875 a Latino, Romualdo Pacheco, was California's governor.
3. Susan Anderson, "Rivers of Water in a Dry Place—Early Black Participation in California Politics," in Byran O. Jackson and Michael B. Preston, eds., *Racial and Ethnic Politics in California* (Berkeley: Institute of Governmental Studies, University of California Berkeley, 1991), pp. 55–69.
4. Ibid, p. 61.
5. "Jim Crow" refers to the institutionalized segregation of African Americans in the South following the end of slavery.
6. Brief from the Center for Educational Telecommunications, *Chinese Exclusion Act*, www .cetel.org/1882_exclusion.html.
7. Brief from the Library of Congress (LOC), *The Chinese in California, 1850–1925*, http:// memory.loc.gov/ammem/award99/cubhtml/chron.html.
8. See Supreme Court Justice Murphy, in his dissenting opinion in *Korematsu v. United States* (1944).
9. Frank J. Taylor, "The People Nobody Wants," *Saturday Evening Post* 24, no. 66 (May 9, 1942): 214.
10. National Organization for Women, *Talking About Affirmative Action*, www.now .org/issues/affirm/talking.html.
11. Ibid.
12. 438 U.S. 265 (1978).
13. See *Wards Cove Packing Co. v. Atonio* (1989), *Patterson v. McClean Union* (1989), *Adarand v. Pena* (1995), and *Hopwood v. University of Texas Law School* (1996).

14. In the conclusion of the *Grutter vs. Bollinger* case, Judge Bernard Friedman delivered the court conclusion: "The University of Michigan Law School's use of race as a factor in its admission decisions is unconstitutional and a violation of Title VI of the 1964 Civil Rights Act. The law school's justification for using race—to assemble a racially diverse student population—is not compelling state interest. Even if it were, the law school has not narrowly tailored its use of race to achieve that interest." See www.vpcomm.umich.edu/admissions/legal/grutter/gru-op.html.

15. Professor Randall of the University of Dayton School of Law summarized the *Grutter* case for the importance of intervention: "Students of color—not university administrators—have the broadest, deepest and most urgent interests in preserving affirmative action. After all, when race can no longer be a factor in admission decisions, it is minority students who are denied access to higher education opportunities." Vernellia R. Randall, *Grutter v. Bollinger: University of Michigan Law School Affirmative Action Case*, http://academic.udayton.edu/race/04needs/affirm14.htm.

16. "In summary, the Equal Protection Clause does not prohibit the Law School's narrowly tailored use of race in admissions decisions to further a compelling interest in obtaining the educational benefits that flow from a diverse student body. Consequently, petitioner's statutory claims based on Title VI and 42 U. S. C. §1981 also fail. See Bakke, supra, at 287 (opinion of Powell, J.) ("Title VI . . . proscribe[s] only those racial classifications that would violate the Equal Protection Clause or the Fifth Amendment"); *General Building Contractors Assn., Inc. v. Pennsylvania*, 458 U. S. 375, 389–391 (1982) (the prohibition against discrimination in §1981 is co-extensive with the Equal Protection Clause). The judgment of the Court of Appeals for the Sixth Circuit, accordingly, is affirmed." See *Grutter vs. Bollinger* (2003).

17. Brief from CNN, *Courts' Affirmative Action Decision Add Fuel to Political Debate*, June 23, 2003, www.cnn.com/2003/ALLPOLITICS/06/23/affirmative.reax/index.html.

18. As a proposed constitutional amendment, the proposition required 693,230 valid registered voters' signatures. The extra margin of over 1 million would guarantee that it would meet the threshold enforced by the secretary of state's office.

19. Ballot text of Proposition 209 (1996), clause 1, lines 1–3.

20. Ibid., clause 3, lines 5–7.

21. Richard Paddock, "Affirmative Action Era Over, Foe Says," *Los Angeles Times* (November 26, 2006): B1.

22. Rachel Gordon, "Supes Extend Affirmative Action Plan," *San Francisco Examiner* (September 23, 1998): A8.

23. Larry Gordon, "UC Regents Move Toward Easing Admissions Requirements," *Los Angeles Times* (February 5, 2009): B1.

24. Ibid.

25. Jeffrey S. Lehman, "At UC, Race Must Matter," *Los Angeles Times* (August 26, 2006): B17.

26. Peach Indravudh, "Events Mourn Death of Diversity," *Daily Bruin* (November 3, 2006): 1.

27. Rebecca Trounson, "UCLA to Blacks: You're Welcome," *Los Angeles Times* (November 11, 2006): B1.

28. Michael B. Preston, Bruce E. Cain, and Sandra Bass, eds., *Racial and Ethnic Politics in California*, Volume II. (Berkeley: Institute of Governmental Studies, University of California Press, 1988).

29. From Terry McHale, *Capitol Morning Report* (February 4, 2002), as quoted at www.sen.ca.gov/womenscaucus/history.htp#RoseAnn.

30. Ibid.

31. Cited in Jonathan Katz, *Gay American History: Lesbians and Gay Men in the USA* (New York: Thomas Y. Crowell, 1976), p. 285.

32. Ibid., p. 292.

33. Ibid., p. 412.

34. Ibid., p. 426.

35. 140 F.2d 289.
36. Hearings before the Subcommittee on the National War Agencies Appropriation Bill for 1945, Part II, pp. 608–726; Lieutenant General J. L. DeWitt, *Final Report, Japanese Evacuation from the West Coast, 1942*, pp. 309–327; Hearings before the Committee on Immigration and Naturalization, House of Representatives, 78th Cong., 2d Sess., on H.R. 2701 and other bills to expatriate certain nationals of the United States, pp. 37–42, 49–58.
37. Lieutenant General J. L. DeWitt, *Final Report, Japanese Evacuation from the West Coast, 1942*. This report is dated June 5, 1943, but was not made public until January 1944.
38. Further evidence of the Commanding General's attitude toward individuals of Japanese ancestry is revealed in his voluntary testimony on April 13, 1943, in San Francisco before the House Naval Affairs Subcommittee to Investigate Congested Areas, Part 3, pp. 739–740 (78th Cong., 1st Session): "I don't want any of them [persons of Japanese ancestry] here. They are a dangerous element. There is no way to determine their loyalty. The West Coast contains too many vital installations essential to the defense of the country to allow any Japanese on this coast. . . . The danger of the Japanese was, and is now—if they are permitted to come back—espionage and sabotage. It makes no difference whether he is an American citizen, he is still a Japanese. American citizenship does not necessarily determine loyalty. . . . But we must worry about the Japanese all the time until he is wiped off the map. . . ."
39. *Final Report*, p. 9, casts a cloud of suspicion over the entire group by saying that "while it was believed that some were loyal, it was known that many were not."
40. *Final Report*, p. vii; see also pp. 9, 17. To the extent that assimilation is a problem, it is largely the result of certain social customs and laws of the American general public. Studies demonstrate that persons of Japanese descent are readily susceptible to integration in our society if given the opportunity. . . . The failure to accomplish an ideal status of assimilation, therefore, cannot be charged to the refusal of these persons to become Americanized or to their loyalty to Japan. And the retention by some persons of certain customs and religious practices of their ancestors is no criterion of their loyalty to the United States.
41. *Final Report*, pp. 10–11. No sinister correlation between the emperor worshipping activities and disloyalty to America was shown.
42. *Final Report*, p. 22. The charge of "dual citizenship" springs from a misunderstanding of the simple fact that Japan in the past used the doctrine of *jus sanguinis*, as she had a right to do under international law, and claimed as her citizens all persons born of Japanese nationals wherever located. Japan has greatly modified this doctrine, however, by allowing all Japanese born in the United States to renounce any claim of dual citizenship and by releasing her claim as to all born in the United States after 1925. See Harrop A. Freeman, "Genesis, Exodus, and Leviticus: Genealogy, Evacuation, and Law," *Cornell L. Q.* 28 414, 447–448, and authorities there cited; Carey McWilliams, *Prejudice*, (1944) 123–124.
43. *Final Report*, pp. 12–13. We have had various foreign language schools in this country for generations without considering their existence as ground for racial discrimination. No subversive activities or teachings have been shown in connection with the Japanese schools. McWilliams, *Prejudice*, (1944) 121–123.
44. *Final Report*, pp. 13–15. Such persons constitute a very small part of the entire group, and most of them belong to the Kibei movement, the actions and membership of which are well known to U.S. government agents.
45. *Final Report*, p. 10; see also pp. vii, 9, and 15–17. This insinuation, based purely upon speculation and circumstantial evidence, completely overlooks the fact that the main geographic pattern of Japanese population was fixed many years ago with reference to economic, social, and soil conditions. Limited occupational outlets and social pressures encouraged their concentration near their initial points of entry on the Pacific Coast. That these points may now be near certain strategic military and industrial areas is no proof of

a diabolical purpose on the part of Japanese Americans. See McWilliams, *Prejudice,* (1944) 119–121; House Report No. 2124 (77th Cong., 2d Session.), pp. 59–93.

46. *Final Report*, pp. 8–9. This dangerous doctrine of protective custody, as proved by recent European history, should have absolutely no standing as an excuse for the deprivation of the rights of minority groups. See House Report No. 1911 (77th Cong., 2d Sess.), pp. 1–2 and House Report No. 2124 (77th Cong., 2d Sess.), pp. 145–147. In this instance, more-over, there are only two minor instances of violence on record involving persons of Japanese ancestry. Carey McWilliams, "What About Our Japanese-Americans?" *Public Affairs Pamphlets*, no. 91 (1944): 8.

47. *Final Report*, p. 18. One of these incidents (the reputed dropping of incendiary bombs on an Oregon forest) occurred on September 9, 1942—a considerable time after the Japanese Americans had been evacuated from their homes and placed in assembly centers.

48. Special interest groups were extremely active in applying pressure for mass evacuation. See House Report No. 2124 (77th Cong., 2d Sess.), pp. 154–156, and McWilliams, *Prejudice,* (1944) pp. 126–128. Mr. Austin E. Anson, managing secretary of the Salinas Vegetable Grower-Shipper Association, frankly admitted: "We're charged with wanting to get rid of the Japs for selfish reasons. . . . We do. It's a question of whether the white man lives on the Pacific Coast or the brown men. They came into this valley to work, and they stayed to take over. . . . They undersell the white man in the markets. . . . They work their women and children while the white farmer has to pay wages for his help. If all the Japs were removed tomorrow, we'd never miss them in two weeks, because the white farmers can take over and produce everything the Jap grows. And we don't want them back when the war ends, either." From Frank J. Taylor, "The People Nobody Wants."

49. See notes 4–12, supra.

50. *Final Report*, p. vii; see also p. 18.

51. *Final Report*, p. 34, makes the amazing statement that as of February 14, 1942, "The very fact that no sabotage has taken place to date is a disturbing and confirming indication that such action will be taken." Apparently, in the minds of the military leaders, there was no way that the Japanese Americans could escape the suspicion of sabotage.

CHAPTER 17

Rethinking California

Featured Reading / Page 228
Philip K. Dick
Do Androids Dream of Electric Sheep?

The Gold Coast

The great gridlock of light.
Tungsten, neon, sodium, mercury, halogen, xenon.
At ground level, square grids of orange sodium streetlights.
All kinds of things burn.
Mercury vapor lamps: blue crystals over the freeways, the condos,
    the parking lots.
Eyezapping xenon, glaring on the malls, the stadium, Disneyland.
Great halogen lighthouse beams from the airport, snapping around
the sky.
An ambulance light, pulsing red below.
Ceaseless succession, redgreenyellow, redgreenyellow.
Headlights and taillights, red and white blood cells, pushed through
    a leukemic body of light.
There's a brake light in your brain.
A billion lights. (Ten million people.) How many kilowatts per hour?
Grid laid over grid, from the mountains to the sea. A billion lights.

—Kim Stanley Robinson, describing Southern
California in 2027, from *The Gold Coast* (New York:
Tom Doherty Associates, 1988)

The Golden State has lost a little of its luster. Rebounding from recession, political turmoil, an energy crisis, and crippling deficits, California finds itself at a crossroads. This raises the prospects for government to draw upon its resources to find solutions to current problems and to fend off the next wave of crises. Governor Arnold Schwarzenegger came into office as a reform-minded activist, riding a wave of voter discontent with the state's fiscal problems and partisan bickering in Sacramento, but he failed to deliver the change he promised. Unable to solve the state's financial

224

problems by working with the legislature, Schwarzenegger hoped the voters would approve five initiatives to help balance the state budget in 2009. They didn't.

The day after voters rejected those measures, Michael Hiltzik noted in *The Los Angeles Times* that the governor began in 2003 with popular support that "would have allowed him to tell the voters the harsh but necessary truths about California governance and force real reforms." Instead, Hiltzik wrote, "he uttered the same lies about state government and proposed the same nostrums as many of his predecessors," including the notion that the budget could be balanced by trimming waste, fraud and abuse. In fact, Schwarzenegger's decision to cut the vehicle registration tax by $2.3 billion per year caused much of the state's financial woes. The challenge for the next generation of leaders, according to Hiltzik, is to prove that California is not "ungovernable" as is commonly said, just that it's been "ungoverned." Real reform, he insisted, would require removing legislative term limits, revising Proposition 13, and changing the two-thirds legislative requirement to pass a budget.[1]

Reversing California's problems will require more than a few ballot initiatives and handshakes in a gubernatorial smoking tent; it will require commitments from California's people and institutions to chart a different future. The choices they make today will determine the quality of life for future generations of Californians. To get a sense of where those choices might bring us, it is instructive to look back at the consequences of the choices made a generation ago.

In 1971, a group of business leaders, environmentalists, and elected officials published a pamphlet that served up two contrasting visions of California's future. The pamphlet, titled *The California Tomorrow Plan*, quickly attracted the attention of planners and officials around the state and the nation. The plan identified a list of urgent problems facing the state in 1971, a time and place dubbed by the authors as "California Zero." They argued that each of these problems, ranging from preservation of agricultural land to civil unrest, was rooted in four dysfunctional public policy issues arrangements that needed to be addressed: (1) a lack of individual political strength, (2) a lack of individual economic strength, (3) a damaging population distribution, and (4) a damaging pattern of resource consumption.[2] California's social and economic viability would be determined, according to the report, by the willingness of policymakers to act in these four areas during the next three decades (1970–2000).

The plan offered two scenarios projecting what California might be like in the twenty-first century. "California One" was a nightmarish scenario that the authors predicted would emerge after 30 years of policies that encouraged unrestrained economic growth. In California One, increased urbanization led to massive sprawl and environmental destruction. These problems were exacerbated by governmental policies that subsidized certain economic enterprises while only sporadically enforcing control regulations. In California One, the state budget reflected separate programs of several single-purpose agencies. Because the budgeting and accounting process was not designed to make full assessments of various policy alternatives, the costs of planning and coordination were overstated. Quality of life in California was severely impaired as growth continued unabated. Sprawling cities joined with one another, devouring open space in between. Air pollution increased, despite tougher air quality standards, as more automobiles appeared on the new freeways and roads that connected the proliferating suburbs. Several species, including the remaining salmon population, were lost due to habitat destruction. The state's national parks became severely congested. There was high crime punctuated by occasional periods of civil unrest, encouraging the affluent to seek refuge in the security of private, gated communities. In other words, California One was the logical consequence of three decades of development, while clinging to 1970 methods of solving problems.

"California Two" was an alternative scenario of the state at the beginning of the twenty-first century, which would come into existence if policymakers followed the authors' proposed path. In contrast with California One, quality of life was much better in this near-utopian vision of the twenty-first century. Coordination replaced governmental fragmentation, and the piecemeal policymaking practices of the past were overcome through rational planning. In this vision, agricultural and open space were preserved, as growth was carefully managed and confined to urban boundaries. Energy-efficient mass transit systems moved people within and between urban centers, and wilderness areas and recreational space remained intact. Looking back after three decades, many of the proposals seemed to reveal a pre-Proposition 13 innocence. Roughly formed illustrations of high-speed bullet trains and monorails showed people zipping between urban centers surrounded by open space. Aggressive landscaping transformed inner-city streets into gardens and downtown areas into pedestrian plazas containing schools and cafes.

Even if the authors' unabashed optimism about the capacity of government to improve California's quality of life seems naive by today's standards, the accuracy of their forecast is chilling. Their recommendations went unrealized, and their warnings of what the state would become have largely materialized. Californians now face several choices about how the state will be governed and how it will grow over the course of another generation. The example of *The California Tomorrow Plan* hints at the long-term repercussions of choices made or not made.

Philip Dick's 1968 novel *Do Androids Dream of Electric Sheep?* portrays a nightmarish world in mid-2021, where androids have been employed as slaves on outlying planets, and police assassins search the earth to retire trespassers.[3] The tension between the real and the artificial allows Dick to tease out a logical twenty-first century conclusion to late twentieth century social dysfunction. Set in San Francisco, the book envisions a society where electronic replicas of pets are affordable alternatives to the extremely rare, and extremely expensive, animals themselves. Androids are indistinguishable from humans, both in form and biology, though they differ in emotional capacity. Police powers include summary execution, and due process is reduced to a questionable series of test questions.

The Ridley Scott film *Blade Runner* adapts the Dick novel, placing it in Los Angeles. The film's prologue grimly lays the framework:

Early in the 21st Century, the Tyrell Corporation advanced Robot evolution into the Nexus phase—a being virtually identical to a human—known as a Replicant.

The Nexus 6 Replicants were superior in strength and agility, and at least equal in intelligence, to the genetic engineers who created them.

Replicants were used Off-world as slave labor, in the hazardous exploration and colonization of other planets.

After a bloody mutiny by a Nexus 6 combat team in an Off-world colony, Replicants were declared illegal on earth—under penalty of death.

Special police squads—Blade Runner Units—had orders to shoot to kill, upon detection, any trespassing Replicant.

This was not called execution.

It was called retirement.[4]

That Philip Dick's imagined twenty-first century California will actually come into being is unlikely. However, several key issues remain a contested terrain, leaving open several plausible outcomes. Novelist Kim Stanley Robinson examines California's future through three starkly different views of the mid-twenty-first century. One vision, *The Wild Shore*, presents a California in 2047 amid the ashes of nuclear war where daily survival is a battle and within which the blurred distinctions between good and evil are constant morality plays.[5] Alternately, *Pacific Edge* envisions an ecotopia in 2065, where harmony and sustainability are in tension with resurgent greed and exploitation.[6] Finally, and perhaps most salient among the trilogy, *Gold Coast* predicts 2027 suburban sprawl run amok.[7]

The *Blade Runner* metaphor suggests that social evils have become so severe that extraordinary police powers are necessary and appropriate. *The Wild Shore* metaphor suggests that human or natural disasters may usher in a period of moral ambivalence. We should not assume that such extraordinary events are necessarily futuristic—we have seen such historical examples as the internment of Japanese Americans during World War II, the Cold War paranoia and Red scare, periodic civil unrest, earthquakes, floods, and fires. The question, ultimately, is of choices made well in advance of the mid-twenty-first century. With this in mind, our current arc of progress is far more likely to arrive at a *Gold Coast*–like scenario then any of the others: "grid laid over grid, from the mountains to the sea. A billion lights."[8]

When looking into the face of the twenty-first century, several choices appear. Not surprisingly, they exist within current policy areas: environment, immigration, education, and civil rights. Environmental degradation is perhaps our most immediate concern, particularly when we include land use, congestion, and urban sprawl. As the state approaches 35 million people, we still insist on land-intensive suburban development. The consequences are severe: continuing reliance on single occupant vehicles, with the associated congestion and poor air quality; less and less open space; and greater pressure to develop adjacent to public parks, ridgelines, and the few miles of pristine coastline left.

As California continues to be a gateway for immigration, there is serious potential for greater demonization of new Californians. Anthropologist Fred Krissman[9] observes that immigrants, both documented and undocumented, have historically provided the next generation of citizens. Yet we provide these new Californians with a civic education grounded in xenophobia and intolerance. Public education will continue to be a contested terrain, particularly as we demand more while providing fewer resources. The civil rights discourse will continue to evolve, as we redefine the notions of inclusion and equity to incorporate the many challenges of twenty-first century statehood. While these pressures will continue to grow, we would be wise to remember Pogo's admonishment: "We have met the enemy and he is us."

"California Two" may yet be possible. The choices discussed throughout this book demand the participation of all stakeholders. The only truism that applies to California's future is, simply, that in a democracy we get the policies we deserve. Greater participation may lead to better choices. This book has explored California politics and policy from a historical, social, and cultural perspective, in an effort to provide a foundation for understanding policy and politics in the Golden State. The rest is up to you.

Do Androids Dream of Electric Sheep?   *Philip K. Dick*

The small beam of white light shone steadily into the left eye of Rachel Rosen, and against her cheek the wire-mesh disk adhered. She seemed calm.

Seated where he could catch the readings on the two gauges of the Voigt-Kampff testing apparatus, Rick Deckard said, "I'm going to outline a number of social situations. You are to express your reaction to each as quickly as possible. You will be timed, of course."

"And of course," Rachel said distantly, "my verbal responses won't count. It's solely the eye-muscle and capillary reaction that you'll use as indices. But, I'll answer; I want to go through this and—" She broke off, "Go ahead, Mr. Deckard."

Rick, selecting question three, said, "You are given a calf-skin wallet on your birthday." Both gauges immediately registered past the green and onto the red; the needles swung violently and then subsided.

"I wouldn't accept it," Rachel said. "Also I'd report the person to the police."

After making a jot of notation Rick continued, turning to the eighth question of the Voigt-Kampff profile scale. "You have a little boy and he shows you his butterfly collection, including his killing jar."

"I'd take him to the doctor." Rachel's voice was low, but firm. Again, the twin gauges registered, but this time not so far. He made a note of that, too.

"You're sitting watching TV," he continued, "and suddenly you discover a wasp crawling on your wrist."

Rachel said, "I'd kill it." The gauges, this time, registered almost nothing: only a feeble and momentary tremor. He noted that and hunted cautiously for the next question.

"In a magazine you come across a full-page color picture of a nude girl." He paused.

"Is this testing whether I'm an android," Rachel asked tartly, "or whether I'm homosexual?" The gauges did not register.

He continued, "Your husband likes the picture." Still the gauges failed to indicate a reaction. "The girl," he added, "is lying face down on a large and beautiful bearskin rug." The gauges remained inert, and he said to himself, An android response. Failing to detect the major element, the dead animal pelt. Her—its—mind is concentrating on other factors. "Your husband hangs the picture up on the wall of his study," he finished, and this time the needles moved.

NOTES

1. Michael Hiltzik, "Schwarzenegger Missed His Golden Opportunity to Give Californians the Truth," *Los Angeles Times* (May 21, 2009): A1.
2. The report was later published in book form as Alfred Heller, ed., *The California Tomorrow Plan: The Future Is Now* (Los Altos, CA: William Kaufmann, 1972).
3. Philip K. Dick, *Do Androids Dream of Electric Sheep?* (New York: Ballantine Books, 1968).
4. Prologue from the Ridley Scott film *Blade Runner*.
5. Kim Stanley Robinson, *The Wild Shore* (New York: Tom Doherty Associates, Inc., 1984).
6. Kim Stanley Robinson, *Pacific Edge* (New York: Tom Doherty Associates, Inc., 1988).
7. Kim Stanley Robinson, *The Gold Coast* (New York: Tom Doherty Associates, Inc., 1988).
8. Ibid.
9. Fred Krissman, "Undocumented Mexicans in California: Disenfranchising Some of Our Best and Brightest 21st Century Citizens." Center for Southern California Studies, Working Papers series, #4. (California State University, Northridge, 2001).

California's Counties

Source: California Geological Survey.

California Resources
on the Web

California Government

Official California homepage
www.ca.gov

Governor
www.gov.ca.gov

Assembly
www.assembly.ca.gov

Senate
www.senate.ca.gov

State agencies (by topic)
www.ca.gov/directory.html

California state and local government (U.S. Library of Congress resource)
www.loc.gov/rr/news/stategov/stategov.html

California County Information

California Department of Finance county profiles
www.dof.ca.gov/html/fs_data/profiles/pf_home.htm

California State Association of Counties
www.csac.counties.org

California Cultural Resources

California Council for the Humanities
www.calhum.org

Japanese American National Museum
www.janm.org

Manzanar Internment Camp, Owens Valley
www.pbase.com/trip/manzanar

California Studies Centers

Center for California Studies, California State University, Sacramento
www.csus.edu/calst

California Geographical Survey
http://geogdata.csun.edu

California Studies Center, UC Berkeley
www.irle.berkeley.edu/californiastudies/

California Studies Association
http://californiastudiesassociation.berkeley.edu/

Pat Brown Institute, California State University, Los Angeles
http://patbrowninstitute.org/about

Institute of Governmental Studies, UC Berkeley
www.igs.berkeley.edu

California Mission Studies Association
www.ca-missions.org

California Studies Program, San Francisco State University
http://bss.sfsu.edu/calstudies

Center for Southern California Studies, California State University, Northridge
www.csun.edu/~cscs

Center for the Study of Los Angeles, Loyola Marymount University
www.lmu.edu/page39865.aspx

Index